POLITICAL HERETICS

political

heretics

From Plato to Mao Tse-tung

BY MAX NOMAD

Ann Arbor   The University of Michigan Press

2/69

ACKNOWLEDGMENT

*My thanks to my friend Herman Singer
for reading my manuscript
and for his valuable suggestions.*

CONTENTS

POLITICAL HERETICS

INTRODUCTION

During the heyday of the McCarthy era, a patron of a small-town library asked for a periodical named *The Progressive*. The librarian had never heard of it and suggested that the inquirer might obtain it in the local radical bookshop, for the title sounded subversive. For all its simplicity there was a kernel of truth in the reply, even though the periodical in question was as much removed from radicalism as the braintrusters of F. D. Roosevelt or the advisers of J. F. Kennedy. The history of human progress can be written in terms of revolts against the status quo prevailing at any given time.

An attempt to record all these struggles would be tantamount to writing a history of the human race since its emergence from primitive tribal life. It would require a life-time effort equal to that of an Arnold Toynbee or a Will Durant to do justice to all the major struggles, successful or unsuccessful, against the masters of the day. It is beside the point whether progress is conceived as a real advancement for the bulk of the human race or as a change from one form of minority rule to another, whether it results in the improvement of the status of merely some of those who had risen against the powers that be, or, to be still more modest, whether the memory of the crushed revolts served to nourish the rebellious spirit of the underprivileged of later generations.

Seen thus, the revolts of the ancient slaves, as symbolized by the names of Eunus and Spartacus, though suppressed, in the long run contributed, with the sabotage practiced by the slaves, to the change of their status from vocal pieces of salable property to the somewhat less burdensome condition of serfdom or the like. The movements and uprisings connected with the names of the Gracchi and Catiline, by eventually converging into Caesarism, had their impact in improving the lot of the impecunious freemen. The rebellions of the serfs under Wat Tyler in England, Thomas Münzer in Germany, and Razin and Pugachev in Russia were, regardless of their outcome, not altogether without effect upon the descendants of the victors when they decided to "emancipate" their bondmen.

The same can also be said about the medieval revolts of the Czechs against the Germans and the Church, of the Poles against the Russians, of the Ukrainians against the Poles and the Russians, of the Italians against the Austrians, of the Greeks and Balkan Slavs against the Turks, of the Irish against the British, and of the non-European populations against the colonial powers. Whether or not they succeeded, whether or not the result was the substitution of new or native crooks and grafters for the old or foreign ones —the course of history was accelerated, carrying with it some improvement of the lot of the underdog, who saw in the rise of new masters an encouragement to fight for his own improvement.

The growth of the cities, the development of modern industrialism, and the concomitant decline of feudalism and agrarianism in general brought to the fore and increased the ranks of three social strata which were henceforth to dominate the historical stage of modern society: the capitalist employer, the hired manual worker, and, between the two, the noncapitalist man of education, the privileged and not-so-privileged managerial and technical employee—in short, the intellectual worker. Of these three forces, the uppermost stratum, the capitalist bourgeoisie, has in the course of the last centuries secured its ascendancy as a result of a number of violent and peaceful revolutions. In that struggle the bourgeoisie was inspired by the ideology of what is now vaguely referred to as old-time laissez faire or Manchester liberalism—an ideology which in many respects stands for the very opposite of the ideas advocated at present by New Deal or Welfare State liberalism. In that struggle the bourgeoisie was also largely assisted by two other strata, the intellectuals and the manual workers, who saw in the defeat of the old masters the dawn of a better future.

The triumph of capitalism put an end to that "alliance." The manual workers, as a mass, evolved no political ideology of their own. Their philosophy, if it may be so called, was a "fair day's wage for a fair day's work" within the existing capitalist system. It was the philosophy of trade unionism, pure and simple, which did not negate the principle of private enterprise.

From its inception the very basis of the profit system was to meet a theoretical and practical challenge issued by many representatives of the propertyless men of education, intellectuals, professionals, technicians, and other mental workers. They questioned the wisdom or the justice of the wealth of the world being concentrated in the hands of a small minority of property owners and suggested various forms of collective ownership under which, as they claimed and believed, the despoiled majority would come into its own.

That challenge found expression in the writings and actions of successive waves of utopian dreamers, romantic conspirators, profound scholars, gradualist politicians, rabid "direct-actionists," and, finally, the Machiavellian superrevolutionists now in control of one-third of the globe.

Will that control spread over the rest of the world? Is the challenge against social injustice slated to convert the dream of individual liberty and universal welfare into the infernal reality of universal collective submission to the all-powerful bureaucracy of the Moloch state?

Are we therefore to accept the aristocratic, or rather plutocratic, gospel of those critics of the coming slavery of totalitarianism who would make us believe that every intervention of the state beyond its role as mere thief-and-murderer-catching policeman is a sinister transgression of the sacred principle of individual liberty, a sinister concession to the infernal idea of socialism, which to those critics is one step removed from what the disciples of Lenin call communism? Or are we to reject their "libertarian" arguments as the special pleading of hired apologists of the sordid interests of the supermillionaires whose "rejection" of the state is the "ideological" fig leaf of their hostility to the income tax, and of their readiness to deliver to private charity—to starvation—all the present beneficiaries of social security?

Or is there any substance in the Cassandra cries of those prophets of doom who believe in the inevitable triumph of the totalitarian brand of socialism the world over? Are we to accept the defeatist idea that dictatorial collectivism, now in the ascendancy, is the only historically possible "inheritor" or "grave digger" of the continually changing modern industrial system?

Those prophets of doom should be reminded of the fact that there is no such thing as inevitability of historical outcomes in the life of human *societies*. (The only thing that is absolutely inevitable is the death of their *individual* members.) Time was, not so long ago, when many defeatists were convinced that the world triumph of Fascism was inevitable. Three generations before Hitler, there were those who believed in Marx's prediction that the capitalist system was going to collapse because of the increasing misery of the masses. This prediction never came true, not only due to the ever-increasing resistance of the workers, but also because intelligent conservative statesmen initiated the use of what is now called by ultrareactionaries "the welfare-state poison of socialism" to mitigate the misery of the masses and thus to consolidate the basis of the existing system. The mass appeal to the workers and the lower middle classes of the semisocialist Chartist movement of the 1840's inspired the author of *Sibyl* with the ideas of the "New Toryism," which had its share in stopping the "inevitable" trend toward superpauperization with its possibly "inevitable" sequel of bloody social revolution. Following Disraeli's example, the German "Iron Chancellor," similarly afraid of the growth of the socialist movement, initiated social reforms which, more than his antisocialist laws, had their share in slowing down the progress of the socialist movement and in quashing the revolutionary spirit of the masses. It is such welfare state measures, on a much larger scale constituting what was called the "minimum program" of socialism, which, after World War I, largely prevented the "inevitable" triumph of both the Western democratic and the Eastern totalitarian version of Marxism in the Western world. It is also the adoption of other "socialist" measures, such as the nationalization of important branches of the national economy, which has likewise contributed to the prevention of that "inevitable" collapse.

It was in recognition of this nonsubversive, or

"conservative" character of "socialist" measures that in the middle of the 1880's, long before the turn of the century, the British moderate Liberal statesman, Sir William Harcourt, exclaimed in the House of Commons that "we are all socialists now." That was at the time when, for all its revolutionary Marxist verbiage (outside of England), the socialist movement had already relegated its "final aim" to the realm of dreams and when the more intelligent statesmen of the capitalist world began to realize that the gradual acceptance of the socialist minimum program would conjure away the idea of the maximum program of which only the most timid beneficiaries of the status quo were still afraid.

It was World War I and the past antidemocratic policy of the tsarist government which set in motion the forces which eventually gave birth to the "maximum program." The circumstances of its birth turned into a monster of iniquity what generations of dreamers, conspirators, scholars, organizers, agitators, and terrorists had hoped or claimed would become the realization of the ideal of justice.

Opposition to the house built by Lenin has called forth two equally wrong reactions. Some defenders of the status quo refuse to make any distinction between totalitarian communism and democratic socialism. And some democratic socialists are doing violence to the cause of historical truth when they insist that the system established behind the Iron Curtain has nothing to do with socialism at large, or when they deny that there can be such a thing as nondemocratic socialism.

For socialism—in the meaning of what is called "public ownership"—is capable of assuming various forms, not unlike the system of private enterprise, which can be carried on either under the "rugged individualism" of the laissez-faire advocates or under the near-socialist aegis of the welfare state, and which could flourish both under the Oriental medievalism of prewar Japan and under the political democracy of the Western world. Hence this volume is going to deal with the various, often contradictory, phases of socialist thought and action.

Chapter I

THE DREAMERS

Prior to the Bolshevik Revolution the world at large was skeptical of the possibility or the practicability of a social system that would abolish the institution of private property. To refute those skeptics the opponents of the status quo often pointed to Plato, the Greek philosopher, who, more than two thousand years ago, in one of his best-known works gave a glowing description of an imaginary social system built upon the allegedly impracticable principle of community of property. To be sure, not all radical thinkers were particularly eager to recognize the Athenian sage as their legitimate ancestor. Some of them pointed out that while modern radicalism is based on a socialized form of production, what Plato suggested was in reality a communism of *consumption* for the ruling elite, while the old individualistic methods of production by the mass of population were not affected at all.

There are other reasons why modern radicals have little reason to be particularly proud of this ancestry. Plato's Utopia was not a plea for the plebeian underdog, but a protest in behalf of the aristocratic intelligentsia, the highly educated offspring of the landed nobility who resented the rule of the "democratic" merchants of Athens, whose policy of importing cheap grain from the colonies cut the profits of the landed aristocracy.

Plato's parasitic communism of the "knows"—for his was an aristocracy of knowledge based neither on birth nor on wealth—shows many similarities to the allegedly proletarian "communism" of the Soviet orbit. Plato's philosophers, who are the top stratum, correspond to the upper layers of the Communist party, whose familiarity with Marx's and Lenin's teachings constitutes the "ethical" basis of their rule, just as the rule of Plato's philosopher-kings is based on the knowledge and the practice of what he called "virtue." Below the top stratum in Plato's Republic are the warriors, who are obviously identical with the Soviet officers' corps. Plato's merchants, who are looked down upon by the philosophers and the warriors, have their counterparts in the technocrats of the Soviet system. In either case their high incomes are a consolation for their inferior status. The great mass of peasants and craftsmen, who were not free and were kept in their place by the warriors, differed from their counterparts in the Soviet orbit in that they were not mocked by the possession of a "vote" under a one-party system and were not told that they were the owners of all the wealth of their "classless" country. In one important respect, however, Plato's "ideal" had a familiar ring. Art and literature were to be tolerated only if considered helpful in the maintenance of the regime. There was to be a state religion which the subjects were forced to accept, though Plato did not believe in it himself.[1] Considering the great intelligence of the present Soviet rulers it is doubtful whether Khrushchev and his partners actually believe in Marxism-Leninism, the official state religion of their regime.

Of Hippodamus of Miletus, who was apparently a contemporary of Plato, Aristotle reports that he worked out a plan for an ideal republic that to a certain extent shows similarities to the "classless" system established behind the Iron Curtain. The entire arable land area was to be divided into three parts. The first part comprised the sacred land, the produce of which was to be used for the needs of the religious cult, that is, for the priests; the second was to be devoted to the needs of the warriors; while the third was to belong to the common run of tillers of the soil (who apparently would have to till the soil for the first two categories of citizens as well). There were to be elections for public office in which all citizens would take part. There is a curious resemblance between this plan and the Inca communism of ancient Peru. It may be assumed that the officeholders were chosen either from among the priests or from the warriors. There is no such tripartite division under contemporary "communism," under which about half of the national income—and not two-thirds—is assigned in the form of higher salaries to the educated upper crust—officeholders, army officers, technicians, and cultural workers —constituting (including their families) about 20 per cent of the population.

A contemporary of Hippodamus was Phaleas of Chalcedon, an ancient Greek port on the Bosporus. In his ideal republic the population was to be divided into two classes—landowners and workers. The principle of equalitarianism would prevail so far as the former were concerned, all owners possessing equal shares of land which they had no right to sell. Otherwise, there was what is now called "communism." All manual workers were to be slaves of the state, which had a monopoly of trade and industry. The works of Phaleas have been lost, and posterity has learned about them from Aristotle. Some of the ideas have a familiar ring.

Another variant of communism was advocated by the Greek mythographer Euhemerus, who lived around 300 B.C., the author of *Sacred History*, of which only a few fragments are preserved. His *Sacred History* reports an island south of Arabia whose population lived under a system of priestly communism. No one owned any property except a house and garden. All produce was handed over to the priests in charge of distribution, who are reported to have given to each one an equitable and satisfactory share.

For all the fantastic features of their schemes the Greek utopians were nevertheless "realists" of sorts in that they stood firmly on the traditional concept of the majority's subjection to a ruling minority which controlled the state. However, a unique position was occupied by Zeno (336-264 B.C.), the founder of the Stoic school of philosophy. One of his ancient biographers reports that in his *Republic*, a lost work, Zeno visualizes an ideal social system that dispensed with temples, courts, mints, and military training schools— a system, in short, which two thousand years later was to find an echo in the works of the radical philosophers designated as anarchists. Zeno's superidealism might perhaps be explained by the fact that, as an "outsider" of sorts—he was a Phoenician by birth—he could rise above the nationalist concepts of the Greeks in whose opinion the best a "barbarian" could hope for was to be a slave of the Greek master race. Zeno's "anarchism" might also have been the extreme protest of a sensitive soul against the military rule established by the generals of Alexander the Great after his death. In this respect Zeno was the very antipode of Plato, whose system was inspired by the aristocratic "communism" of Sparta, where the military caste held the majority of the population in the most cruel subjection. Plato's "virtue" did not rebel against the treatment of the helots. As Karl Kautsky, an anticommunist Marxist, put it, he merely wanted to substitute the "philosophers"—the intellectuals—for the army officers, as the ruling stratum.

THOMAS MORE's *Utopia*

The question has often been asked as to why, over a period of nearly two thousand years, no attempt was made by philosophers or poets to present the image of an ideal state. The answer may perhaps be that during this period men resentful of the injustices of their time were inspired first by the teachings of Stoicism, which combined humanitarian ideas with resigned submission to fate. This attitude restrained those who might have striven beyond the inhuman reality. Then came the Christian idea of salvation with belief in the second coming and the thousand years of the kingdom of Christ on earth, which was a perfect Utopia of sorts and apparently needed no minute elaboration. And when that too lost its attraction, the theological constructions of the countless heretical sects and their struggles against the all-powerful Church may likewise have submerged all the potential authors of political romances.

A break came early in the sixteenth century with the appearance of *Utopia* (1516) by Thomas More, who achieved fame both as an author of this epic of a perfect society and as the martyred chancellor of King Henry VIII. That break coincided with the great change then occurring in the economic and social conditions of England. The change was characterized by the cruel "enclosures," the procedure by which thousands of families were driven off their farms because it was more profitable to the landed noblemen to convert them into grazing land and to engage in the wool export business. More's indignation was aroused by the reduction of those peasants to the status of homeless vagabonds who could find no work and were mercilessly executed when, to escape starvation, they were forced to steal. More's indignation found expression in his famous phrase about "sheep eating men," referring to the sacrifice of human lives for the sake of the wool trade.

The ideal system recommended in More's opus is a curious mixture of economic radicalism, political authoritarianism, and cultural totalitarianism. The basic principle is the negation of private property because, as the spokesman of that book puts it, under a regime of property and money, "all things will be divided among a few," and "the best things will fall to the share of the worst men." The absence of private property is to be accompanied by complete equality of all citizens in the enjoyment of the good things of life. All products are at the disposal of those who need them. There is, of course, a general obligation to work; only those exceptionally gifted are exempted so as to have a chance to follow some intellectual pursuit. Those who do not come up to the expectations must rejoin the ranks of the workers.

Some of the other features of More's Utopia bear the marks of its author's puritanical outlook on life. In his youth More aspired to become a Franciscan monk and to submit to the strict discipline of monastery life, a concept he introduced into his Utopia, whose inhabitants had to wear uniform clothes; however, provision was made so as to distinguish men from women and the married from the unmarried. Once established, fashions were never to change.

There were distinguishing symbolic insignia on

the uniforms of the priests who, to all practical purposes, were the ruling class. More was a devout son of the Church, but he was more tolerant than the clergy of his time. Adherents of other creeds were not molested in his Utopia; even nonbelievers were permitted to live, but they were not permitted to hold public office. Nearly five centuries after More's death, there are sections in the United States in which atheist lawyers are not permitted to practice and in which the testimony of atheist witnesses is not considered valid evidence.

As in the case of many other idealistic advocates of social change, More combined humanitarianism with some features of a citizen of the non-Utopian world. He believed in the conquest of neighboring lands as a cure for overpopulation, and in the use of mercenary armies for that purpose. One of the weapons of Utopian warfare was also the now familiar policy of organizing fifth columns and of having the ruler of the enemy country assassinated by his own subjects. There is nothing new under the sun.

All in all, More was a philanthropist rather than a practical social reformer. When, years after the appearance of his book, More was appointed lord chancellor by Henry VIII, he made no attempt to carry out any of the changes which he had suggested. He died on the scaffold because, as a good Catholic, he opposed the King's divorce. It is most likely that he hardly believed in the possibility of an equitable regime such as was presented in his work. His dream of equality was apparently the protest of a highly cultured intellectual against the luxury and cruelty of a parasitic nobility.

More's *Utopia*, written in Latin, was soon translated into various languages of Western Europe. Needless to say it made a very deep impression on many intellectuals, who felt the way More did during the period of transition from feudalism to capitalism, and in whom the decline of the power of the lords of the manor subconsciously stimulated the dream of the decline of the lords of the moneybags as well.

TOMMASO CAMPANELLA's *City of the Sun*

One of the conscious or unconscious disciples of More and of Plato for that matter, was the Italian monk Tommaso Campanella (1568-1639). His *City of the Sun* was written in prison, to which he had been confined for twenty-seven years because he had headed a conspiracy aimed at wresting southern Italy from the rule of the Spaniards. As in More's *Utopia*, the inhabitants of Campanella's dreamland live in community houses, take their meals in public halls, and work together. And as in *Utopia* the whole roost is ruled by a hierarchy of priests and savants—an aristocracy of knowledge as against the ascendancy of birth and wealth. That new aristocracy bases its power on the omnipotence of the state, to which every individual must be unflinchingly devoted. In this respect Campanella went much further than More. There is a community of wives and children—not the result of the lecherous imagination of a sex-starved imprisoned monk, but as a prop for the authority of the state, which might not attain full power if individuals were devoted to their own families. Here one clearly sees the influence of Plato, except that the latter wanted to see his sex theory applied solely to the ruling minority of savants, while the masses lived on in the traditional manner. At bottom, Campanella's views in this respect were not such mad heresies as they seem at first sight. In support of his views the author of the *City of the Sun* quotes Saint Clemens who, in Campanella's words, "thought, in conformity with the teaching of the Apostles and of Plato, that there should be community of women as well as that of possessions."

Campanella was less tolerant than More, for he wrote his book in the heat of the struggle between the Church and the various branches of Protestantism. In Campanella's state all dissenters or nonbelievers are simply exterminated.

It would be a mistake to see in Campanella's vision merely the freakish fancy of a monk. What he wrote was undoubtedly symbolic of the protest of the lower clergy against the privileges of the upper classes, who at that time had begun to treat the clergymen as their flunkeys. It was also a prophetic dream of a totalitarian-communist society ruled by the clergy of an all-powerful church.

GERRARD WINSTANLEY

In direct contradiction to Campanella's authoritarian communism was the libertarian communism of a younger contemporary of his, Gerrard Winstanley (1609-52), who lived during the time of the Cromwellian revolution. The ultraradical religious and political sect of the "True Levellers" or "Diggers" took its inspiration from his ideas. In his *New Law of Righteousness*, Winstanley preached a system of communism under which there would be "no buying or selling of the earth, nor of the fruits thereof." There was to be no money. "If any man or family," he wrote, "want corn or other provisions, they may go to the storehouse and fetch without money. If they want a horse to ride, they may go into the fields in summer or to the common stables in winter, and receive one from the keepers, and when the journey is performed, bring him back." Similar ideas, short of Winstanley's religious mysticism, were to be encountered two and two-and-a-half centuries later in the writings of William Godwin and Peter Kropotkin. Winstanley is considered by some writers as one of the precursors of anarchism. In Winstanley's time these ideas were doubtless the expression of the protest of the strata at the bottom of the social ladder, propertyless peasants and urban workers or impoverished members of the lower middle class like Winstanley, who had been completely ruined during the Civil War.

MABLY AND MORELLY

The Age of Enlightenment, which set in after the religious wars of the seventeenth century, brought forth a large crop of utopian writers of which only the most important can be mentioned here. They are the French political philosopher, Gabriel Bonnot de Mably (1709-85), and another writer of the eighteenth century about whom nothing definite is known except his surname—Morelly.

Mably, who had studied for the ministry, renounced a clerical career to enter the service of the government. As secretary in the Ministry of Foreign Affairs he became a leading expert on international relations. At first a staunch defender of the old regime, he experienced a complete change of heart in 1757 when he left government service to write a number of books in which he presented his political philosophy.

Accepting equality as the basic law of nature, he believed that real equality implied economic equality, that is, equality of incomes and not merely political equality. He assumed that communism was the original condition of mankind, and his ideal was a social system in which private property has been abolished and in which societies consisting of small numbers of families tilled the land in common. Everything produced was to be brought to public storehouses to be distributed according to the needs of the individuals. However, he did not believe that such a system could be realized under prevailing circumstances; he therefore made various proposals for the mitigation of injustice. He advocated the abolition of the right of inheritance by collaterals (brothers, nephews), the state to become heir where there were no lineal descendants. Thus, the state would eventually take over all private property.

Speaking about the possibility of a revolution, Mably thought it would be justified. He believed it would be best if the majority of the human race perished in the process, as long as a million happy people survived. Under the influence of Plato, he expressed great admiration for the simplicity of the Spartans and for what he thought was their communism, without considering that the aristocratic communism of the Spartans was built upon a foundation of the most abject slavery of the majority of the population.

Some of Mably's ideas exerted a great influence upon Babeuf, the organizer of the Conspiracy of the Equals. Mably's communist ideas are presented in his *Des droits et des devoirs du citoyen* ("On the Rights and the Duties of the Citizen") and in his *Ordre naturel et essentiel des sociétés* ("The Natural and Essential Order of Societies").

Somewhat related to the ideas of Mably are those of Morelly, whose *Le Code de la nature* (1755) has become one of the most famous classics of utopian literature. The gist of his code is the idea that private property is the cause of all evil; to eliminate evils the state becomes the owner of all land and of all industries. Everyone works for the state, those between twenty and twenty-five years of age being employed in agriculture, while those above that age do less strenuous work. The state takes care of everybody. There is no trade or exchange; everyone receives everything he needs. Foreign trade is carried on by the government. The nation is divided into families, tribes, cities, and provinces. Government changes on the principle of rotation. The administration of cities is carried on by a senate composed of heads of households who are over fifty years of age, while the executive power is wielded by a civic officer who is the head of a tribe. After a year his office is taken over by another head of a tribe. In a similar way every province is ruled in rotation by an officer supplied every year by another city, while the various provinces supply successively the head of the state, who holds his office for life. There is a supreme senate holding authority over the entire nation. It is composed of representatives of the various cities, and its membership changes every year. Marriage is obligatory, and divorce is permitted only after ten years of marriage. It is the duty of every mother to nurse her child. The government takes care of the general and vocational education of the children.

Morelly's *Code* made a great impression. Having appeared anonymously, it was attributed to Diderot, one of the most outstanding writers of the period. It was even included in a collection of his works published in 1773. The influence of Morelly's work reached far beyond his own generation. One of his outstanding disciples was Gracchus Babeuf, whose equalitarian communism was based entirely upon Morelly's ideas. Babeuf, in turn, served as inspiration for the various French communist groups of the first half of the nineteenth century, known under the collective name of

"Babouvists." And from the Babouvists the line goes directly to Auguste Blanqui, whose ideas of a revolutionary dictatorship made their imprint upon the early ideas of Karl Marx.

From the egalitarianism of Morelly and the near-egalitarianism of Mably there is a historical leap of more than two generations to those representatives of French anticapitalist thought who are usually designated as utopian socialists and the basis of whose social philosophies was the very opposite of economic equality. These were the followers of Saint-Simon and Fourier.

THE SAINT-SIMONIANS

At the very outset, it must be stated that most historians are guilty of gross negligence when they classify Claude Henri de Saint-Simon (1760-1825) as a socialist. A scion of the old French aristocracy and a prolific writer, Saint-Simon gave rise to and lent his name to a school of socialism whose adherents were called Saint-Simonians, even though there is no trace of any definite socialist concepts in his works. In spite of his background—he was a count and a relative of the famous Duc de Saint-Simon, the author of the *Memoirs*—he identified himself with the rising bourgeoisie—the industrial and commercial classes whose virtues he extolled as against the parasitism of the aristocrats. Hence, he has been called the prophet of big business, whose representatives he tried to inspire with a sense of social responsibility. His writings contain ideas which might have served as inspiration for the "technocrats" of our time. He championed the idea of a working aristocracy of merit in control of social processes, as against the feudal aristocracy of birth.

The aristocracy of merit would include the chiefs of industry—owners and managers—and the scientists. He envisaged an industrial state whose spiritual administration was in the hands of men of science, while its industrial chiefs were to be educated or compelled to use their wealth in the interest of the entire nation. He expected the workers to submit voluntarily to a hierarchy of industrialists, managers, and savants who, in his opinion, were their natural masters. Individual property was to be respected, and there was no thought of collectivism, that is, of public ownership, in his mind. That idea was introduced into his philosophy after his death by his two outstanding disciples, Bazard and Enfantin, who thus became the originators of what is called Saint-Simonian socialism. Saint-Simon's most important works were *Letters of an Inhabitant of Geneva*, and *New Christianity*. (The title of this last work apparently misled Bertrand Russell, in his *Freedom Versus Organization*, p. 178, into asserting that "Saint-Simon was essentially a medievalist who disliked industrialism and the modern world, and sought renovation in a purified Christianity." Even the greatest and most charming philosopher of our time should not be exempt from the duty of reading the books he is writing about.)

Originally, Saint-Amand Bazard (1791-1832) was a liberal republican in whose ranks he fought against the Bourbons who had returned to power after Napoleon's fall. During the 1820's he became acquainted with the teachings of Saint-Simon, which he developed in the direction of socialism. After the death of his teacher in 1825, he became with Enfantin one of the two chief exponents of Saint-Simonian socialism. Aside from the mysticism which pervaded the theories of the Saint-Simonians, the concrete views of Bazard and his followers could be summed up in the following three propositions: The abolition of the right of inheritance and the transfer of all means of production to the State. The application of the principle that every person should be employed in accordance with his abilities and rewarded according to his works—a principle which took for granted the inequality of rewards. The recognition of a hierarchical organization of society and what is called nowadays the "Fuehrer-Prinzip."

In a document addressed by Bazard and Enfantin to the Chamber of Deputies on October 1, 1830, in reply to the accusations directed against the Saint-Simonian school—a document which is generally credited to Bazard—the ideas of the school are expressed as follows: "The system of community of goods means an equal division among all the members of society either of the very means of production or of the fruits of the toil of all. The Saint-Simonians reject this equal division of property which in their opinion would constitute a more reprehensible act of violence, a more revolting act of injustice than the unequal division which has been effected originally by the force of arms, by conquest. For they believe in the natural inequality of men, and consider this inequality as the very basis of association, as the indispensable condition of social order. They reject the system of community of goods; for this community would be an obvious violation of the first of all the moral laws which it is their mission to teach, and which demands that in the future every one should rank according to his ability, and be rewarded according to his works. But in virtue of this law they demand the abolition of all privileges of birth without exception, and consequently the destruction of the right of inheritance, the principal among these privileges, which today includes all the other privileges, and the effect of which is to leave to chance the distribution of the social advantages among the small number of those who can claim them, and to condemn the most numerous class to deprivation, ignorance and misery. They demand that all the tools of production, land and capital, which today are distributed among individual owners, should be united into one single social capital and that this capital should be exploited in a collective (*par association*) and hierarchical way so that every one should be assigned a task in accordance with his ability and that every one's wealth should correspond to his works. The Saint-Simonians attack the institution of property only in so far as it perpetuates, for the few, the ungodly privilege of idleness, that is, the privilege of living off the labor of his fellow men; only in so far as it leaves to the accident of birth the determination of the social status of the individual."

In 1831 a conflict of opinions concerning the question of marriage and of sex relations led to a break between Bazard and Enfantin, whereupon Bazard attempted to form a new school of his own, of which he proclaimed himself chief.

In his writings Bazard anticipated many slogans of present-day socialism and communism, such as the phrase "exploitation of man by man." His insistence on the principle of hierarchy and the absolute authority of the leader seems to have found an echo in the theory and practice of both Fascism and communism.

It was under the influence of Prosper Enfantin (1796-1864), Bazard's cofounder of the Saint-Simonian school, that the Saint-Simonian movement evolved from a school of political thought to a religious sect with special rites and a clergy, with Enfantin as the "Father." Enfantin was convicted of "immorality"; the subsequent ridicule was also instrumental in bringing about the ruin of the movement.

Generally speaking, it may be said about the Saint-Simonians that their sympathy for socialist ideas was not an outcome of their devotion to the working class, but the result of their fears lest the horrors of the Revolution of 1789 recur if no reforms were adopted to mitigate the misery of the masses. They were *not* underpaid or unemployed déclassé lower middle-class intellectuals, but middle- and upper middle-class professionals, like the British Fabians of half a century later, who, *mutatis mutandis,* were motivated by similar considerations.

The Saint-Simonians showed no particular partiality toward forms of government. They were ready to collaborate with any government which would organize a public school system for the masses and would undertake the establishment of credit institutions and the construction of public works, railways, canals, etc., which would further the industrialization of the country. Hence, they were ready to support Louis Philippe, the "citizen-king" (1830-48) and later Napoleon III. Several cabinet members under the Second Empire were former Saint-Simonians. "These practical men," says the French historian Georges Weill in his *Histoire du mouvement social en France* (p. 51) in referring to the Saint-Simonians under Napoleon III, "had not entirely renounced their erstwhile generous aspirations; some of them often repeated the formula of the Saint-Simonian school about the physical, moral, and intellectual amelioration of the most numerous and most destitute class; but while to some of them this meant a complete reconstruction of the social system in a remote future, the others were dreaming only about the ever-increasing development of trade and industry (*circulation et production*). Thus they were drawing close to the position of the liberal economic school, without, however, sharing its aversion to government intervention. Saint-Simonian inspiration is often perceptible in the doings of the Second Empire, particularly at its outset."

CHARLES FOURIER

While the aristocrat Saint-Simon was extolling the idea of the new era of industrialism, and his upper middle-class followers were looking toward government ownership as a remedy against its evils, a humble bookkeeper and commercial traveler by the name of Charles Fourier (1773-1837) was writing volume after volume stigmatizing the evils, the misdeeds, and the corruption of the new commercial system that was emerging from the ruins of feudalism. His life was uneventful. Prosperous in his youth, he lost his inherited fortune during the French Revolution and was most of his life engaged in the humble occupations of traveling salesman or clerk. He wrote several volumes about the irrationality and waste of the existing competitive system and about an ideal society which he described in complete detail. He believed that if he could find one rich philanthropist ready to advance the means for the construction of the first "phalanstery," miniature sample of his ideal society, the human race would immediately proceed with the reorganization of the social system in accordance with the example given by him. He never lost hope that the expected philanthropist would appear some day, and he was always at home at noon in order not to miss the rich visitor whom he expected at that time. The imagination Fourier displayed in some of his writings justified the suspicion that his mind was unbalanced. Yet for all that, his books are full of ideas which are of interest and which have fructified the minds of his contemporaries.

There are some points in common between his philosophy and that of the Saint-Simonians. Both were opposed to violence as a method of effecting social change, and both accepted the idea of human inequality and the ensuing inevitability of unequal rewards. They were, however, at opposite poles when it came to the basic ideas of remedying the evils of nascent capitalism. At variance with the Saint-Simonians, Fourier ignored the state and expected salvation from voluntary organizations, for which he used the expression of *phalanstère* and *phalanx*. In his vocabulary and that of his followers, the *phalanstère* was the central building inhabited by all the members of a "phalanx," the name Fourier gave to the socialist communities, cultivating about 5,000 acres of land, which he hoped to see established in accordance with his plans. A phalanstery was to house between 1600 and 1800 persons with unequal accommodations in accordance with ability to pay, for there is no equality of income in the socialism conceived by Fourier. The entire income of the organizations was to be distributed among "capital" (those who had invested their money in the organization of the phalanx), "talent" (the men of education engaged in managerial, technical, and other intellectual functions), and physical labor. Labor, though constituting the majority, would get five-twelfths of the total product, while of the remaining seven-twelfths, "capital" would be awarded three and "talent" four.

Fourier believed that all human passions and inclinations were essentially beneficent and would contribute to the common welfare once society was reorganized in a "rational" way—in accordance with his suggestions. Nature in his opinion was benevolent, and all evils were the result of ignorance and the ensuing faulty organization of society.

Fourier's teachings found many followers in France and the United States. They influenced the ideas of the Brook Farm group, which included among others such men as Ralph Waldo Emerson and Charles Dana. Albert Brisbane (1809-1890), an American Fourierist, founded a number of "phalanxes" in this country.

The revolution of 1848 turned the minds of many of Fourier's followers in another direction. Two of his French followers achieved a sort of freakish fame or notoriety. One of them, Victor Considérant, a gifted popularizer of Fourier's ideas, published in 1845 the *Manifeste de la démocratie*, many passages of which, as some unfriendly critics of Marx claimed, reappeared three years later in a somewhat "rewritten" form in the *Communist Manifesto*. (In reality, these ideas were in the "air" at the time and were shared by most radicals of the period.) Another of his disciples, Alphonse Toussenel, became in his time widely known for an anti-Semitic classic—entitled *Les Juifs rois de l'epoque*—directed against the influence of Jewish financial capital.

With his emphasis upon voluntary organizations, such as his *phalanstères*, Fourier became, in a way, one of the precursors of the movement which expected producers' and consumers' co-operatives to play an important role in the elimination of the capitalist system. For the same reason the champions of some anarchist schools, particularly that of Peter Kropotkin, the theorist of communist anarchism, likewise consider him as one of their forerunners. There are also those who, half-jocularly and half-seriously, point out that some of his ideas concerning community life in the *phalanstères* have actually been realized in modern large apartment hotels.

The millionaire on whose financial help in the organization of the first *phalanstère* Fourier built his hope for the world's salvation never made his appearance—even though a man likely to advance the necessary money for any noble project was at that time very much alive in England. Unfortunately for Fourier, that Englishman had his own ideas for promoting the welfare of the human race. His name was Robert Owen (1771-1858). He shared the Saint-Simonian and Fourierist rejection of violence as a method of social change and also their belief that it would be possible to remove existing social evils by persuasion. He was, however, motivated chiefly by his compassion for the poor, while the writers of the two French schools maintained a sort of aloofness, if not contempt, as far as the masses were concerned, as evidenced by their uninhibited insistence upon inequality of rewards which would maintain the manual workers at the bottom of the social ladder.

Born in the family of a small shopkeeper, Robert Owen started earning his living at the age of nine. He showed great skill as an organizer and became an independent manufacturer at a very early age. A philanthropist by nature, he converted his factory in New Lanark, Scotland, into a model enterprise in which the conditions of the workers were better than anywhere else. He was a champion of social legislation and particularly an opponent of child labor. He also advocated the formation of "villages of co-operation" to be established by the government for the relief of the unemployed who, under this scheme, would be engaged in industrial and agricultural occupations. However, neither the government nor private philanthropists were interested in helping him carry out this scheme. Hoping to be more successful in his plans to help the poor, he went to the United States in 1825, where he established a communist colony called New Harmony in Indiana. After the failure of the project he returned to England in 1829.

The ideas which he had been preaching during the previous years had in the meantime taken root among workers and intellectuals. Co-operative organizations had sprung up all over the country, and the repeal of the Combination Acts (1824), which prevented the formation of labor organizations, facilitated the formation of trade unions. Those active in these two movements looked forward to the establishment of a co-operative commonwealth based upon a combination of producers' co-operatives and trade unions. One of the results of Owen's propaganda was the spread of consumers' co-operatives, whose founders were imbued with his ideas. Owen himself was not interested either in the practical aims of the consumers' co-operatives or in strikes for higher wages. He did not believe the position of the workers could be considerably improved within the existing system and looked upon both trade unions and co-operatives as instruments for effecting a peaceful transition from capitalism to socialism. In pursuance of this aim he founded in 1832 the Equitable Labor Exchange, a sort of banking institution whose members could deposit in it the goods they produced, receiving in exchange "labor notes," the value of the goods to be determined by the cost of the raw materials and the average time necessary for the production of the given merchandise. The enterprise collapsed.

Owen was not interested in political activities of any kind. He expected the triumph of his ideas to come from his appeals to the ethical sentiments of all men regardless of social status and from the example given by the colonies which he financed. An important component of his philosophy was his conviction that "man's character is made for and not by him." This meant that changed social institutions would change man's character. This point of view has been accepted by most later socialists and communists as well. One of the organizations formed under his influence was the "Association of All Classes of All Nations," whose members called themselves "socialists" since 1839. The very name of the organization shows that—in contradistinction to the revolutionary socialists, both contemporary and of a later period—the Owenites, true to their teacher, did not believe in the class struggle. Throughout his active years Owen was interested in making propaganda for a sort of rationalist or materialist religion. In his declining years he became a mystic and a believer in spiritism. Some of his attitudes—such as his attempt to persuade members of the ultra-reactionary Holy Alliance to accept his ideas for relieving the plight of the poor—show that his characterization by the Marxists as a utopian in the meaning of a visionary, impractical thinker was fully justified.

One of Owen's best-known projects was the establishment, in the United States, of the aforementioned communist colony called New Harmony for which he had acquired the site of the former Rappist community, Harmony, in Indiana. The colonists were unable to make a success of it, and Owen, who lost most of his fortune in the experiment, was forced to give it up after three years. Various causes contributed to its failure, not the least of them being the fact that its managers were unable to rid the colony of the parasites who had joined it and took advantage of the principle of complete equality of rewards regardless of the contributions or accomplishments of the individual.

Some of Owen's ideas had repercussions on the thinking of a number of French malcontents who were to become known as "Icarians." They were followers of Etienne Cabet (1788-1856), author of the utopian novel *Voyage en Icarie*. A lawyer by profession, Cabet had participated in the liberal movement directed against the Bourbons who had been restored after the fall of Napoleon. After the Revolution of 1830 he opposed in parliament the plutocratic regime of Louis Philippe. Because of his attitude he was forced in 1834 into exile in England; an amnesty permitted him to return to France five years later. In England he had become familiar with Thomas More's *Utopia* and with Robert Owen's views. Converted to communism, he wrote *Voyage en Icarie*, which was the starting point of the Icarian movement. The basic idea of his theory was government ownership of all industries with equal rewards to all, and government control of the nation's cultural life as well. Only books approved by the government were to be printed, while newspapers were to be edited by government officials. (They were to print only facts and the reports of the sessions of parliament.) Cabet was opposed to violence and believed in the triumph of his ideas by persuasion. In 1848 a number of his followers went to the United States, where a few colonies embodying his principles were founded. They all failed because of internal quarrels and the dictatorial attitude of their teacher.

Cabet was not concerned with evolving a theoretical system. His reply to objections on that score was as follows: "When they ask us to what science we adhere, our answer is: the science of brotherhood! What our basic principle is? Brotherhood! What our doctrine? Brotherhood! What our theory? Brotherhood! What our system? Brotherhood!"

To the question as to whether higher ability, intelligence, or genius should not be specially rewarded Cabet replies in his *Voyage en Icarie:* "No, are they not merely gifts of Nature? Would it be just to punish in any way him whom fortune has meanly endowed? Should not reason and society redress the inequality produced by blind chance? Is not the man whose superior ability makes him more useful fully recompensed by the satisfaction he derives from it?"

Cabet's views, a curious combination of the most idealistic and philanthropic egalitarianism with a cultural totalitarianism, outdoing even that of the Stalin regime, seems to confirm Schopenhauer's remark that "many things can exist alongside each other within the same man."

LOUIS BLANC

Another egalitarian, though of an altogether different kind, was Louis Blanc (1811-82), whose interest in radical ideas may have been aroused by the fact that the fall of Napoleon put an end to his father's position in the upper ranks of the Empire's bureaucracy. The Revolution of 1830, which overthrew the reactionary Bourbons and ushered in the comparatively liberal Orléans dynasty, enabled him to enter on a journalistic career and to contribute to various progressive publications. Under the influence of socialist and communist ideas then current in France he developed a system of his own which in 1839 he presented in *Organisation du travail* ("Organization of Work"). The gist of his system was that every human being has the right to live (*droit à la vie*) and that this right could be realized

by the establishment of "social workshops"—co-operative associations of producers equipped and financed
by the government out of the resources it would obtain
from the nationalized public utilities and enterprises
such as railways, mines, insurance establishments, and
banks. The government would not be the owner of
these "social workshops" but merely their regulator. It
would manage them during their first year; after that
the workshops would take care of their own management. Remuneration should be realized according to
the principle of equality of rewards. Louis Blanc's guiding ideas were, in the words of the Austrian political
scientist Anton Menger, "not the right to the whole
produce of labor, but the right to subsistence; not an
economic principle, but the philanthropic conception
of brotherhood."[2] Louis Blanc expected that his "social
workshops," established by the state, would successfully
compete with private enterprises, driving them to bank-
ruptcy and thus forcing them to establish themselves
as "social workshops" as well. With regard to agriculture
Blanc—borrowing the idea of Mably—believed in the
abolition of collateral succession, so that eventually all
land would be taken over by the government and organized on the principle of "social workshops." Louis
Blanc did not expect to bring about his system by
violent methods. He hoped the state—which, in his
opinion, existed to protect the poor—and the rich
would help in bringing about these reforms. It was
he who coined the slogan "from each according to his
capacity; to each according to his needs." He based his
postulate of economic equality upon the ethical idea
that those who were stronger and more gifted owed a
debt to those who were not so endowed. The slogan of
the "right to work"[3]—the right to have a job—has been
connected with his name. However, the idea and the
slogan originated long before Blanc. It has been pointed

out that to him the "right to work" was a corollary of the right to exist.

The Revolution of February 1848 raised Louis Blanc to a position of political power. He became a member of the Provisional Government and was put in charge of a commission for the study of economic conditions. Many historians believe that the government, afraid of his popularity among the workers and anxious to discredit his idea of the "social workshops," organized what was to be called the "national workshops," which were a caricature of Blanc's idea. The turbulent events of May and June 1848 strengthened the influence of the conservative element; as a result Blanc was forced into exile to escape an indictment and probable conviction. He remained in England throughout the reign of Napoleon III and returned to France only after his fall in 1870. Elected to the National Assembly in February 1871, he represented in that body a moderate concept of socialism. His radical reputation was tarnished by his violent opposition to the Paris Commune of 1871. He was, however, opposed to the cruelty with which that uprising was suppressed. During the 1870's until his death in 1882, he was a member of the Chamber of Deputies, where he represented the views of the extreme left wing of the "Radical" republicans. ("Radical" in French corresponds to "liberal" or "progressive" in other languages.)

EDWARD BELLAMY AND WILLIAM MORRIS

Toward the end of the nineteenth century two more Utopias appeared in literature. It is worthy of note that they were written in the United States and England, countries in which socialism had not become a mass movement. One of them, *Looking Backward*

2000-1887 by Edward Bellamy (1850-98), sold about half a million copies in America. It did a great deal to familiarize his contemporaries with the ideas of socialism. The novel, which was published in various languages throughout the world, pictures an ideal socialist commonwealth such as the United States might become in the year 2000 if all national resources and industries were to be taken over and run by a government regulating everything while maintaining the principle of full political and economic equality.

The success of the book encouraged its author to "cash in" politically on its vogue. The word "socialism," lacking popularity in America because it smacked of foreign importation, Bellamy chose the inoffensive though meaningless label of "Nationalism" for a movement which he hoped would become a powerful radical third party. If objective circumstances are not favorable, however, even the most popular book cannot produce more than royalties.

The author of *Looking Backward* visualized the realization of his Utopia as a result of a peaceful process. He anticipated that a benevolent government would simply take over the industrial fabric as soon as the entire economic life of the country had become dominated by a small number of big corporations. This view was not shared by William Morris (1834-96), a radical English poet and artist whose dreamland, as presented in the utopian romance *News From Nowhere* (1891), was the outcome of a violent revolution. There was also this difference between the two Utopias: to Bellamy socialism represented the triumph of technical efficiency; his libertarian English counterpart anticipated in it the blossoming of individual craftsmanship and artistic endeavor.

In neither of the two utopian romances is there an inkling as to the bureaucratic-totalitarian potentialities of a socialized economy. It took the Bolshevik Revolution and its aftereffects to inspire three novelists of note—two of them disenchanted radicals—to write what is called "anti-utopias," giving an ultra-pessimistic view of man's fate under the iron rule of an all-powerful state.

The first was Eugene Zamiatin's *We*. Written in Russian during the heat of the Civil War of 1918-20, it gave a picture of the world as it would be a thousand years hence. Obviously, a lampoon on the house that Lenin built, it had to be published abroad. The author was a leftist but not a Bolshevik. His book was translated into English, but nobody paid any attention to it. To the rightist enemies of new Russia it was too subtle, and to the leftist sympathizers it seemed a gross exaggeration and a malicious libel. It was doubtless the inspiration of Aldous Huxley's *Brave New World* and of George Orwell's *1984*.

As if to counteract the impact of this prophecy, Khrushchev, in his report to the Soviet Communist Party Convention of 1961, painted an enthralling picture of what Russia would be in 1980, four years before Orwell's sinister figure. In the meantime, however, the statistical yearbooks of the Soviet regime still refuse to publish any figures concerning the wages and salaries paid to the "owners of the national wealth."

Chapter II

THE REBELS

There are malcontents and malcontents. Some would write down their dreams of a perfect society and hope that the logic of their reasoning would in the end persuade both the beneficiaries and the victims of an evil system to work in peace and harmony toward the realization of heaven on earth. These were and are the utopians. Whether they are prompted by pity for the downtrodden, by fear of an inevitable bloody cataclysm, by envy, or by a hopeless lust for power—they are as a rule not men of action; they console themselves either with the Oriental adage that "the ink of the savant is more valuable than the blood of the martyr," or with the mostly correct realization that they are far ahead of their times, that a courageous example on their part would meet with no emulation, and that at any rate it is better to be a living philosopher than a dead rebel.

In contrast to these purely platonic champions of subversion, the conditions of the last two centuries have brought forth a number of outstanding malcontents of an altogether different caliber, men ready to risk their lives for the sake of their dreams, or, what in most cases means the same thing, their will to power. Men of this kind make their appearance only under circumstances of particular stress affecting both their social group and their private lives.

Circumstances of this kind were the revolutions, civil wars, economic depressions, and political tyrannies accompanying or following each other during the years of the great French Revolution and of the post-Napoleonic reaction not only in France but in all European countries.

The social group which at that time, next to the manual workers, suffered most under the changing conditions comprised the impecunious, educated members of the lower middle class—men whose situation and prospects were comparable to those of the bulk of the unemployed or underpaid intelligentsia in the emerging but still industrially undeveloped or underdeveloped countries of the Asian, African, and South American continents.

Under such conditions submission to fate becomes meaningless to many who have noticed that things are in flux in their own or neighboring countries and have seen or have heard of the toppling fortunes of yesterday's political grandees or economic tycoons and their replacement by parvenus. So they turn against the new status quo, particularly if they come under the spell of a man of superior energy, will power, ambition, courage, eloquence, personality appeal, intelligence, integrity, or cunning.

Some of these qualities exclude others, but a combination of some of them is likely to create a type of leader who can sway men and women to follow his daring example, even if the conspiracies and expeditions be undertaken "with only three men and four stones," as some contemporaries of Mazzini put it in criticizing some of his patriotic-revolutionary ventures.

The ideas in behalf of which the men of action rose varied according to circumstances: Where, as in the case of the Italians or the Poles, the main or the most visible source of discontent was the rule of foreign

conquerors, the ideology would be nationalism somewhat blended with vague sympathies for the uneducated rural and urban underdog; where, as in France, a
revolution has supplanted the aristocratic old rich by a
class of bourgeois newly rich, the militant malcontents
among the educated would adopt a vocabulary of anticapitalist revolt in order to attract the great mass of the
disinherited. However, the cloven foot of their sometimes unconscious desire for their own advancement to
the seats of power would appear, one way or another,
either in their pronouncements or in their actions. For
men of action are more often than not "domineering in
temper, jealous of the influence of others . . . with more
of anger in their heart, albeit righteous anger, than of
love." What Mazzini, in these phrases, said about
Marx holds for most men of action, rebels as well as
conservatives. These characteristics explain why most of
the active rebels are less consistent, as far as their
"principles" are concerned, than the utopians. For, with
their "domineering temper" they are always prone, for
the sake of their "dominion," to treat the ideals they
professed at the outset of their careers either as dreams
or as propaganda necessary for winning a following.
Objectively, this is a fraudulent game, but it is not always so subjectively—in the consciousness of the leading personalities concerned. It is natural for a leader to
identify his power with the ideal he once preached to
his followers or, to be more exact, with the period of
transition before that ideal can be realized.

BABEUF AND THE "EQUALS"

A case in point, yet somewhat apart as far as the
eponymous hero and martyr of the revolutionary undertaking was concerned, was that of the "Conspiracy of

the Equals" of 1796-97, which was directed against the post-Robespierrist masters of revolutionary France. The apparent head of it was François Noel ("Gracchus") Babeuf, a simple-minded dreamer rather than a revolutionary leader and politician. The "Conspiracy of the Equals," the communist ideas Babeuf expressed in his *Tribune of the People*, and his tragic death have helped to weave a tissue of legends around an enterprise which was even less "proletarian" in character and intent than the Bolshevik Revolution of 1917.

The material brought to light by the great historians of the French Revolution, Aulard and Mathiez, has contributed a great deal toward separating the elements of romantic myth from the cold facts and has helped to distinguish between the propagandist professions and the actual intentions of the "Equals."

Babeuf himself, whose name has been immortalized by the conspiracy, was a communist equalitarian in his beliefs, firmly opposed to the system of private property. He was influenced by communist philosophers, such as Mably and Morelly, by Rousseau, Linguet, and Brissot, and by a prolific contemporary journalist, Sylvain Maréchal, who was to go down in history as the author of the *Manifesto of the Equals*. Yet there was little connection between Babeuf's philosophical communism and the purpose of the conspiratorial activity that was to bring him to the scaffold.

Babeuf's career as equalitarian conspirator began after the defeat of Robespierre at the hands of that section of his own party which later came to be known as the "Thermidorians." Like most of the other Jacobins, Babeuf did not realize immediately the social significance of this overturn. He saw in it merely the triumph of liberty over the unbearable despotism of the "tyrant." At that time he was still a "free-lance" journalist, without any following and without any definite program. His communist aspirations were a personal religion with him rather than a political platform. A communist for the distant future, he was a fellow traveler of the Thermidorians for the immediate present.

Soon enough it became clear that Robespierre's fall meant not only the end of the Terror, but also the ascendancy of the upper middle-class profiteers who had enriched themselves as a result of the demise of the feudal system. The losers were not only the followers of the "Incorruptible" but also many other Jacobins who, while opposing Robespierre's terror, were not ready to accept the rule of the plutocratic elements represented by the corrupt Barras, the man who launched Bonaparte on his career and was later pushed aside by this ungrateful husband of his discarded mistress.

A number of Robespierre's followers were meeting in the house of Amar, a wealthy ex-member of the Convention, who had been affected by the fall of Robespierre. A few of them constituted what was called the "Amar Committee," which was later to play an important part in what has gone down in history as Babeuf's Conspiracy.

It was their common opposition to the plutocratic policy of the Directory that brought about a sort of united front of the radicals professing the communist views of Babeuf and of the followers of Robespierre who were thirsting for revenge. It was the latter who, according to Mathiez, one of the outstanding historians of the Revolution, supplied the financial backing for the *Tribune of the People*, a periodical edited by Babeuf. That financial backing was reflected in the contents of that publication, which could blow both hot and cold, and would defend, in turn, the principles of communist egalitarianism and the policies of Robespierre, who was a rabid opponent of communism.

An explanation of this seeming incongruity is not hard to find. An analysis of the social status of its 650 subscribers—a very large figure for that period—shows that all of them belonged to the well-to-do classes. Mathiez comes to the conclusion that they were certainly not interested in Babeuf's communism, but that they had all been, one way or another, connected with the overthrown Robespierre regime and that they had an ax to grind against the beneficiaries of the Thermidorian reaction. As practical men they readily understood that propaganda for an earthly paradise may be useful in inducing the poor to rise against the hated regime.

The general mood of the population was favorable to a revolutionary undertaking, and the Insurrectional Committee, a secret body composed of Babeuf and some of his closest associates, such as Darthé and Buonarroti, conducted a skillful propaganda campaign among the masses.

One thing, however, stood out in this communist propaganda: it was not concerned with the practical, everyday needs of the workers. Strikes were going on at that time in Paris—yet the Equals did not pay attention to them. Babeuf spoke continually to "the men of the people, to the workers of all classes (*états*)." To be sure, the Equals tried to win over the workers, and it was for their consumption that equalitarian propaganda was spread in the poorer sections of the capital. But the wage workers were still a small fraction of the population. In order to be successful the Equals had to win over the middle and the lower middle classes, many of whose members were employers of labor.

While the Equals were getting ready for their insurrection, the amnestied followers of Robespierre were likewise making preparations for the coming events. On May 7, 1796, the two groups—the Amar Committee of Robespierrists, and the Insurrectionary Committee of the Equals—agreed on a joint program of action and on the distribution of functions after the seizure of power. Three days later all the leaders of the conspiracy were arrested. They had been betrayed by one of the leading members, Captain Grisel, military "revolutionary agent" of one of the districts of Paris.

Babeuf and Darthé were condemned to death and executed. Five of the conspirators, including Buonarrotti, were deported to the penal colonies. It is worthy of note that, according to Aulard, the outstanding historian of the French Revolution, Babeuf's socialist opinions were *not* the subject of the indictment against the conspirators. He had, so to speak, signed his own death warrant by his advocacy of a "plebeian Vendée"; for this was an open appeal to civil war, threatening to break up that policy of union of all republicans which the Directory considered necessary against the mounting royalist tide.

The others were acquitted. The Directory, apparently, was reluctant to deepen too much the gulf between itself and the left wing of the republican camp, for the possibility of a Bourbon restoration had never ceased to haunt them.

To contemporaries the conspiracy was merely an episode in the family quarrel among various republican clans rather than a serious attempt to usher in a communist form of society. To the practical politicians of that period the communist professions of the conspirators were mere propaganda, the like of which they had seen before. It is significant that the Act of Insurrection —the last document in which the conspirators called upon the people to rise—did not contain a word about communism. Babeuf himself and Buonarrotti, though sincerely believing in the gospel they preached, apparently realized at the moment of action that the time for their ideal had not come as yet.

The revelation that equalitarian, that is, truly communist slogans were used as a means for attempting the rehabilitation and the return to power of a group of ousted bourgeois politicians of the French Revolution, may come as a shock to those who are used to taking principles and programs at their face value. They should be reminded of the fact that the radical political movements of the last one hundred and fifty years have been one long succession of the exploitation of socialist and communist slogans either for the elevation of ambitious politicians to positions of power within the capitalist system or for the establishment of an all-powerful totalitarian bureaucracy on the ruins of private capitalism, just as the religious communism of the first semi-educated Christian preachers served as a stepping-stone for the rise of the powerful hierarchy of the Church.

SYLVAIN MARÉCHAL

The assumption that Babeuf's communism was not taken seriously by his Robespierrist backers is evidenced by the fact that the *Manifesto of the Equals,* which was an epitome of Babeuf's communist views, was not accepted as an official document of the Conspiracy. That *Manifesto* was written by the poet and journalist, Sylvain Maréchal, who was a sympathizer of the "Equals" rather than an active member of the Conspiracy. For that reason he escaped persecution when the leaders of the "Equals" were arrested. At first one of the champions of the antireligious Cult of Reason, he sympathized with the extreme Left as against the politicians in power; but he was at heart a believer in a sort of idyllic, pastoral, or as the anarchist historian Nettlau put it, "patriarchical" anarchism, rejecting all authority, except that of the father. For the attainment of his ideal he advocated a peaceful general strike of all those who worked for the rich. He was thus one of the first champions of the idea of the general strike. Maréchal's concept of communism as a system of complete equality of incomes is expressed in the following sentence: "Let us convert the earth into the common property of all its inhabitants. If there is any one among you who has two mouths or four arms, it is just that we give him a double portion. But if we are all made after the same pattern, we will give every one an equal share of the cake."

The point of departure of Maréchal's *Manifesto* was the rejection of the purely formal equality as expressed in the Declaration of the Rights of Man and the insistence on real equality in the enjoyment of the good things of life. That equality, according to the *Manifesto,* can only be realized if the great majority no longer works for a small minority, if the distinction between rich and poor is abolished, if the land ceases to be private property, and if the fruits of the earth belong to all. For this purpose it is necessary to establish a Republic of Equals. "We claim," says the *Manifesto,* "henceforth to live and to die equals, as we have been born equals. We demand real equality or death; that is what we must have. And we will have this real equality, no matter at what price. Woe to those whom we meet, coming between it and us! Woe to whomsoever offers resistance to so determined a desire. The French Revolution is only a forerunner of another revolution, still greater, still more solemn, and which will be the last. . . . We must have this equality, not merely transcribed in the declaration of the rights of man and of the citizen: we must have it in our midst, under the roof of our houses. We consent to everything for its sake, to make a *tabula rasa* so that we may cleave to it alone. Perish, if need be, all the arts, provided there remains to us real equality!"

One of the sentences of his *Manifesto of the Equals* in which Maréchal advocated the disappearance of "the revolting distinction between those who rule and those who are ruled" was ridiculed and rejected by Buonarrotti, Babeuf's fellow conspirator and during the 1830's the inspirer of the communist movement known as Babouvism.

BUONARROTTI

Filippo Michele Buonarrotti (1761-1837), believed to be a lineal descendant of Michelangelo's brother, was at first active in the liberation of Italy from the domination of her various despotic rulers. Forced to flee from his native country he eventually went to Paris, where in 1792 he joined the republican opponents of the monarchy and was granted the honorary title of French citizen. In 1796 he participated in the "Conspiracy of the Equals." Arrested and convicted, he spent ten years in prison. Banished from France, he lived first in Geneva and later in Brussels, where in 1827 he published his *History of Babeuf's Conspiracy*. This book was to become the inspiration of various "Babouvist"-communist groups and sects active in France during the 1830's and 1840's. One of his disciples was the famous conspirator Auguste Blanqui.

As mentioned before, Buonarrotti had rejected as ridiculous Maréchal's sentence about "the revolting distinction between those who rule and those who are ruled." He had accepted the *Manifesto*'s ideal of complete equality of rewards, but his romanticism did not go so far as to assume that all government would become superfluous on the morning after the revolution. He firmly believed in the necessity of a dictatorship by the victorious conspirators, for he was convinced that, if permitted to vote after a revolution, the masses would invariably bring back the reactionaries. Skeptical of the intelligence of the masses, he had no doubt about the good intentions of their liberators. During the 1820's he actually called one of his secret organizations *Sublimes maîtres parfaits* ("Sublime Perfect Masters").[1] It may not be amiss to mention here that, prior to 1848, the terms "communism," "democracy," and "revolutionary dictatorship" were practically interchangeable, communist slogans being used for the purpose of establishing a revolutionary dictatorship which was meant to be a transitional period prior to the establishment of a democratic regime. It was not considered good manners to ask how this transition from a dictatorial to a democratic regime would be effected.

AUGUSTE BLANQUI

Out of the maze of the various, often mutually hostile, "Babouvist" groups manned chiefly by educated déclassés and a sprinkling of self-educated workers, there emerged during the 1830's the personality of Auguste Blanqui (1805-81), who, for several decades, was to impose the stamp of his name and of his ideas upon the activities of France's revolutionary intelligentsia and who was to fructify the minds of many rebels in other countries as well.[2]

A man of extraordinary gifts, an indomitable will, and a domineering temper, Blanqui was the very opposite of a utopian dreamer. He never discussed the structure of the ideal system he wished to see established after the overthrow of the existing regime. He apparently preferred not to antagonize the followers of any of the various radical sects whom he hoped to win over. His political creed could be condensed in two simple propositions: the forcible overthrow of the monarchy was to be followed by the establishment of a "Parisian dictatorship" over the rest of France (i.e., the rule of Blanqui's party of conspirators); that dictatorship was to perform the task of breaking the hold of the Church over the minds of the masses.

He was firmly convinced that as long as the masses were under the sway of religion, they would, under a democratic setup, always return reactionary majorities to parliament, thus undoing the victory of the revolution. Once in power, the revolutionists would proceed with gradual reforms. In short, what Blanqui actually wanted was a benevolent anticlerical dictatorship that would usher in a sort of New Deal—with socialism as a distant goal when the economic conditions were ripe for it.

Blanqui spent nearly half of his long life in various prisons because of the many uprisings in which he was the leading figure, yet, ironically, the Republic emerged not because of the revolts of his followers but as a result of the victory of Prussian arms in 1870 and of the disunity of the monarchists, who could not agree on the dynasty to rule France. The revolutionary dictatorship to which he had been aspiring since the 1830's was no longer needed to save the country from the double incubus of monarchy and priest rule. Such social changes as were necessary, he concluded, would be accomplished gradually within the framework of the Republic. He became convinced that "the abolition of exploitation of man by man" would be accomplished by "the future generation thanks to the instrument which we have bestowed upon it since 1848: universal suffrage." The progress of public education had converted him to very moderate gradualism.

However, it is not this septuagenarian well-nigh right-wing socialist Blanqui that is usually thought of whenever his name is mentioned. His reputation is based upon his "putschism," on the idea that a small, even very small, determined minority could accomplish a social revolution by a daring coup leading to the seizure of power. The lever to that revolution Blanqui saw in the educated déclassés, or as Alan B. Spitzer put it in *The Revolutionary Theories of Louis Auguste Blanqui*: ". . . in the existence of a small group whose knowledge of the roots of oppression was not coupled with the desire to profit by it. Since the great mass was too ignorant to free itself, the instructed and altruistic few would have to strike the first blows in the battle for the freedom for all."

The idea that the "instructed few" would display "altruism" after the seizure of power was the great "life-lie" of Blanqui and all similarly minded post-Blanquist revolutionists. When the latter-day Russian followers of the early Blanqui, who preferred to call themselves Marxists-Leninists, won "the battle for the freedom for all," their "altruism" converted one-third of the globe into one big police state.

WILHELM WEITLING

Blanqui's career shows how time and democratic liberties may convert even the most fiery social insurrectionist into a mild-mannered gradualist. Such was also the evolution of a German pre-Marxist communist rebel of the 1830's and 1840's who, like Blanqui, had taken his original inspiration from the Babouvists. His name was Wilhelm Weitling (1808-71). The illegitimate son of a German servant girl and a Napoleonic officer, he had tasted both the humiliation of his "irregular" birth and the miseries of an underpaid manual worker—he was a tailor by trade. Self-educated, he had concocted a sort of ultraradical communist theory of his own, the result of a combination of Babouvist dictatorial ideas with primitive Christian thunderings against the rich. One peculiar aspect of his gospel was his hope that the denizens of the criminal underworld might become an effective ally of the manual workers in their guerrilla warfare against the bourgeoisie. It would seem that this idea greatly impressed Michael Bakunin, the later champion of anarchism, who had met him in Switzerland during the early 1840's.

Like Blanqui, Weitling had a very high opinion of himself. In a not too veiled form, he hinted that he was "a second Messiah, greater than the first"[3]—a megalomania which was probably a compensation for his lowly origin, just as Blanqui's conviction that he was the dictatorial man of destiny might have been an overcompensation for the fact that, for all the risks he was taking, his physical courage was not on a par with his other qualities.

Disappointed with his loss of influence among the German radical malcontents, particularly due to the growing prestige of Karl Marx, Weitling went to the United States, where the conditions of political liberty and economic opportunity turned the once fiery rebel to harmless utopian schemes of communist colonies and industrial exchange banks. The only element that remained of his European past was his domineering character and his belief in his dictatorial indispensability in whatever enterprise he was engaged in. Are those correct who suspect that, next to the hatred of tyranny, the lust for power is the greatest stimulus of revolt?

To Karl Marx, Weitling's successful rival in the leadership of the early German communists, belongs a place apart in the gallery of champions of nineteenth-century radicalism. He was a rebel, of course, but he was also the spiritual fountainhead of three generations of radicals of various schools. It is for this reason that his role will be appreciated in the following chapter which deals with those opponents of the capitalist system who made a dent in history primarily as critics of the status quo.

MICHAEL BAKUNIN

Speaking in Marxian terms, there is a "class angle" for explaining the revolutionary ardor of a Babeuf, a Blanqui, or a Weitling—the first two impecunious intellectuals in an era of a rising commercial and industrial bourgeoisie, while the self-educated tailor was born into a world which as yet had no labor unions that might appreciate his talents. But there is no such economic interpretation for the career of Michael Bakunin (1814-76), who was one of the most heroic figures among nineteenth-century rebels. Bakunin was a member of tsarist Russia's ruling aristocratic caste, the scion of a family of wealthy landed noblemen. Reasons of a purely psychological character made him declare war not merely on the system prevailing in his country but on all the powers of the world. There are those who explain his titanic revolt by his sex frustration—his "sister-fixation" and ensuing total impotence or indifference toward all other women. Be that as it may, after serving for three years as an officer in the imperial army, Bakunin gave up his military career to devote himself to the study of philosophy in Germany, Switzerland, Belgium, and France. He became acquainted with the views of Proudhon[4] and Marx[5] and assimilated in his mind elements of both philosophies, accepting from the former the libertarian outlook and the "negation" of the state, and from the latter the "materialist interpretation of history" and the idea of the class struggle. These concepts were to become the basis of his revolutionary anarchist philosophy. Yet almost throughout his life his anarchism was shot through with a powerful admixture of democratic Slavic nationalism, a sort of revolutionary Pan-Slavism fortified with a chauvinistic aversion to Germans and Jews.

During the revolutionary years of 1848 and 1849 he participated in the uprisings of Prague and Dresden. Arrested and condemned to death, he was finally handed over to the Russian authorities. After six years of imprisonment, he was exiled to Siberia, from where he escaped in 1861.

Back in Western Europe, he preached the gospel of revolutionary Pan-Slavism and in 1863 gave his active support to the Polish insurgents who struck out for their independence from Russia. By the middle of the 1860's, his nationalistic ardor cooled. Bakunin devoted himself entirely to general revolutionary activities in Western Europe and to the elaboration of his anarchist theories. However, for all his prolific writings, he never published a comprehensive work setting down his theories.

After a few years in Italy, where he won many followers among the déclassé intellectuals, he settled in Switzerland in 1867. There he joined first the League for Peace and Liberty, a society of middle-class pacifists which he tried to win over to his ideas. A year later (1868) he left it to join the Geneva section of the International Workingmen's Association (the First International), which was at that time controlled by Marx, although his followers were a minority within that agglomeration of political groups and trade unions professing a variety of social philosophies. Bakunin, when joining the International, actually planned to wrest its control from Marx and make it into an instrument for his own revolutionary plans. The struggle for power between Bakunin and Marx came to a head in 1872, when Bakunin and his followers were expelled from the International, although they constituted at that time an actual majority within the organization.

Bakunin's ideas were subject to continuous changes, or, to be more exact, to a continuous evolution. In its final version his social philosophy was a combination of "anarchism" and "collectivism." Under anarchism Bakunin understood the negation of the state as a matter of principle and its immediate abolition after the victorious revolution. However, numerous documents from his pen—letters and secret circulars to his close followers—point unmistakably to the fact that Bakunin believed in the necessity of a revolutionary dictatorship by his own following, apparently as a transitional phase before the final liquidation of all forms of government. (At bottom this did not differ at all from the Marx-Engels concept of the "withering away of the State" as a sequel of the "dictatorship of the proletariat".) Under "collectivism" Bakunin understood the seizure of the means of production by the *workers' associations*, a concept which he opposed to what he called the "communism" of Marx and of other socialists who advocated the seizure of the industries by the *government*. In *this* respect there is a substantial difference between the concepts of Bakunin and those of Marx.

At the time when Bakuninism was in vogue, during the later 1860's and the 1870's, its followers came from the same stratum as those of Blanqui—the impecunious, déclassé lower middle-class intellectuals, the proverbial lawyers without clients, physicians without patients, underpaid or unemployed journalists, college graduates or undergraduates without prospects for jobs. They were badly in need of an immediate radical social change, in short, of a social revolution that would secure them *immediately* a place in the sun. To the Italian, Spanish, Balkan, and Russian following of Bakunin the immediate abolition of the state meant the same thing that the "Parisian dictatorship" meant to their French fellow déclassés, except that Bakunin, by insisting—in his *public* pronouncements, that is—on the *immediate* destruction of all government power, was much less candid than Blanqui. The Russian rebel's double game was an outcome of his rivalry with Marx, whom he endeavored to outdo in radicalism by launching a slogan that sounded more radical than the "dictatorship of the proletariat."

Bakunin's followers were not utopian sectarians who could actually believe in the *immediate* abolition of all state authority. This was clearly demonstrated by his Spanish disciples shortly after the proclamation of the first Spanish Republic in 1873. During the turbulent days of that period the Spanish Bakuninists, who were influential among the lower middle-class intellectuals and who also had a following among the workers, participated in the provisional governments established in a number of cities by left-wing republicans—their theoretical "anti-statism" notwithstanding.

Bakunin's following in France was not as numerous as in the other countries outside England and Germany, where favorable economic conditions fostered the development of gradualist (or "reformist") movements, such as trade unionism and democratic socialism. Blanqui's prestige in France was an obvious handicap to the spread of Bakunin's competing gospel in that country. Yet two of French radicalism's most illustrious figures, Paul Lafargue and Jules Guesde, were during the 1870's in the camp of the Russian rather than of the

French superrevolutionist. As time went on, both the economic evolution of the industrially backward countries and the liberalization or democratization of political institutions weakened the appeal of extreme radicalism and paved the ground for the spread of a political creed which combined radical, irreconcilable verbiage of hostility to capitalism with a moderate, law-abiding, gradualist practice—in short, the democratic socialism advocated by Marx since the organization of the [First] International in 1864. In the course of that development both Lafargue and Guesde joined the Marxist camp, the former to become its outstanding theorist, while the latter, because of his oratorical and journalistic gifts, became the eponymous leader of the French democratic Marxists (the "Guesdists"), as distinguished from those French socialists who did not use the Marxist vocabulary. Lafargue's and Guesde's example was followed by the Bakuninist intellectual elite in most countries except Spain. Andrea Costa became the founder of the Italian Socialist party, while Plekhanov and Axelrod went down in history as the founders of Russian Marxism.

It may not be amiss to mention here that, after the collapse of the revolutionary hopes of 1848, Marx for a while accepted wholeheartedly not only Blanqui's ideas of a revolutionary minority dictatorship, but even his tactical methods. With the followers of the French conspirator and some English revolutionaries he joined the secret Universal Society of Revolutionary Communists. The first article of the by-laws of that superrevolutionary and superconspiratorial body read as follows: "The purpose of the association is to do away with the privileged classes, to submit these classes to a dictatorship of the proletarians by maintaining the revolution in permanence until the realization of communism which is to be the last form which the human family will assume." This was also essentially the conception of the later Bakunin, except that, instead of speaking of a "dictatorship of the proletarians," he used, in his confidential missives, the expression "invisible dictatorship."[6]

NECHAYEV: THE "TIGER CUB"

A separate niche in the Pantheon of famous revolutionists is for Sergei Nechayev (1847-82), the original of the younger Verkhovensky in Dostoyevsky's *The Possessed*. A student at the St. Petersburg University in 1868-69, he had become acquainted with the writings of various Western and Russian revolutionists and considered himself a follower of Bakunin, although it is more likely that he had been just as much or even more impressed by the ideas of Babeuf and Blanqui and their concept of a revolutionary dictatorship. (It must not be forgotten that Bakunin himself, while preaching the destruction of *all* government, was at the same time firmly convinced of the necessity of the dictatorship of his own group.) To the teachings of his masters, Nechayev added the fanatical conviction—not original by any means—that in the pursuance of a good cause, revolutionists are justified in having recourse to any methods regardless of whether they are considered unethical or repulsive by the common run of humanity. It was the application of these methods in his dealings with his own comrades that established his fame, or rather notoriety, among the revolutionists of the world, as well as those of Russia. When, after a short fling at propaganda among students at the University, he was forced to go abroad in order to escape the dragnet of the police, he created the legend that he escaped from the prison of St. Peter and St. Paul—a feat commonly held impossible of achievement. Later, after his return from abroad, he murdered one of the members of his group because he refused to submit unquestioningly to his authority. Eventually, he was repudiated and execrated by his own teacher, Bakunin, who had at first admired his energy. Nechayev is believed by many to have been the author of the *Catechism of the Revolutionist* which in a way was the code of ethics followed by him.[7] In 1872 he was arrested in Switzerland and delivered to the tsarist authorities. He died in the prison of the Fortress of St. Peter and St. Paul after ten years. Nearly forty years after his death some of the Bolshevik historians proclaimed him a "superrevolutionist" and a paragon for the younger generation of communists. There is no doubt that "Nechayevshchina"—as the old-time Russian revolutionists called the ways of that fanatic—is now the only code of ethics followed by both the Soviet government and its fifth columnists the world over.

A few of the twenty-six articles of that controversial Bakunin-Nechayev code of revolutionary Machiavellian ethics follow:

"1. The revolutionist is a doomed man. He has no personal interests, no affairs, sentiments, attachments, property, not even a name of his own. Everything in him is absorbed by one exclusive interest, one thought, one passion—the revolution.

2. In the very depth of his being, not merely in word but in deed, he has broken every connection with the social order and with the whole educated world, with all the laws, appearances, and generally accepted conventions or moralities of that world which he considers his ruthless foe. Should he continue to live in it, it will be solely for the purpose of destroying it the more surely.

4. He despises public opinion. He despises and hates

the present-day code of morals with all its motivations
and manifestations. To him whatever aids the triumph
of the revolution is ethical; all that which hinders it
is unethical and criminal.

5. The revolutionist is a doomed man. He is merciless
toward the state and toward the entire system of
privileged educated classes; he need in turn expect no
mercy from them. Between him and them there is a
continuous and irreconcilable war to the bitter end—
whether it be waged openly or secretly. He must be
ready to die at any moment. He must train himself to
stand torture.

15. The whole ignoble social system must be divided
into several categories. . . .

19. The fourth category consists of ambitious officeholders and liberals of various shades. One may con-
spire with them in accordance with their programs,
making them believe that one follows them blindly and
at the same time one should take hold of them, get
possession of all their secrets, compromise them to the
utmost, so that no avenue of escape might be left to
them, and use them as instruments for stirring up
disturbances in the State.

20. The fifth category—doctrinaires [refers to Bakunin's opponents within the revolutionary camp], conspirators, revolutionists talking idly in groups and on
paper. They must be continually pushed and pulled
forward, toward practical neck-breaking statements, the
result of which would be the complete destruction of
the majority and the real revolutionary training of a
few.

25. Therefore, in getting closer to the people, we must
first of all join those elements of the masses which, since
the foundation of the Moscow state power, have never
ceased to protest, not in words alone but in deed as
well, against everything which is directly or indirectly

connected with the state: against the nobility, the bureaucracy, the clergy, the guilds [meaning the merchants and capitalists in general], and against the parasitic kulak. Let us join hands with the bold world of bandits—the only genuine revolutionists in Russia."

The defection of many of Bakunin's followers to the camp of the gradualist socialists marked the end of the insurrectionist phase of anticapitalist radicalism in the Western world. The post-Bakuninist anarchism and the crypto-Bakuninist Bolshevism were phenomena of a different kind, to be dealt with in Chapters V and VI.

A phenomenon *sui generis* was the revolutionary underground which continued to operate in tsarist Russia long after Western insurrectionism had found a pleasant grave in parliaments and trade union mansions. At variance with the law-abiding verbal non-Russian anticapitalism, Eastern radicalism was, up to 1917, its various socialist theories notwithstanding, a revolutionary movement whose objectives were strictly bourgeois-democratic.

Paradoxical as it may seem, the first revolutionary champions of bourgeois democracy, wearing the cloak of democratic socialism in Russia, were the daring "dynamiters" erroneously called "Nihilists."[8] They were the survivors of what amounted to a Children's Crusade of a whole generation of idealistic young students who, early in the 1870's, "went to the people" to arouse the peasants against the tsarist regime in the name of a naive anarchoid philosophy according to which it might be possible to leap from semifeudalism straight into the paradise of a stateless socialism without the transitional phase of capitalist industrialism.

Most of those crusaders—they were called Narodniks ("Populists")—had been delivered to the police by the peasants themselves, who suspected an intrigue of the big landowners to restore serfdom against the tsar's will.

The so-called Nihilists of the "People's Will" organization set themselves a much more modest aim. All they wanted was to convert Russia into a democratic republic or a constitutional monarchy in which peaceful socialist propaganda and activity in behalf of democratic and social reforms would be possible. The peasants having failed as a potentially revolutionary force, those revolutionists decided to rely exclusively on their own daring, on their terrorist guerrilla warfare against the tsar and his highest dignitaries.

ENTER PLEKHANOV

When this tactic too failed to achieve results some of the survivors of the revolutionary movements of the 1870's and the early 1880's concluded that there was no short cut in Russia to socialism or even political democracy Western style until, as a result of the country's economic development, there appeared on the scene a numerous industrial working class that would constitute the mass basis in the struggle for the overthrow of the tsarist regime. With the tsarist regime disposed of in a rather distant future as a result of a revolution of the urban masses, there would no longer be any need for revolutionary underground activities. The socialists of democratic Russia would then carry on the same law-abiding, parliamentary, and trade-union struggle against capitalism as did the democratic socialists in the Western countries. There would, of course, be eventually a "social" (or "socialist") revolution in accordance with Marx's prediction as to the inevitable collapse of capitalism, but that contingency was so far off that it was considered a purely academic question which it was idle to discuss.

The outstanding preacher of this theory, a former disciple of Bakunin, was George Plekhanov (1857-1918). At the outset of his revolutionary career, he was an active participant in the "Populist" (*Narodnik*) movement of the 1870's, which sought a short cut to socialism. Converted to Marxism, he became a founder of the group called "Emancipation of Labor" (1883), an embryonic stage of the Russian Social Democratic Workers party organized in 1898. Living abroad, he wrote a number of philosophical works which, when published in Russia under various pseudonyms, won many members of the Russian intelligentsia to the cause of Marxism. One of his disciples was Lenin. During the struggle between the followers and the opponents of the latter within the Russian Social Democratic Workers party, Plekhanov, who at first had sided with Lenin, eventually turned against his most famous disciple and remained his foe until his death. During the Russo-Japanese War (1904-5) he took the same attitude as all Russian revolutionists, wishing for a victory of Japan from which they expected a revolution in Russia. However, during World War I his views differed from those of most of the other Russian revolutionists. As against the defeatism of the latter who expected the downfall of the tsarist regime as a result of a military defeat, Plekhanov took a "defensist" attitude, for he believed that a world triumph of German militarism would be a greater evil than the survival of tsarism. When after the democratic revolution of March 1917 he returned to Russia, his attempts to rally a following around a program of national unity against the German foe met with little response among the revolutionists of the various schools.

Before the Revolution there were various currents within the camp of the Russian Marxists. Highly respectable scholars, mostly university professors, acclaimed Marxism as the theoretical justification of Russia's entrance upon the road of capitalist development. They were called the "legal Marxists" and did not participate in any underground activities, although they sympathized with them. Foremost among the active underground militants were Vladimir Ilyich Ulianov, better known as Lenin (1870-1924), and Julius Martov (1873-1923), at first Lenin's friend and co-worker in the St. Petersburg revolutionary underground during the 1890's, but later, in exile in Western Europe, the leader of the Russian Marxists opposed to those methods which led eventually to Lenin's complete break with democratic socialism. After his return to Russia as a result of the collapse of the tsarist regime in 1917, Martov opposed the seizure of power by Lenin's followers and had to leave the country in 1921.

THE "ECONOMISTS"

At the turn of the century both Lenin and Martov opposed a group of influential heretics within the party who were to become known as "Economists" because of their support of strikes for higher wages—a struggle which was called "economic" because it had no direct political implications. The "Economists" believed that the socialists could win the confidence of the workers *not* by trying to indoctrinate them with socialist ideas or by putting emphasis upon the struggle against absolutism, but by leaving politics to the liberal bourgeoisie and by concentrating efforts on helping workers in their bread-and-butter struggles. They argued that only after the violent suppression of strikes by the tsarist regime, proving to the workers that it was impossible to obtain any improvements under it, would the time be ripe for approaching the masses with *political* propaganda. It was a subtle plan, but the other Marxists sensed danger in it. Without saying so, they realized—so some of their critics suspected—that the workers, fighting for higher wages only and ignorant of any political issues, might eventually get out of hand; the movement might lead to wild, chaotic wage revolts, in the course of which the workers would be more anxious to force as much as possible from their employers than to ask for a more civilized form of government. Or, if in the course of the fight the tsarist government should find it expedient to grant political liberties, the workers—if not indoctrinated by the Social-Democrats—having obtained the right to organize, might become steeped in nonpolitical trade-unionism, pure and simple. In any case the Social-Democratic party, which sought political influence and power, would come out empty-handed.

The "Economists" were attacked violently in a volume entitled *What Is To Be Done?* written in 1902 by Lenin, then the outstanding personality of the Russian Social Democratic Workers party founded in 1898.

"WHAT IS TO BE DONE?"

The R.S.D.W.P. was a "workers' party" only in a Pickwickian sense, for most of its members were college-bred intellectual workers in search of a working-class following. Taking its inspiration from Marx, that party was distinguished from the other revolutionary groups in that it saw in the industrial workers the force which eventually would break the backbone of the hated tsarist system. Other opponents of Russian absolutism, such as the "Socialist-Revolutionists" (or "SR's"), expected the accomplishment of that task from the dissatisfied peasant masses. Organized in 1900, the Social Revolutionists combined elements of both old-time "Populism" with the terrorist tactics of the "People's Will" (the so-called "Nihilists").

At first all sections of the Russian Social-Democratic Workers party were in full agreement as to the character the hoped-for revolution was to assume. It was to give power to the middle-class parties, including the representatives of the peasantry; the Social-Democratic leaders of the working class were to constitute the law-abiding opposition, following the example of the social-democratic, socialist or labor parties of the democratic Western European countries.

Soon after the turn of the century, however, the harmony among the Russian Marxists was disturbed by the ideas put forward by the dynamic personality of Lenin. These ideas concerned primarily the organizational nature of the party and only later came to affect the very character of the Revolution itself.

In *What Is To Be Done?* Lenin laid down his specific conception of the methods of revolutionary activity. The crucial point of his argument was insistence upon the paramount importance of a body of professional revolutionists to direct the whole movement in an efficient manner. This was coupled with a belief in the necessity of recognizing as party members only those who were active participants in the party's underground activities. This would leave out all middle-of-the-road sympathizers from among the educated middle class—professional men, university students, and high-school boys and girls—who did not have the courage to burn their bridges behind them. In Lenin's opinion this course would avert the danger of swamping the party with weak-kneed adherents who might dampen its combative spirit.

With this object in view Lenin insisted on the greatest possible extension of the powers given to the Central Committee of the party, which was to direct all revolutionary activities. These powers included confirming the personnel of the local committees and even of nominating their members. These proposals met with the strongest opposition on the part of most of the old-time militants of Russian Marxism. Instead of a movement based on mass support, they asserted, Lenin wanted an organization of conspirators—his attitude implying a belief that revolutions could be planned in advance—as opposed to the genuine Marxist viewpoint that revolutions occurred but were not made. Some of Lenin's opponents, indeed, went so far as to call his postulates Bonapartist, because, if carried out, his scheme would have concentrated all the power in his hands. Among his opponents at that time was Leon Trotsky, who admitted no necessity for such a centralization of power and was inclined to suspect Lenin of ambitions for personal dictatorship. Denouncing this ambition, Trotsky wrote in 1904 that "for the dictatorship of the proletariat Lenin wanted to substitute the dictatorship of the party over the proletariat, for the dictatorship of the party—the dictatorship of the Central Committee over the party, and for the dictatorship of the Central Committee—the dictatorship of Lenin over the Central Committee."

Lenin's position was based upon two fundamental concepts: his very realistic understanding of the mentality of the working masses who, in his opinion, could think only in terms of wages and hours, but not in terms of social systems; and his quite unrealistic faith in, or hypocritical presumption of, the infallibility, good intentions, and messianic role of revolutionary leadership, as personified by himself and those intellectuals who accepted his views. (To be sure, among these intellectuals were also included exceptional, self-taught ex-workers who had succeeded in absorbing certain elements of education enabling them to assume leadership.)

This skepticism with regard to the ability of the masses to evolve socialist concepts out of their own midst, found its expression in a famous passage contained in the aforementioned *What Is to Be Done?*: "The history of all countries shows that, by its own efforts, the working class can develop only a trade-union consciousness—that is, the realization of the need of getting together in unions in order to fight employers and to demand from the government the passing of laws necessary for the workers."

As against this inability of the masses to overcome, by their own efforts, their subordination to "bourgeois ideology" (i.e., the acceptance of the legitimacy of the existing system), Lenin emphasized the fact that "the theory of socialism grew out of the philosophic, historical, and economic theories that were elaborated by the educated representatives of the propertied classes, the intellectuals. The founders of modern scientific socialism, Marx and Engels, belonged to the bourgeois intelligentsia . . ." (*ibid.*).

To a large extent this view of Lenin's was derived from an opinion expressed in 1901—a year before the appearance of Lenin's book—by Karl Kautsky, chief exponent of Marxian orthodoxy in Germany. In an article published in the theoretical organ of the German Social-Democratic party (*Neue Zeit,* 1901-2, XX, I, No. 3, p. 79) Kautsky wrote: "Socialism and the class struggle [Kautsky has in mind the wage struggles of the manual workers] arise side by side and not one out of the other; each arises out of different premises. Modern socialist consciousness can arise only on the basis of profound scientific knowledge. . . . The vehicles of science are not the proletariat but the *bourgeois intelligentsia* [emphasized in the original]: It was out of the heads of the members of this stratum that modern socialism originated, and it was they who communicated it to the more intellectually developed proletarians who, in their turn, introduced it into the proletarian class struggle where conditions allow that to be done. Thus socialist consciousness is something introduced into the proletarian class struggle from without and not something that arose within it spontaneously."

It is beside the point here whether this view of the nonworking-class origin of socialism was in keeping with the original concepts of Marxism. Kautsky may have advanced this view merely in order to put in their place those ex-horny-handed trade union leaders within the social-democratic movement who, in their rivalry with the college-bred leaders, occasionally tried to prejudice the masses against lawyers, journalists, and professors holding top positions within the socialist movement. The fact remains that Kautsky and Lenin, two outstanding thinkers of modern socialism (including communism), took it for granted that a set of ideas introduced into the labor movement from a nonworking-class stratum, was nevertheless the true expression of the interests of the manual workers. To be sure, individual heretics within the radical intelligentsia, turning against their own group, suspected that the gift of socialism was a Trojan horse of the underprivileged, declassed lower middle-class intelligentsia, and that at bottom, the idea of socialization was nothing but the substitution of a new privileged class of managerial and political officeholders for the individual entrepreneurs and stockholders of private capitalism. But naturally enough, their logical arguments were powerless to overcome the interested rationalizations of those who were out to "emancipate" the working class by taking their historical turn as a ruling elite.

Lenin's insistence upon a strictly centralized, near-military form of organization led in 1903 to the historical split within the ranks of the Russian Marxists. The followers of Lenin, known as "Bolsheviks," were henceforth arrayed against the "Mensheviks" whose views were more or less identical with those of the traditional European socialist parties. Eventually, the rift between the two groups was to go beyond the mere organizational concept of the movement. It became a conflict between democratic "gradualism"— aiming at peaceful transition from capitalism to collectivism—and dictatorial revolutionism employing the methods of conspiracies and armed uprisings. At the time when the Bolsheviks ceased to call themselves social-democrats and assumed the "communist" label (1918), the difference between the communists and socialists had become a class conflict between the more impecunious and hence more adventurous section of the intellectual and white collar workers (with a sprinkling of well-to-do neurotics in search of a new religion) on the one hand, and the more sedate labor politicians with a "proletarian" vocabulary, whose ambitions did not go beyond the laurels of a parliamentary career or of a cabinet post within the capitalist system, on the other.

The unsuccessful Russian Revolution of 1905 deepened the original split by expanding it from the field of mere organizational to that of tactical methods. As the upheaval approached—the disastrous war with Japan had brought the downfall of the hated regime within the sphere of imminent probabilities—the Mensheviks began to get ready, so to speak, for the modest role they expected to play in the future parliament of a democratic Russia. They saw themselves as a party of parliamentary opposition to a regime headed by middle-class liberals. A government of this kind was in their opinion the only solution under the prevailing economic conditions.

Lenin's solution was different. He believed that the liberal bourgeoisie was too pusillanimous to take the energetic measures needed to hold what had been won. The forces of reaction, in his opinion, were bound to come back—as they had done in Western Europe in 1848—if the government were to be left in the hands of the liberals. His way out was a "democratic dictatorship of the proletariat and the peasantry." These two classes would have to assume power and by ruthless measures destroy all vestiges of tsarism and render its return impossible. This, however, was not to be a social revolution. The "proletariat and the peasantry" were to exert their dictatorship only for the purpose of establishing an honest-to-goodness bourgeois-democratic system on the Western-European model. The big landowners, the mainstay of absolutism, were to be dispossessed and their land was to be distributed among the peasants. Some concessions with respect to wages, hours, and other conditions of labor would be made to the workers. Stripped of its specific terminology ("dictatorship of the proletariat and of the peasantry"), what the Bolshevik program of that period called for was the establishment of a coalition government of representatives of the Bolshevik professional revolutionists active among the industrial workers, and of those non-Marxian socialist intellectuals, lawyers, journalists, politicians, and ex-conspirators, known under the name of "Social Revolutionaries" or "Socialist Revolutionists," who were influential among the peasant masses.

During the Revolution of 1905 neither of the two Marxist factions nor the "Populist" Socialist Revolutionists were able to marshal enough popular forces to bring about the downfall of the initially shaken tsarist regime. So the factional strife, conducted mainly by refugees in periodicals published outside of Russia, continued until the Revolution of 1917, when the tsarist regime collapsed under the blows of the German army, which brought about the mutiny and the fraternization of the garrisons of Petrograd and Moscow with the war-weary and hungry population that demonstrated on the streets of the two capitals.

1917

The provisional government established in March 1917 by the liberals and the right-wing near-Socialist Revolutionists headed by Kerensky was supported by the right-wing Mensheviks, who jointly with the Socialist-Revolutionists and the liberals were in favor of continuing the war and of driving the Germans out of the occupied territories. It is the belief of many critics that their reluctance to conclude a separate peace with the kaiser gave Lenin's party in November 1917 the opportunity to ride into power on the crest of the general war weariness and of the land-hunger of the peasant-soldiers.

Neither the Mensheviks nor the Socialist Revolutionists were willing to accept the dictatorship of the Bolsheviks. As long as there was still some semblance of political liberty the Mensheviks conducted a vigorous campaign against the new regime which they often embarrassed by encouraging strikes on the part of the workers under their influence. By 1920-21 their press was silenced, and they were either imprisoned or forced to leave the country. The Socialist Revolutionists resorted to the old weapon they had used against the tsarist regime—terrorism. One of their members, Fanya Kaplan, seriously wounded Lenin in an attempt upon his life. Another member killed the chief of the Soviet secret police in Petrograd (renamed Leningrad after Lenin's death). They were particularly incensed against the new regime, for the general elections had given them a large majority of representatives to the Constituent Assembly, which the Bolsheviks dispersed on the very day of its opening. They could actually claim to be the legitimate rulers of the country by all standards recognized by democratic socialists. The Soviet government put a stop to their terrorist activities by holding all their leaders as hostages and threatening to execute them if there should be a recurrence of political assassinations.

Since that time the Socialist Revolutionists have either disappeared or merged with the Mensheviks in exile. Some of the Menshevik intellectuals who had remained in Russia and withdrawn from all political activity were permitted by the Soviet government to hold positions in various cultural and economic institutions. In 1932 Stalin, harassed by economic difficulties, used these men as scapegoats at one of the first "Moscow trials." They were offered the alternative of being shot or of "confessing" to acts of sabotage and counter-revolutionary plots. They "confessed."

There are no reports about present-day Menshevik activities in the U.S.S.R. The two most prominent survivors of the Old Guard—both of them in New York —are still active as critics of the regime—the octogenarian Raphael Abramovich, the editor of the monthly *Socialist Courier* (in Russian), and Boris Nicolaievsky, a well-known historian.

Chapter III

THE CRITICS

Criticism of economic inequality has been the basic feature of social discontent in all ages. A combination of such criticism with remedies negating the principle of private ownership of land and the *means of production* has been the essence of anticapitalist radicalism for the past few centuries.

The utopians and the rebels dealt with in the preceding chapters contributed a large share to this criticism. Their protest was joined during the last century by a number of scholarly economists and social theorists who anticipated many of the ideas constituting the basis of what Gregor Strasser, one of the victims of Hitler's blood purge of June 30, 1934, called "anticapitalist longing."

WILLIAM THOMPSON

One of the forerunners of such modern socialist ideas was William Thompson (1783-1833), a prosperous Irish landowner with a progressive and humanitarian outlook, who was greatly influenced by the ideas of Jeremy Bentham and later by those of Robert Owen. In his opinion "the greatest happiness of the greatest number" (Bentham) could be obtained only under a social system which has done away with the unearned income of the landowner and the capitalist. In criticizing the existing system, he argued, as Anton Menger puts it,[1] that both the land rent of the landowner and the profit of the capitalist represent deductions from what had been produced by labor, deductions made to the detriment of the worker and which are only possible because the landowner's and the capitalist's right of the stronger is recognized by law. Much of Thompson's early criticism of capitalism was taken over by such socialist economists as Rodbertus and Marx; the term "surplus value," one of the most frequently used expressions in the Marxist vocabulary, was used by Thompson as far back as 1825 (when Marx was seven years old) in his *Inquiry into the Principles of the Distribution of Wealth*.

Thompson opposed the beneficiaries of rent and profit because, in his opinion, these two forms of income contradicted his concept that the worker was entitled to obtain the whole product of his labor, or, as he put it, to "secure to the producer the free use of whatever his labor has produced."

To do away with the injustices which he thought were inherent in the capitalist system, Thompson proposed Owen's remedy of the organization of co-operative settlements—the land necessary for these settlements either to be bought or rented. He visualized those settlements as co-operative communities of 500 to 2000 persons engaged in agricultural and industrial work. The principle upon which these communities were to be built is *man's right to exist*, for everyone would be supplied with food, clothing, and housing, while the children were to be brought up in common. In writing about Thompson's views Anton Menger assumes that Thompson's insistence upon the "right to the whole product of labor" was meant as a protest against "surplus value" and private property and that it was not to be applied to a system in which these two were abolished. In a communist society the "right to the whole produce of labor" was apparently to apply not to the individual but rather collectively to the sum total of all individuals, all persons able to work being equally obliged to do so.

JOHN FRANCIS BRAY

Another critic of the capitalist system, whose ideas anticipated many of the concepts of Proudhon and Marx, was John Francis Bray (1809-95), an American-born English socialist, the author of *Labour's Wrongs and Labour's Remedy* (1839). "The capitalists and proprietors," Bray wrote, "do no more than give the workingmen, for his labor of one week, a part of the wealth which they obtained from him the week before." Speaking about the privileged classes, he says that their wealth "has all been derived from the bones and sinews of the working classes during successive ages, and it has been taken from them by the fraudulent and slavery-creating system of unequal exchanges." He did not believe that a mere change of government would remedy the situation, for in his opinion "every form of government, and every social and governmental wrong, owes its rise to the existing social system—the institution of property as it at present exists." Hence he concluded that "community of possessions is in every respect the most perfect form of society which man can institute." However, he believed in the necessity of a transitional phase between the system of private enterprise and full communism. That "intermediate resting place," as he called it, he visualized in the form of producers' co-operatives. He hoped these aims might be achieved by persuasion rather than by violence and compulsion. But he was not quite sure that the governments would permit such peaceful changes.

PROUDHON, THE AN-ARCHIST

The names of Thompson and Bray are hardly remembered today—even by scholars. Somewhat luckier was another champion of early nineteenth-century anticapitalism—Pierre Joseph Proudhon (1809-65). Most educated laymen are familiar with the famous phrase "property is theft," constituting Proudhon's answer to the title of his first book, *Qu'est ce que la propriété?* ("What Is Property?") published in 1840. This phrase, by the way, the author had purloined from an earlier French writer, the Girondist Brissot de Warville who, in using it, had in mind only feudal property, of course. It is ironical that these three words should be the only thing that survived from the threescore volumes of his collected works and correspondence.

Proudhon was an enemy of capitalism, but what he opposed to it was not what the other schools of anticapitalism understood by socialism or communism. His answer to capitalism was the organization of a "people's bank" that would grant free credit to all those willing to become independent producers.

Proudhon was the first writer ever to call himself an anarchist, though, to explain what he had in mind, he placed a hyphen between "an" and "archy" thus conveying the idea that, etymologically speaking, the "anarchy" he aspired to meant "without government" or "self-government," and not "disorder" as the word is usually understood.

Proudhon was given to verbal fireworks, and his learned admirers among anarchist historians were often at a loss to understand what he really meant. His writings abound in contradictions, so that he actually could become all things to all men. He "negated" the state; hence he was venerated as the "Father of Anarchy" by two generations of anarchists, the followers of Bakunin and those of Kropotkin, who preached the complete destruction of all government authority. Yet what Proudhon actually advocated was local or regional autonomy obtained by "breaking up France into twelve independent states and demoting Paris" [from its role as capital].[2]

Proudhon called himself a revolutionist—yet he was opposed to violence, while to practically all later anarchists (except those of the Tolstoyan school) violence was the main stock in trade as opposed to the "legalism" of the democratic socialists. He was an enemy of economic privilege, yet he was opposed not only to expropriation but even to strikes and to labor unions. A champion of progressive ideas, he was a rabid opponent of feminism; he was full of contempt for universal suffrage (one of the reasons why the French monarchists, at the time when Georges Sorel had his short-lived flirtation with them, forty years after Proudhon's death, suddenly discovered a great affection for him). He was also given to observations about the Jews and the Negroes which were just as disconcerting as the casual remarks made on the same subject by Karl Marx. His glorification of war for its own sake was as shocking as anything that Oswald Spengler perpetrated on the same theme.

No wonder then that even serious thinkers who take up the study of his works nearly a century after he had written them often come to curious conclusions about the actual role played by the once famous founder of the now extinct school of "mutualist anarchism." One of these scholars, Professor J. Salwyn Schapiro—the author of otherwise very valuable contributions to modern history—arrived at the strange conclusion that the "Father of Anarchy" was in reality a herald of Fascism. Proudhon's hostility to both capitalism and the various schools of socialism of his time, reflected, in Professor Schapiro's opinion, the fact that he spoke on behalf of the middle class whose interests he saw threatened both by the financiers from above and by the rebellious workers from below. It was on this point that Professor Schapiro saw an analogy between Proudhonism and Fascism, which he quite correctly calls a movement of the [lower] middle classes.

The paradox implied in the discovery that one of the most famous exponents of libertarian opposition to the state was in reality the proto-champion of the gospel according to Mussolini is certainly breathtaking and highly amusing. But fortunately for the reputation of Proudhon, who after all was not a villain, that discovery is based on a misunderstanding. The lower middle classes championed by Proudhon were quite different from those who constituted the chief support of Fascism. The author of *What is Property?* had in mind the interests of the small independent producers and of those who aspired to join their ranks, that is, of the skilled workers who hoped to open their own little shops. That was the *old* lower middle class. It was in line with Proudhon's championship of this social group that he was opposed to labor unions and to the class struggle. For these had no meaning to a group of aspiring independent producers.

On the other hand, the *new* middle and lower middle class of the Mussolini-Hitler era consisted chiefly of the *educated and semi-educated scions of the old middle classes.* Their ambition was not cheap credit for attaining economic independence as small producers in an era dominated by big industry, but a chance to get a salaried job with the central or local governments, or with the various nationalized or municipalized enterprises controlled by either of them. Hence, the basic principle of Fascism was the deification of the state with its millions of jobs covering every aspect of the nation's life. In direct contradiction to this view, Proudhon's "anarchism" or "anti-statism" was at bottom only a utopian or paradoxical formulation of the small producer's hostility to a voracious, ubiquitous, and all-powerful bureaucracy swallowing up a substantial part of the nation's income.

In contradistinction to Blanqui's followers who were mostly déclassé intellectuals anxious to get hold of the job-dispensing government machine, those who for nearly two decades professed and spread the views of Proudhon were mostly highly skilled workers anxious to achieve economic independence, or those stray intellectuals who were repelled by the Blanquists because they saw in their radicalism only the mask for the job-hunger of impecunious students and underpaid or unemployed journalists or other professionals.

Eventually, most of Proudhon's followers deserted the gospel of their teacher. The growth of large-scale industrialism had demonstrated to them the futility of the skilled worker's hopes for economic independence to be realized by the bootstrap scheme of people's banks or mutual credit societies. They gradually turned either to Bakuninism, Marxism, or plain trade-unionism.

Professor Schapiro admits that "there is no hint of the totalitarian corporative state in Proudhon's writings." By admitting this he virtually abandons his thesis. For *totalitarianism* is the essence of Fascism. With that essence absent from Proudhon all his reactionary vagaries are not sufficient to stamp him as a precursor of Mussolini and Hitler.

For all the harmless, nonrevolutionary methods which Proudhon advocated, he was a precursor of revolutionary anarchism in that he supplied the followers of Bakunin and Kropotkin with an "anti-statist" vocabulary and with a horror- and dread-inspiring label, which hardly contributed to the growth of the movement. In the eyes of the general public, which the anarchists tried to win, that label branded them as either villains or crackpots, even though they counted among their champions such paragons of nobility, courage, and scholarship as Kropotkin, Malatesta, and Reclus. But such is the curse of every faith that a label once adopted (or imposed from outside), no matter how damaging or preposterous, remains sacred to its followers.[3]

RODBERTUS—THE TORY SOCIALIST

More neglected than the writings of Proudhon are those of his German contemporary Johann Karl Rodbertus (1805-75). An economist of note who acknowledged labor's claims as against capital, he was the very opposite of Proudhon because of his views about the primacy of the state as against the individual. A radical Tory—he is sometimes called a conservative socialist—and a supergradualist, as it were, he rejected the class struggle and accepted—for the next five centuries—the existence of the privileged classes under a regime of a paternalistic monarchy before the state would be able to regulate every aspect of production and distribution.

His importance lies chiefly in the fact that some of his ideas (along with those of Marx) undoubtedly impressed the mind of Ferdinand Lassalle, the first champion of a socialist mass movement in Germany during the early 1860's. They may have also impressed the German Chancellor Bismarck with the idea that certain measures, such as nationalization of certain branches of industry or services, far from being subversive, could serve the purpose of strengthening the existing state and consolidating the status quo.

It is very unlikely that Rodbertus, who was a humanitarian at heart, would have enjoyed the fact that some of his ideas were made use of by the theoreticians of German national socialism. Nor is it likely that Rodbertus' younger contemporary Karl Marx would enjoy his deification by those who now call themselves communists in deference to the designation which he had chosen for himself as a gesture of defiance of the status quo.

KARL MARX

Karl Marx (1818-83) was born into a German-Jewish middle-class family which had become converted to Christianity when he was still a child. He studied at the universities of Bonn and Berlin, where he was graduated as a doctor of philosophy. Prevented from entering upon an academic career he turned to journalism, becoming in 1842 editor of the *Rheinische Zeitung*, a Liberal daily published in Cologne. Because of its vigorous democratic stand against the reactionaries at the helm of Prussia's government, the paper was suppressed in 1843. Marx, who had become familiar with the literature of the various socialist and communist schools of the period, went to Paris, where Arnold Ruge, a radical German democrat, decided to publish with him a radical magazine, *Deutsch-*

Französische Jahrbücher ("German-French Yearbooks"). There Marx published the first essays which were the fruit of his conversion to communism. They were entitled "The Jewish Question" and "Critique of Hegel's Philosophy of Law." "The Jewish Question" represents a sort of curiosity to the twentieth-century reader of Marx's works, for in it the founder of modern socialism takes the anti-Semitic stand of many mid-nineteenth century radicals who identified Jewry with capitalism. The second article contained in a germinal state, as it were, the economic interpretation of history which was to become one of the cornerstones of Marx's philosophy. He says that "juridical relations, like state forms, cannot be explained by the progress of the human mind; they are rooted in the material conditions of life." Speaking about the coming revolutionary struggle in Germany, he makes the remark that the "head of [German] emancipation is philosophy, its heart the proletariat." This has been variously interpreted to mean that in a revolution headed by philosophers, that is intellectuals, Marx needed the workers. In other words, that it was not Marx who joined the workers in *their* need for a revolution, but that it was the workers who were needed in *his* revolution. One of the critics who gave this interpretation was the former leading communist Arthur Rosenberg, who had observed how in Russia a party of professional revolutionists, mostly of lower middle-class origin, and professing the views of Marx, had used the workers in order to establish the rule of a new middle class composed of officeholders and technical managers.

While in Paris in 1844 Marx met Friedrich Engels, who was to become his life-long friend, collaborator, and benefactor. Expelled a year later from France upon the demand of the Prussian government, Marx went to Brussels, where he stayed until the outbreak of the French Revolution of February 1848. Before his expulsion from Paris he had written jointly with his friend a philosophical opus entitled *The Holy Family*, which is indicative of Marx's gradual elaboration of the economic interpretation of history and of the class-struggle theory. In Brussels he further developed his views in a book entitled *The Poverty of Philosophy*. During that period he also wrote *The German Ideology*, a philosophical work that was only published half a century after his death. However, the most important publication of that period was the pamphlet known as the *Communist Manifesto*, which has been translated into practically every language of the civilized world. The *Manifesto*, written in conjunction with Engels, was to be the statement of the ideas of the Communist League, which the two friends had joined in 1847. (That League had been in existence for several years as a secret organization of German radicals living in Belgium, England, France, and Switzerland. It had also members in Germany.)

The French Revolution of February 1848 enabled Marx to return to Paris, where all German refugees expected the outbreak of a similar revolution in Germany. When that event actually occurred Marx returned to Cologne, the place of his early radical activities, where he had edited a liberal daily six years before. He again became the editor-in-chief of a daily paper, the *Neue Rheinische Zeitung* ("New Rhenish Gazette") whose publication had been undertaken by a group of middle-class democrats and communists. Marx and his followers joined the German Democratic Party. Standing at the extreme left wing of that party, he hoped to drive the German middle classes forward to an energetic stand against the Prussian monarchy which was biding its time and waiting for the opportune moment to crush Germany's incipient democracy. Convinced that the victory of the democratic middle-class revolution had to be secured first and that to achieve this result it was necessary to avoid antagonizing and frightening the middle class, Marx during 1848 published no reports about strikes and other manifestations of the incipient labor movement. He considered that the Revolution had not been victorious as yet, that the Junker reaction still could come back, and that for this reason it was necessary not to antagonize the middle classes.

During the same period Marx supported the nationalist campaign directed against Denmark on account of two strips of territory with a predominantly German population which were claimed by Denmark. During that campaign Marx larded his criticism with chauvinistic insults against Scandinavians in general, speaking of their "permanent drunkenness," of their "brutality toward women," and of their intellectual inferiority. Chauvinistic invective—strange in a man hailed as the founder of the modern international socialist and communist movement—expressed both in his public statements and in his private correspondence, was to characterize his political utterances, whether public or private, throughout his life. When Austrian democracy was defeated in 1848-49, due to the help given the reactionaries by the various Slavic nationalities forming part of the Habsburg Empire, Marx wrote about "the Croats, Pandurs, Czechs, and similar scum" and demanded the complete "annihilation" of those "reactionary races." He even justified the subjection of eight million Slavs to four million Hungarians on the ground that the Hungarians had "more vitality and energy." In the early 1860's, he was in the habit of referring to Lassalle, the first successful founder of a socialist mass movement in Germany, as "Baron Itzig" and "the Jewish Nigger" and to his movement as the "Itzig movement"—because he personally disliked his somewhat heretical disciple. (Marx, having been baptized in his childhood and having married a Prussian noblewoman, did not consider himself a Jew.) When in 1870 the Russian revolutionist Bakunin, also a heretical disciple of his, attempted an uprising in Lyons (France), Marx objected to it because Bakunin was a "foreigner," yet he was full of praise for the two Poles, Dombrowski and Wroblewski, and the Hungarian Jew, Leo Frankel, who held high positions in the Paris Commune of 1871, of which Marx approved. (It is worth noting that in print he referred to Leo Frankel as a "German," while in his private correspondence he called him *das Jüdchen*—the little Jew.)

During his activities in Germany in 1848, he was in favor of a war against Russia, which he considered the greatest enemy of, and a permanent threat to, the survival of European democracy. A war against Russia, he wrote later in a retrospective article published in the *New York Tribune* of 1851, "would have called more active and energetic men to the helm." In other words, Marx and his friends expected to ride into power on the crest of a war.

The breakdown of the German revolution forced Marx to seek refuge in England, particularly as the reaction had triumphed in France as well. Years of misery followed, especially since his friend Engels was still unable to provide for him and his growing family. For about two years after the defeat of the revolution Marx still hoped for a return of the revolutionary wave, and during that period he took a leading part in the revived activities of the Communist League which had been held in abeyance during Marx's collaboration with the German Democratic Party. In the address to the members of the Communist League, published in March 1850, Marx encouraged his followers to collaborate with the most radical section of the progressive-republican lower middle classes, but not to permit their allies to bring the revolution to a stop; on the contrary, the revolution should be made "permanent until all the more or less possessing classes are driven from power" and the communists have taken possession of it, and the revolution, involving the nationalization of the most important industries, has spread to "all the dominant countries of the world." In short, in 1850 Marx hoped for a revolution of the kind which about seven decades later was to be carried out in Russia under the leadership of Lenin and Trotsky. The same aim was expressed, likewise in 1850, in the bylaws of the Universal Society of Revolutionary Communists, a secret organization which admitted only the chief leaders of the German communists, the French Blanquists, and of the revolutionary wing of the British Chartists. "The purpose of the organization," it was said in the bylaws, "is to do away with the privileged classes, to submit these classes to a dictatorship of the proletarians [that is, of the communist parties] by maintaining the revolution in permanence until the realization of communism which is to be the last form which the human family will assume."

Democratic socialist biographers have tried to explain Marx's "Bolshevik" utterances of that period by the fact that his "judgment had been affected by the breakdown of his immeasurable hopes." There are those, however, who believe that Marx's change of attitude toward conspiratorial activities—activities to which he had previously been opposed—could be explained by the sudden change in his social status. He had sunk into the *Neue Rheinische Zeitung* the whole of his paternal inheritance, and the breakdown of the revolution left him a penniless déclassé. Revolution to him was now the only salvation from a most desperate material situation. He began to look at it not primarily as an automatic, spontaneous process, but as the handiwork of energetic men—the view characteristic of Blanquist and, later, Leninist, but not of traditional Marxist conceptions.

Marx gave up his "ultra-leftist" position when the economic crisis, which he expected to occur in August 1850, did not materialize. There was a general economic upswing which, as Marx fully realized, sounded the death knell to his revolutionary hopes. Marx's opinion that all hopes for an early revolution were gone was not acceptable to the majority of the exiles constituting the Communist League. There was a split which led to the eventual dissolution of the League. Marx withdrew from all activities among the revolutionary emigrants and tried hard to provide for his family. An offer to write for the *New York Tribune* enabled him to earn a scant living, but his attempts to supplement his meager income by means of other literary work failed. During that period he wrote a large pamphlet entitled *The Eighteenth Brumaire of Louis Bonaparte* which deals with the French Revolution of 1848 up to the *coup d'état* of December 1851, through which Louis Bonaparte, later Napoleon III, seized absolute power. It is generally considered the most brilliant work among his political pamphlets. However, that piece of writing was only an incident in the gigantic work that was to absorb him during the 1850's and most of the 1860's. It was the preparation of his magnum opus known under the title of *Capital—A Critique of Political Economy*. The first volume was published in 1867. The other two volumes were published after his death.

In 1864 Marx reappeared on the international political scene by becoming instrumental in the foundation and the conduct of the affairs of the International Workingmen's Association, usually referred to as the

First International. He was entrusted with working out the bylaws and the program of the International, a document which became known as the Inaugural Address. In that organization he tried to steer a middle course between the extremely moderate elements, as represented by the British trade unionists and to some extent the Proudhonists, on the one hand, and the conspiratorial and insurrectionist elements, as represented by the Blanquists and the Bakuninists, on the other. He was instrumental in having Bakunin and his followers expelled from the International.

The uprising of the Paris Commune of March-May 1871 was defended and glorified by Marx in his pamphlet entitled *Civil War in France*. There are those who believe that Marx greatly overshot the mark by calling the regime a "working-class government" and by weaving a proletarian-socialist myth around the Commune.

During the last decade of his life, Marx saw the gradual decline of the influence of the other schools of socialism (including anarchism) and the rise of the socialist mass parties which took their inspiration from his teachings.

The misery and privations Marx had to endure for nearly twenty years after the downfall of the Revolution of 1848, came to an end in 1868, when his friend Engels was able to bestow upon him an annuity which secured him a life of comfort and security.

Many of Marx's personal character traits have been criticized as being those of a vindictive, power-hungry would-be dictator, unscrupulous in the choice of his methods. There are even those who speak of two different personalities living within the same man: the philosopher of genius and the dreamer who visualized a new world that has done away with exploitation, oppression, race prejudice, and all the other vestiges of the past, and the thwarted statesman who was a "Real-politiker," altogether undistinguishable from a typical bourgeois politician.

In Marx's defense one might plead that radical politics, just as all politics, is a struggle for power—a struggle in the course of which it is just as impossible to abide by the principles of ethics and fair play as it is impossible to keep one's hands from being soiled with innocent blood in the course of wars or revolutions.

MARXISM

In the following pages an attempt is made to present, in a condensed form, those philosophical, economic, and political ideas which are comprised by the term "Marxism" and which, since the middle of the last century, have served as the theoretical basis for various political parties and sects calling themselves either socialist or communist, and applying to their ideas the designation of "scientific socialism." These ideas, elaborated by Karl Marx and his alter ego Friedrich Engels, were formulated over a period of about fifty years, from 1843, when Marx published his first philosophical essays, to 1895, the year when Engels, shortly before his death, wrote his last article. It was inevitable that, in the course of half a century, the two men occasionally expressed views which were at variance with opinions they had held under other circumstances. The result of those discrepancies was a certain confusion within the Marxist camp, the moderate groups or parties taking their inspiration from ideas advanced by Marx or Engels at a more mature age, while the more radical groups, and particularly those calling themselves communists, gave their preference to the "younger Marx."

Neither Marx nor Engels left a systematic presentation of their views, which are dispersed in various books, pamphlets, addresses, and private letters. However, their most important ideas are contained in two works, the *Communist Manifesto* and *Capital*.

The Philosophical Basis. The philosophical method constituting the basis of Marxism is called dialectical materialism, a method which has defied all attempts at a clear, unequivocal definition. According to Lenin, "dialectics is the study of contradictions within the very essence of things." Applied to politics, dialectical materialism gives its believers the assurance that socialism (or communism), being the contradiction of capitalism, is inherent in the latter and is therefore bound to succeed it, since all things in the process of change produce their own contradictions. Accordingly, the American philosopher Sidney Hook called that method "a cosmic evolutionary optimism according to which the dialectic process in nature and society make the realization of communism inevitable." According to Karl Kautsky, the outstanding theorist of the democratic wing of Marxism, "every social system produces contradictions and struggles which work toward the substitution of something that is superior to the status quo. Socialism will overcome the contradictions created by capitalism, and thus produce something superior to it, but not a condition which will represent the end of all social development. New contradictions, new problems, new struggles will arise under the socialist system. However, it is absolutely impossible to foresee what will be the nature of these problems and struggles. Hence it is useless to talk about them." There were also those who, even in Marx's lifetime, predicted that the elimination of capitalism did not necessarily imply the substitution of something "superior," that is, the abolition of exploitation of man by man. They anticipated the bureaucratic police state (as embodied now by the Soviet system) under which the officeholder and manager would take the place of the capitalist property owner.

The Materialist Conception of History. Called also "historical materialism," "economic interpretation of history," "economic determinism," and "economic materialism," this theory explains the historical process as the outgrowth of economic conditions, or more exactly, of the technical methods of production, the latter being the foundation determining the character of what Marx called the "superstructure," that is, the political, juridical, and cultural aspects of a given form of society. "The hand-loom," Marx's collaborator Engels wrote, "created the feudal system, while the mechanical loom created the capitalist system."

The Class Struggle. Another basic idea of Marxism is contained in the sentence of the *Communist Manifesto* which says that "the history of all hitherto existing society is the history of class struggles." Marx did not claim that he discovered "the existence of classes in modern society or of their struggles against each other." His contribution, he wrote, consisted in proving that "the class struggle was inevitably leading to the dictatorship of the proletariat." The bourgeoisie, according to Marx, included the urban propertied classes (financiers, industrialists, merchants), while the "proletariat" was the collective term for all those receiving only wages or salaries. The class antagonism in modern society, as Marx saw it, is one between employers and employees. This concept has given rise to the criticism that, consciously or unconsciously, Marx was concealing the actual or budding antagonism between the manual workers and the "new middle class" of salaried men (professionals, engineers, technicians, managers). These critics have emphasized the fact that the social fabric of the U.S.S.R., in which the manual workers and lower white collar employees are subjected to a privileged stratum of officeholders and managers, has demonstrated Marx's error in stressing the question of *property* rather than that of *income* in drawing his distinction between the classes. According to Marx the class struggle within the capitalist system is bound to result in the victory of the "proletariat" which, in turn, would result in the "abolition of classes" and the establishment of a "classless society." There are those who, by pointing to the countries behind the Iron Curtain, claim that the abolition of the capitalist system, far from establishing a "classless society," has substituted a new elite of officeholders for the old elite of property owners.

Dictatorship of the Proletariat. This is a term which both Marx and Engels used only on two occasions and which neither ever elaborated. In a letter written in 1852 to his friend Weydemeyer, Marx said that the "class struggle necessarily leads to the dictatorship of the proletariat" and "this dictatorship is itself only a transition to the ultimate abolition of all classes and to a society without classes." It has been pointed out that as workers lack the education necessary for exercising political power—dictatorial or otherwise—this "dictatorship of the proletariat" would in fact be a dictatorship of ex-workers and professionals, and that, Soviet-style, those exercising dictatorship would not be in a hurry to liquidate their own rule. Marx used that term once more in 1875 in a letter which contained the following passage: "Between the capitalist and communist society lies the period of the revolutionary transformation of the one into the other. To this there corresponds also a political transition period, in which the state can be nothing else than the revolutionary dictatorship of the proletariat." This quotation was to become the cornerstone of communist revolutionary theory as opposed to the gradualism of the democratic socialists.

The Socialist Aim. Marxism is not concerned with giving a detailed picture of the socialist system it means to substitute for capitalism. It considers all such attempts as utopian. According to the Marxists, the main task at hand is to discern the tendencies of capitalist development and to show that a socialized, noncapitalist form of production will be the inevitable outcome of capitalism's breakdown, allegedly taking place before our eyes.

Transition to Socialism. The democratic school of Marxism, as represented by the various socialist parties, differs from the Leninist school as to their teacher's views about the transition from capitalism to socialism. The followers of Lenin usually quote the passage from Marx's letter of 1875 given in a preceding paragraph. This passage is counterbalanced by the democratic-socialist advocates of a gradual transition in the following sentence, from a speech delivered by Marx after the close of the Convention of the First International held at The Hague in 1872: "We do not deny that there exist countries like America, England, and if I knew your institutions better, I would add Holland, where the workers may be able to attain their ends by peaceful means. If that is true, we must also recognize that in most of the countries of the Continent force must be the lever to which it will be necessary to resort for a time in order to attain the dominion of labor." There are those who, on the basis of this sentence, explain that Marx's passage about "revolutionary dictatorship" was meant exclusively for nondemocratic countries, such as prevailed on the European continent. This view is confirmed by an article published by Engels in 1894 in which he wrote: "We do not consider the indemnification of property-owners as an impossibility under all circumstances. How often did Karl Marx express to me the opinion that if we could buy off the whole gang [of capitalists] it would be the cheapest way of getting rid of them."

Withering Away of the State. In the Marxist concept the state has been an institution for the maintenance of the oppression and exploitation of the masses —slaves, serfs, or wage workers—for the benefit of the privileged classes—slave owners, feudal lords, or capitalists. The elimination of the privileged classes by expropriation and the conversion of the means of production into public ownership, would automatically result in the "withering away of the state," according to an expression coined by Friedrich Engels. The organization in charge of production would no longer be a "state" or a "political power." "In the place of the government over persons," said Engels, "steps the administration of things and the management of the process of production." There are those who point out that the elimination of the propertied classes, as effected in Russia by men calling themselves Marxists, has not led to a "withering away of the state" but on the contrary to a "government over persons" much more tyrannical than any government previously in existence.

Theory of Exploitation and Surplus Value. According to Marx the inevitable breakdown of the capitalist system of production, with the ensuing enthronement of socialism, is inherent in the exploitative nature of that system. Labor, in the Marxist terminology, is a commodity whose value is determined by the amount necessary for maintaining the worker in existence. However, the values created by the worker are in excess of the amount paid him in the form of wages for the maintenance of his labor power. This difference between what the worker has produced and what he receives in the form of wages, Marx calls surplus value. This surplus value is pocketed by the capitalist and constitutes what is referred to as exploitation.

Theory of Cyclic Crises. Exploitation, expressed in low wages, and hence in underconsumption, gives rise to overproduction, because the workers, due to their low buying power, cannot absorb the goods they have produced. That situation results in periodically recurrent breakdowns, crises, or "depressions," accompanied by mass unemployment. Increased purchasing power of the workers, expressed in higher wages, always causes capitalists to recoup their reduced profits by the introduction of labor-saving machinery; this, in turn, causes unemployment, which in turn results in the accumulation of unsold stocks. According to Marx this vicious circle is inherent in the capitalist system, public ownership being the only way out of the situation.

Theory of Increasing Misery and Theory of Collapse. Along with the transformation of part of the surplus value into new capital (machinery and equipment), a process called accumulation and concentration, there is the process of continuous "centralization" of capital, owing to the fact that "one capitalist always kills many." This dual process, according to Marx, eventually leads to a situation where "a few usurpers" are in possession of all the wealth of the nation, while the enormous majority of the population is reduced to ever-increasing misery. Once the whole population has been expropriated by a few supercapitalists, then the whole edifice collapses under its own weight. This is what is usually called Marx's "theory of collapse." At that point, it becomes an easy matter to bring about "the expropriation of a few usurpers by the mass of the people." Marx presented the theory of collapse as follows in his *Capital*:

"Along with the constantly diminishing number of magnates of capital, who usurp and monopolize all the advantages of this process of transformation, grows the mass of misery, oppression, slavery, degradation, exploitation; but with this too grows the revolt of the working class, a class always increasing in numbers and disciplined, united and organized by the very process of capitalist production itself.

"The monopoly of capital becomes a fetter upon the mode of production which has sprung up and flourished along with it and under it. Centralization of the means of production and socialization of labor at last reach a point where they become incompatible with their capitalist husk. This husk is burst asunder. The knell of capitalist private property sounds. The expropriators are expropriated."

There were those, even within the socialist camp (cf. Eduard Bernstein), who on the basis of statistical data, disproved the theory of the increasing misery of the workers and of the disappearance of the middle layers of society which, according to Marx, were sinking into the ranks of the working class. Critics have also pointed out that where, as a result of war or depression, the capitalist system either collapses or is crippled to a considerable extent, the result is not the "emancipation of the working class" predicted by Marx, but the establishment of either "communist" or Fascist dictatorships, or at best, a democratic welfare state which has nationalized many public utilities and key industries without, however, removing the class barriers between the manual workers and the educated office-holders and property-owners.

One of the critics of Marx's views within the radical camp was the German social philosopher Eugen Dühring (1833-1921). An author of many works on philosophy, politics, and economics and a lecturer at the University of Berlin during the 1860's and 1870's, he exerted some influence on the Berlin socialists during the 1870's. His violent attacks against Marx called forth a reply from Marx's friend and collaborator Engels, whose book, known under the abbreviated title of *Anti-Dühring*, has perpetuated Dühring's name in socialist literature. The socialist views which Dühring advocated during that period attracted attention because of the author's insistence on the importance of trade-union struggles for higher wages and shorter hours, his rejection of the "iron law of wages," and his opposition to the idea of government ownership and advocacy of producers' co-operatives as owners and managers of the nation's economy. Dühring achieved a certain notoriety by the violence of his anti-Semitism and by his megalomania which pointed to a lack of mental balance in the mind of the gifted scholar who had become totally blind at an early age. Completely forgotten and unread during the last four decades of his long life, he achieved fleeting posthumous fame when the Nazis resurrected him because of his anti-Semitic outbursts.

HENRY GEORGE

Less fierce than the gospels of either Marx or Dühring was the teaching of another enemy of poverty who was a radical of sorts, though he could not be called a socialist. In his writings, particularly in *Progress and Poverty* (1879), Henry George (1839-97), an American economist, suggested as a sort of nostrum the adoption of a single tax that would deprive the land owners of the benefits accruing as a result of what is called the "unearned increment" of land values. He had been exposed to the boom period of California, when investors became wealthy overnight through land speculation, and held that the state should derive all its tax revenues through a levy on the surplus realized on automatic increases in value of land caused by the general appreciation of values in the area. George felt that such a tax would not only supply the state with enough revenues to conduct its operations, but would release land to those who would expend productive labor upon it.

George's book, a passionately written description of the evils inherent in the ownership of land by speculators, was particularly influential in England, where George Bernard Shaw, among others, was led in the direction of social analysis by its emphasis on contrasts between wealth and impoverishment, existing side by side.

Critics of the "single tax" theory hold that it would not be broad enough to cope with the more complex problems imposed by a society in which land-based values are not pre-eminent. Karl Marx called Henry George's scheme "the last attempt to save the capitalist system," while expressly insisting that this was certainly *not* that reformer's conscious intention.

George's views enjoyed a certain popularity around the turn of the century in the United States, Australia, and a number of other countries. The movement has since ebbed away.

While Henry George was chiefly concerned with the question of land and its impact upon modern society, another American economist, Thorstein Veblen (1857-1929), nearly two decades younger, had a better chance to observe the gigantic development of American industrialism. He evolved a sociological system which, original in the form of its presentation, restated and also anticipated many ideas of his predecessors and contemporaries. While Marx saw all history as a succession of class struggles, and Pareto visualized the same process as a "circulation of elites," Veblen distinguished in history one uninterrupted conflict between the predacious and the producing elements of the population. He pointed to the hypocrisy of the former who would hide their parasitism behind lofty principles and no less dishonest references to the general interest. This referred both to the pirate chief and the robber baron of the pre-industrial era, and to the present-day industrial and financial tycoons. Like Marx and many other opponents of capitalism, he visualized the eventual disappearance of the system of private enterprise. But at variance with most radical thinkers, he rejected the idea that the "proletariat" would take the place of its former masters. Instead, he anticipated a system controlled by engineers and other technical experts, who, he believed, may some day come to power as a result of a general strike of the engineers.

While the concept of a general strike of the engineers was original with Veblen, the idea about the managerial personnel taking the place of the eliminated capitalists was anticipated by Michael Bakunin and the Polish revolutionary thinker Waclaw Machajski (see pp. 238-40).

Chapter IV

THE GRADUALISTS
Part I
The European Continent

The disintegration of the movements inspired by the ideas and the personality of Bakunin resulted in the predominance of Marxist or near-Marxist concepts in the radical movements throughout Europe except Spain and Great Britain. In Spain, the fact that the followers of the Russian rebel had been the first on the spot to help in the organization of labor unions and in the conduct of their strikes secured for the anarchists a well-nigh indestructible reputation of labor champions. Hence neither persecutions by reactionary governments nor Marxist counter-propaganda succeeded in breaking their grip on the majority of organized labor. In England, as in the United States, the labor unions had been a "natural" growth. They had been formed by workers themselves with little outside help from radical-minded educated déclassés. Hence there was no bond of gratitude that might have made the native workers in those countries prone to listen sympathetically to the various gospels of anticapitalism, particularly as basically the workers' mental horizon does not go beyond the very nonideological questions of hours and wages. Moreover, there were in England and America during most of the second half of the last century, few educated déclassés or near-déclassés whose hopeless status would make them, as it did on most of the Continent, ready to rebel against the status quo.

Essentially, the radical movement of the last century was a result of a united front of two social groups, each of which had its own distinct grievances against the rising capitalist state and its semifeudal survivals. The rank and file of that front were the manual workers whose ambitions, generally speaking, did not go beyond higher wages and shorter hours. Its leading political cadres consisted largely of educated "outs," impecunious intellectuals, or déclassé professionals who thought and spoke in terms of political power—with definitely revolutionary connotations at the time of Blanqui, Bakunin, and the early Marx. As time went by and as economic conditions improved, the erstwhile revolutionary intentions of Marx's followers cooled down to a striving toward democratization of or participation in the administrative apparatus of the country, and toward a peaceful substitution of public ownership for private capitalism. Assistance to the workers in their bread-and-butter struggles was the price the socialist leadership paid for the support of the masses.

FERDINAND LASSALLE

The first European country in which that alliance, as it were, made its appearance as a mass movement was Germany. The reaction which followed the collapse of the Revolution of 1848 had practically stamped out all radical activities until the early 1860's. However, the rapid industrialization of the country during that period created a situation which Ferdinand Lassalle, a not quite orthodox disciple of Marx, deemed favorable for the revival of radical propaganda among the masses. Lassalle[1] (1825-64) was the highly gifted son of a prosperous German-Jewish businessman, who had taken an active part in the Revolution of 1848. "Armed," as he said about himself without exaggerating, "with all the knowledge of the century" and driven by a well-nigh demonic ambition, he was determined to use the working masses as a stepping stone for his advancement to supreme power. Until his appearance on the political scene in the early 1860's the German workers, as yet organized only in educational societies, had been politically merely an appendage of middle-class liberalism. In a whirlwind campaign begun in 1863, Lassalle founded the General German Workers Union, the first large workers' organization in Germany to raise the banner of socialism. Lassalle's socialism was a combination of German nationalism—the desire for unification of Germany was common to all German socialists—with the democratic demand for universal suffrage and a hazy socialist formula of "producers' co-operatives with State credits," which he had borrowed from Louis Blanc. The immediate needs of the laboring masses gave Lassalle little concern; their struggles for higher wages were outside the scope of his activities or even of his thoughts. On the contrary, he believed in the "iron law of wages" and regarded as illusory the attempts of the workers, so long as the capitalist system endured, to raise their wages to any considerable extent above the minimum level required for their subsistence. His great popularity among the workers despite his disbelief in the efficacy of the struggle for higher wages is a testimony to the charismatic character of his personality.

After Lassalle's death the General German Workers Union succeeded in having several of its candidates elected to the German Reichstag. The leadership of the German workers by the Lassalleans was challenged by another socialist group, the "Social-Democratic Workers party," usually designated as the "Eisenachers," after the place (Eisenach) where it held its first convention in 1869. That party took its inspiration from Karl Marx. The struggle between these two socialist parties was not merely a sectarian dispute as to the greater merits of their respective teachers or prophets. The Lassalleans took rather a contemptuous attitude towards the trade unions, and while they helped to organize them, treated them as duplications of their political party organization. Their leaders were politicians above all, with a strong nationalistic bias in favor of Prussia, whose hegemony they supported in case of Germany's hoped-for unification. The Lassalleans were ready to support Bismarck and his Junkers against the bourgeoisie. Their Marxist opponents, active mostly in the non-Prussian sections of Germany, were opposed to Prussian predominance; they fought the autocratic methods of the Lassalleans and advocated intraparty democracy. They were in favor of collaboration with the various democratic parties and were ready to grant a modicum of independence to the trade unions which they vigorously helped to organize. The two socialist parties finally merged in 1875 as a result of the changed political situation after the unification of Germany; moreover, the workers were becoming fed up with the unsavory quarreling among their leaders.

BEBEL AND LIEBKNECHT

The united Social-Democratic party enjoyed only a short period of open activity. The German government became disturbed by its continuously increasing poll of votes—it had reached 500,000 in 1877—and in the following year, it found in the terrorist attempts of two unbalanced individuals a pretext for passing antisocialist laws which forbade any kind of radical activity. The growth of a democratic force that threatened

Junkerdom and monarchy had to be checked at all costs.

The antisocialist laws were in operation from 1878 to 1890. During that period the Social-Democratic party was outlawed and worked underground. The party publications were smuggled in from abroad, first from Switzerland and later from London. When smuggling became difficult they were occasionally published secretly at home. The trade unions, at first suppressed along with the party, were permitted to function again in 1883; in them the socialists found a propitious field for propaganda. As a result the socialists garnered more and more votes at each election, reaching a total of nearly one million and a half in 1890. In the same year, a few months before the general elections, the antisocialist laws were repealed.

From its founding the united Social-Democratic party was dominated by two outstanding personalities, Wilhelm Liebknecht (1826-1900) and August Bebel (1840-1913). A wood turner by trade, Bebel had no formal education outside of elementary and Sunday school. Active in the German labor movement since 1862, at first under the influence of Wilhelm Liebknecht, a friend and disciple of Karl Marx, he was elected (1871) to the Reichstag, of which he remained a member until his death. The leader of the German Social-Democratic party, Bebel was considered one of the outstanding orators in the country. In the party Bebel represented what was called the "Marxist center," that is, he accepted all the tenets of traditional Marxism, which he defended both against the ultraradical Left and the ultramoderate Right within the party. He was the author of many books and pamphlets. The best known of his works is *Woman and Socialism* (1879), which had an enormous circulation and was translated into many languages. Shortly before his death he wrote his autobiography (in three volumes), a work which is a history of the German socialist and labor movement.

Wilhelm Liebknecht[2] (1826-1900), one of the founders of the party, was, unlike Bebel, of middle-class lineage and university education. A militant opponent of absolutism, he participated actively in the German Revolution of 1848, after whose collapse he went into exile in London where he came under the influence of Karl Marx. After the amnesty of 1861 he returned to Germany, where he became one of the two leaders of those socialists who opposed the policies of the pro-Prussian Lassalleans. Sentenced in 1872 to two years' imprisonment because of his opposition to the annexation of Alsace-Lorraine, he was elected to the German parliament in 1874 and regularly thereafter until his death in 1900.

Though enjoying great prestige among the masses because of his revolutionary past and his eloquence, Liebknecht was not highly regarded either by his teacher, Marx, or by his comrade and erstwhile disciple, Bebel. The latter called him "a man of iron will and the heart of a child." That about "the heart of a child" apparently referred to Liebknecht's theoretical confusion and general imprudence. For while accepting and fanatically defending revolutionary Marxian orthodoxy against its critics, he would also occasionally blurt out the *unofficial* but de facto concept of the party to the effect that "the State of today is growing into the State of the future, just as the State of the future has its roots deep in the State of today." This was rank ultragradualism, written in 1895, two years before the ultramoderate Eduard Bernstein came out with his criticism of Marxist orthodoxy. This passage, contained in an article written for a progressive middle-class periodical,[3] was meant both to curry favor with the advanced section of the middle classes and to ward off the attacks of those ultrareactionaries who clamored for new persecutions of the party, which they denounced as "subversive." Liebknecht had forgotten that, at *that* time, when the anarchists were still competing with the socialists, it was still necessary to keep up the revolutionary enthusiasm of the masses by offering them the apocalyptic feature of Marx's "theory of collapse" as a substitute for the old-time religion which promised to reward the poor and to punish the wicked rich.

BERNSTEIN AND KAUTSKY

The period between 1890 and 1903 was the most momentous in the development of German socialism. It was a period of continuous growth, unhampered by antisocialist legislation. It was also a period of theoretical disputes which nearly split the party into two hostile camps. By 1890 a strong radical opposition to the old leaders had made its appearance in the party. It was led by young elements—and hence dubbed "die Jungen"—who found that the movement had degenerated into a "petty-bourgeois party of reform," entirely too engrossed in parliamentary activities. At the opposite extreme of party policy was a group of outspoken moderates, like Georg von Vollmar. These—a counterpart of the French "Possibilists" —wanted to abandon the revolutionary phraseology which still pervaded the party utterances, to give up the socialist aim and to concentrate the party's efforts upon certain practical democratic postulates; in other words, they wanted what in radical terminology is called "class collaboration" rather than the class struggle. The rest of the Old Guard, intellectuals and former workers alike, formed the party center, as represented by Bebel and the leading Marxist theoretician, Karl Kautsky. They wanted a combination of revolutionary theory and moderate action. They were afraid lest the revolutionary tactics recommended by the extreme Left provoke persecution and reaction, while renunciation of revolutionary theory advocated by the right wing might strengthen the imprudent Left, or even furnish grist to the anarchist mill. The Center won. The "Youngsters" were expelled from the party; most of them later joined the anarchists. The opportunists of the right wing were humiliated by the accusation, uttered by the party chief Bebel, that the improvement of their material situation had quenched their revolutionary spirit.

Old Liebknecht's momentary "lapse" from revolutionary orthodoxy was vindicated by Eduard Bernstein (1850-1932), the father of what is called the "revisionist" school of socialism. He was born in Berlin, where he was at first employed as a bank clerk. At the age of twenty-two he joined the German Social-Democratic party, in which he remained active until his death. When the party was forced underground by Bismarck's antisocialist laws, he went abroad to edit the party's organ, *Der Sozialdemokrat*—first in Zurich and later in London. He remained in England even after those laws had been dropped. A close follower of Karl Marx and Friedrich Engels and a personal friend of the latter, he gradually evolved from an orthodox Marxist to a position of his own which was critical with regard to most of the fundamental concepts of his teachers. He presented his views, beginning in 1897, in a number of articles and books, the most important of which was translated into English under the title of *Evolutionary Socialism*. In this book he adduced a large array of statistical data to disprove Marx's theory of "increasing misery," according to which the living standard of the masses is bound to deteriorate continuously. Bernstein also refuted another Marxian tenet regarding the disappearance of the middle classes into the ranks of the workers. "What happens to the surplus product," he asked, "which the industrial workers produce beyond their own consumption that is limited by their wages? The 'magnates of capital' might have ten times as big bellies as popular humor credits them with, and they might have ten times as many servants as they really have, their own consumption would be like a feather in the balance, as compared with the mass of the annual national output, for capitalist large-scale production is chiefly *mass production*. One might say they export the surplus. Good, but in the last analysis the foreign buyer likewise pays in merchandise. The circulating metal money plays an insignificant role in world trade. What, then, happens to the mass of goods which the magnates and their servants do not consume? If in one way or another it does not go to the proletarians, then it is being absorbed by other classes. Either there is a relatively growing decrease in the number of capitalists and a rising well-being of the proletariat, or a numerous middle class—this is the only alternative which is left us by a continuous increase of production."[4]

Having demonstrated that the standard of living of the workers was not growing worse and that the middle classes, far from disappearing, were growing in numbers—even though the character of the middle class was changing—Bernstein argued that the refutation of these two tenets of Marx's theory implied also the refutation of Marx's theory of the inevitable collapse of the capitalist system. Bernstein's conclusion was that once the economic development of the capitalist system does not lead automatically to an inevitable collapse involving a violent revolution, the Socialist party should logically abandon the old revolutionary slogans and admit frankly that it was not a revolutionary party but what it actually was—"a democratic party of reforms." He epitomized his view in the epigram: "To me the final aim is nothing, the movement everything," adding, "unable to believe in finalities at all, I cannot believe in a final aim of socialism."

In the discussion which his views called forth within the German Socialist party, his heresies were officially rejected by his party in 1903. In reality, however, Bernstein was the winner, because in practice the Socialist party proceeded in accordance with his views. This became particularly obvious after the establishment of the democratic Weimar Republic (1918), when all talk about an anticapitalist revolution under a system of political democracy was shelved even by his theoretical chief opponent, the spokesman of Marxist orthodoxy, Karl Kautsky.

In 1900 Bernstein returned to Germany after an absence of twenty-two years. Though heading the "revisionist" wing of the Socialist party, he was not in agreement with those right-wing elements of the organization who were ready to throw overboard all the internationalist traditions of socialism. A pacifist and a determined opponent of imperialism, he antagonized many of his own followers during World War I (1914-18) by leaving the ranks of the old party and joining the Independent Socialists, a minority group which split off from the official Social-Democratic party because the majority of the latter gave its support to the Kaiser's imperialist war policy.

In joining the Independent Socialists, Bernstein found himself, ironically, in the same Leftist group with his main opponent, Karl Kautsky (1854-1938), who had likewise rejected his party's pro-imperialist policy. Born of Czech parents, Kautsky lived most of his life in Germany, where he was the founder and the editor of the *Neue Zeit* (1883-1917), theoretical organ of the German Social-Democratic party. He popularized the economic doctrines of Karl Marx and was the author of many books dealing with the various aspects of ancient and modern social movements, among others: *The Precursors of Modern Socialism: From Plato to the Anabaptists*; *The Foundations of Christianity*; *Thomas More and His Utopia*; *War and Democracy*; *Socialists and War*. In his *Bernstein and the Social-Democratic Program*, he defended the official Marxist position against the "revisionist" criticism of Eduard Bernstein. The outstanding titles among his theoretical works written prior to World War I are *The Social Revolution* and *The Road to Power*. His two giant volumes, *The Materialist Interpretation of History*, published in 1929, constitute a sort of compendium of philosophy, sociology, and anthropology viewed from the Marxist point of view. The Bolshevik revolution called forth a number of polemical books and pamphlets from his pen. *Terrorism and Communism, Bolshevism at a Deadlock*, and the *Proletarian Revolution* are outstanding. Many of his books have been translated into most civilized languages.

Prior to World War I, Kautsky's chief task consisted in finding the theoretical justification for the political "line" which the German Socialist party was following at any given period. Critics of that "line" maintained that it consisted of carrying on as a democratic reform party, while maintaining among its following a sort of quasi-religious faith that the party was out to destroy the existing system and that sooner or later the social revolution would put an end to the exploitation of man by man.

During the Bernstein controversy Kautsky took up the cudgels in defense of revolutionary Marxian orthodoxy. There are those who believe that his intransigent radicalism was dictated by the consideration that such an attitude was necessary as long as Germany still had a semiabsolutist regime with the reactionary Prussian Junker caste in the possession of political power. This assumption is borne out by the fact that after Germany's defeat in World War I had brought about the downfall of junkerism, Kautsky took the same reformist or "gradualist" stand as Bernstein, however he might differ from him on the fine points of pure philosophical or economic theory.

When democracy was at last established in Germany (1918-33), Kautsky definitely said farewell to the traditional revolutionary slogans of Marxism. Where Marx had spoken of a "revolutionary dictatorship of the proletariat" as the transitional phase between capitalism and socialism, Kautsky advanced the thesis that it was not a dictatorship but rather a coalition government of bourgeois and proletarian parties that was to fill that transitional period. The communists used this as an argument for their contention that Kautsky had definitely become a renegade to Marxism. Yet, at bottom, Kautsky took the same stand that Marx had taken in 1872 with regard to the Anglo-Saxon democracies, when he expressed the opinion that in those countries socialism could be introduced through peaceful methods. Kautsky also pointed out that there were no indications in Marx's works as to the form the class struggle would assume after the establishment of full-fledged political democracy.

The last twenty years of Kautsky's life were filled with his struggle against Bolshevism. For his criticism, he incurred the most violent abuse on the part of Lenin, Trotsky, and Bukharin. The fate of the three men was in part a justification of Kautsky's attacks. For Lenin died implacably hostile to his successor, whose removal from the secretaryship of the party he demanded in his testament; the other two defenders of the Bolshevik dictatorship were to become its victims.

The seizure of power by the Nazis (1933) forced Kautsky to seek refuge abroad. He died in Holland.

Bernstein's success in weaning the party from the last remnants of its theoretical and purely verbal intransigence was due to the support of two important groups within that organization: the younger set of ambitious politicians and the trade union leaders. The latter were frightened lest revolutionary talk have unfavorable repercussions on the safety of their own organizations. These were even more moderate than the politicians in Bernstein's camp. Indeed, some of the latter, in principle at least, accepted the idea of a political strike for obtaining democratic suffrage in Prussia or for defending universal suffrage, should it be threatened. The trade union leaders refused to take any such chances under any circumstances whatsoever.

As time went by, the Marxist "Center" and the Bernsteinian (or revisionist) Right became very much alike, their doctrinal differences having lost all practical importance. Only some lone firebrands of the extreme Left, such as Dr. Rosa Luxemburg and Karl Liebknecht (the son of Wilhelm Liebknecht, one of the founders of the party) would from time to time sound the old revolutionary tocsin. To the bulk of the party they were merely gifted freaks to whom no attention was paid. Their day was to come only during the war and the stormy events following the breakdown of the empire.

When World War I broke out, the parliamentary deputies of the German Social-Democratic party voted for war credits and declared that in the hour of stress they would not leave their country in the lurch. There are those who believe that this capitulation to German imperialism was dictated either by the fear of losing popularity with the masses, which had been seized by a nationalist frenzy, or by the fear of being crushed by the government if they opposed it; it might even have been genuine conviction. The party functionaries, some of their critics would say, were no longer impecunious déclassés ready to risk their life or liberty, but members of a well-paid hierarchy of an enormous combination of political, trade union, and newspaper organizations and enterprises. In this capacity they represented a vested interest with a stake in their country. Some of these leaders, and there were Marxist theorists among them, such as Heinrich Cunow, even elaborated a special "Marxist" theory justifying Germany's imperialist policy.

However, the attitude of the party majority did not remain unchallenged. A small minority within the parliamentary group submitted to the majority decision not to oppose the war, but they objected to voting war credits. They were not revolutionists out to overthrow the government or to get the soldiers out of the trenches. However, they thought that even a mild opposition would have certain repercussions among the people at large, sufficient to disrupt the complete unity necessary for aggressive war. This, they believed, would hasten the end of the war and also impel the government to grant some democratic reforms. Among the dissenters there were a few still more determined elements, headed by Rosa Luxemburg, Karl Liebknecht, and a few others. These, as the war progressed, inspired the organization of various revolutionary groups, such as "Spartacus" and "Internationale," the precursors of the Communist Party which was formed after the War. They were of the opinion that "victory or defeat in the War was equally ruinous to the German people" and that it was necessary immediately to put forward the most radical demands, such as "popular decision over war and peace" and "control of the government by Parliament and of Parliament by the people."

The Russian Revolution of 1917 in its first democratic phase emboldened the antiwar opposition to sever all ties with the old Social-Democratic party and to constitute itself as the Independent Social-Democratic party. It also emboldened the official Social-Democratic party, whose leaders began to clamor for more democracy and for a peace without annexations. When after the Bolshevik Revolution of November 1917, the ratification of the peace forced upon the Russians came to a vote in the Reichstag, the Social-Democratic party abstained from voting, thus declaring its mild dissatisfaction with the annexation of vast Russian territories.

POWER

During the last few weeks before the final breakdown of Germany's military power, Philip Scheidemann, the leader of the German Social-Democratic party, was invited to join the Kaiser's government. It was the first step toward the seizure of power by the socialists as soon as the old regime collapsed and a republic was established on November 9, 1918. The socialist government included an equal number of representatives of the official Social-Democratic party (sometimes called the "majority socialists") and of the Independent Social-Democratic party, with Philipp Scheidemann and Fritz Ebert of the old party as the most powerful figures of the new regime. This, however, did not result in the complete liquidation of the old aristocratic elements hitherto in charge of the German government. The old army commanders, all the judges, and most of the heads of the civilian administration were left at their old posts. As many liberals pointed out at the time, the socialists could have broken completely the power of the old-time conservatives if they had called a constituent assembly immediately after November 9, 1918, when there was a possibility of their obtaining a majority in the nation's representative body. This the two socialist parties failed to do. It is sometimes explained that they were afraid of provoking a civil war if they were to use to the full extent their newly acquired power. The moderation of the larger of the two parties led to conflicts within the socialist ranks, and the majority socialists resorted to the help of the remnants of the old army to subdue the radical—but not communist—dissenters. This led to a break within the ranks of the government and the independent socialists withdrew from it. There were further clashes which eventually resulted in the "Spartacus" uprising of January 1919.

The Spartacus League, at the extreme Left of the socialist movement, consisted of those elements which, fascinated by the Bolshevik Revolution, wanted to emulate its example in Germany. The majority of its members paid no attention to the decisions of the All-German Congress of Soldiers and Workers Councils which was controlled by the Social-Democratic party and had come out in favor of elections to a constituent assembly. The majority of the "Spartacists" also ignored the advice of their own leaders, Rosa Luxemburg and Karl Liebknecht, who warned them against an immediate uprising which could not possibly succeed. The uprising was crushed by the government with the help of military formations recruited from among nonworkingclass elements under the command of monarchist officers. It is believed by many that both the senseless revolt of the "Spartacists," that is, the communists, and the use of monarchist troops by the socialist government with the ensuing rift within the leftist camp and the strengthening of monarchist elements, laid the basis for the triumph of the Nazis.

In the elections to the Constituent Assembly held on January 19, 1919, the Social-Democrats obtained 163 seats and the Independents 22, a total of 185 for a socialist bloc as against 235 for all the other parties. As the nonsocialist majority consisting of liberals and conservatives was unable to organize a government, the Social-Democrats formed a coalition cabinet with parties of the Center and left of Center. Since the Social-Democrats were the strongest party, Ebert and Scheidemann, were given the highest posts of the Republic, the presidency and the chancellorship. Chancellor Scheidemann soon resigned. He refused to sign the Versailles Treaty because he did not want to have his name attached to a document symbolizing Germany's defeat and humiliation. Another socialist, Gustav Bauer, followed him as chancellor and signed the document. He soon resigned, making place for Hermann Müller, likewise a socialist.

The leniency which the Social-Democratic party, while in power, displayed toward the monarchists was criticized by a minority within the Social-Democratic party—it was headed by the ex-Chancellor Scheidemann—who were in favor of a more energetic attitude against the Right. But they could not prevail against the right-wingers represented by the socialist President Fritz Ebert and his socialist War Minister, Gustav Noske, who were accused of bending over backwards to placate the Right. The elections to the Reichstag held in June 1920 brought to the helm a new coalition of Center and left-of-Center parties in which the socialists were not included.

In 1922 the ranks of the Social-Democratic party

were increased by its unification with the Independent Social-Democratic party, or more precisely with the minority of that party which had refused to join its majority in affiliating with the communists. Though no longer at the helm of the national government, the socialists remained the strongest party.

In 1928 the Socialists, having polled an increased number of votes, were again given an opportunity to form a cabinet, Hermann Müller becoming chancellor again. The socialists remained in power for less than two years—June 13, 1928, to March 27, 1930—when they were replaced by a coalition of parties of the Right. New elections were held during the same year at which the socialists obtained 143 seats. These elections revealed a serious threat to the existence of the republic, the Nazis and the communists returning 107 and 77 members respectively, while practically all moderate republicans lost heavily.

When the 1929-30 depression set in, proposals to socialize industry and to establish a planned economy came from the trade unions, which were largely dominated by the socialists. Hostility between socialists and communists prevented any joint action in behalf of such a program. Fear of the extreme Right, which was supporting the Nazis, induced the Social-Democratic party to support Chancellor Brüning of the conservative wing of the Catholic Center party, whose deflationary measures contributed to drive many workers into the camp of the communist or Nazi extremists.

At the presidential elections of March 1932, the socialists voted for the monarchist Field Marshal Hindenburg, who on that occasion was opposed by Hitler.

Hindenburg, however, whom all the republican parties had supported in the hope of thus stemming the Nazi tide, soon double-crossed his democratic supporters by entering upon a policy of handing over all power to the extreme reactionaries who were out to destroy the republic. As a result, the government of Prussia, which was headed by the Social-Democratic party, was removed by a *coup d'état* on July 20, 1932. The socialists offered no resistance, apparently because they were not certain of the support of either the great mass of the workers, a substantial part of whom had gone over to the communists, or of their own police force. At the Reichstag elections held a few days later the Social-Democratic party lost a number of seats; it returned only 133 candidates as compared with 143 at the preceding elections. A few months later Hindenburg appointed Hitler as chancellor of the republic.

Shortly before Hitler's appointment, the last pre-Nazi chancellor, General Kurt von Schleicher, a conservative, who better than the other rightists realized the meaning of Hitlerism, tried to prevent a Nazi dictatorship by forming a coalition of the army with the Catholic Center and the socialist trade unions. His suggestion that the trade unions call a general strike was rejected by Leipart, the head of the socialist trade unions, on the grounds that such a strike would be "unconstitutional." At the elections of March 5, 1933, the only elections held under Hitler before Germany was made into a one-party state, the socialists polled 7,200,000 votes, returning 120 members to the Reichstag. The attempts of the Social-Democratic party and of the socialist-controlled trade unions to continue to operate under Hitler were of no avail. Both party and trade unions were outlawed and their leaders either arrested or forced to flee abroad. Socialist literature was smuggled into Germany from Czechoslovakia,

France, and Holland, but otherwise there was little underground activity. Rank and file members of the Social-Democratic party and of the socialist-led trade unions who had escaped arrest and remained faithful to their convictions, succeeded in impressing their views upon their fellow workers in the factories. Some of the socialist leaders who had not been molested and had ostensibly made peace with the new system, were later, during World War II, to participate in the inter-party conspiracy to overthrow Hitler in 1944.

THE BONN REPUBLIC

After Hitler's defeat and the re-establishment of political liberty following the occupation of the major part of Germany by the Western powers, the activities of the Social-Democratic party were resumed, and some of the leaders returned from exile or the concentration camps. (Dr. Kurt Schumacher, who became leader of the party, spent ten years in a Nazi concentration camp.) The 1949 elections to the Bundestag, the parliament of Western Germany, returned the Social-Democrats as the second strongest party, with 131 seats out of a total of 371. Its popular vote was 6,932,272, or 29.4 percent of the total number of votes cast. It drew its strength mainly from organized labor whose unions are largely led by socialists. Though in opposition to the regime headed by the Christian-Democratic party, it has consistently refused to have any dealings with the communists. Its general principles are identical with those of all democratic socialist parties.

All the repeated attempts made by the party during the 1950's and early in the 1960's to obtain a majority at the elections to the federal parliament proved unavailing in view of the great popularity en-

joyed by the Christian-Democratic Chancellor Adenauer. It never polled much more than one-third of
the vote cast. To be sure, it did not have to contend
with the competition of the communists, who were
suppressed as Russian agents and hopelessly discredited
because of the bestialities committed by Red Army
soldiers during the occupation of Germany by the Allied
forces. However, the quick economic recovery of the
country—due to American help and comparatively low
military expenditures—had the effect of strengthening
the spirit of conservatism among the majority of the
population. The welfare state measures of the Adenauer
regime gave the masses a sense of social security, while
what was considered the chief plank of the socialists—
nationalization of industries—repelled all those who
had resented ubiquitous government interference and
control during the Nazi regime.

It is in view of this attitude of the electorate that
the German socialists have gradually abandoned the
idea of nationalization, just as, since the establishment
of the Weimar Republic in 1918—to win the middle-
class vote—they have gradually abandoned the idea of
class struggle. They have thus become a progressive
party of reforms intent not upon the overthrow of the
existing system but upon its gradual improvement.

There is no Social-Democratic party in East Germany, which is under Soviet occupation. It has been
forcibly merged with the German Communist party,
the communist-controlled body being called Socialist
Unity party. Those Socialist leaders who opposed the
merger were either arrested or had to flee to the western
part of Germany. One of the socialist leaders who
consented to that "shotgun marriage," Otto Grotewohl,
was appointed prime minister in 1949. The real power,
of course, is in the hands of the communists. The

Western zone of Berlin, which is governed according to democratic principles, has a socialist administration.

THE AUSTRIAN SOCIALISTS

The socialist movement in Austria—both before and after the breakup of the Habsburg Empire—was largely inspired by its German counterpart. However, its unique history can be epitomized in the lives of three of its outstanding champions.

Though it can trace its origin to the late 1860's and early 1870's, socialism did not begin to make a dent in Austrian political life until the appearance in its ranks of Victor Adler (1852-1918), who is considered the actual founder of the Austrian Social-Democratic party.

Born into a prosperous family, Adler studied medicine in Vienna. During the 1880's he became interested in the socialist movement, then sorely split into a radical, near-anarchist and a moderate faction. At the convention held in Hainfeld in 1889 he succeeded in reconciling the leaders of the two factions which henceforth joined their efforts in a united Social-Democratic party, whose program was adopted at that convention. It was due to his efforts and financial support that the party was able to create a daily paper, the Vienna *Arbeiter-Zeitung*, generally recognized as one of the best edited of socialist newspapers. The leader of his party until his death, Adler was admired and feared because of his eloquence and biting wit. Elected to Parliament by the workers of Vienna, he remained a member of that body for the rest of his life. He was a practical politician rather than a theorist. During World War I he supported the policy of the government, guided by his maxim that there is something that is even worse than war, namely, a lost war. As a result he did not object to the annexations planned by the Habsburg regime. When in 1918 it turned out that the defeat and the breakup of the Austro-Hungarian Empire was inevitable, he turned his efforts to the establishment of a republic in the German-speaking sections of Austria, and he favored their unification with Germany when he became minister of foreign affairs of the republic. He died shortly after assuming office.

In distinction to the founder of the party, who had the reputation of being an opportunist and a skeptic as far as the final aims of socialism were concerned, his son Friedrich Adler (1879-1960), a scholar and a theorist of note, was of a fanatical disposition. During World War I he took the same position as the Independent Socialists of Germany and insisted that his party should protest against the annexationist intentions of the Austrian government. His point of view did not prevail against that of his father. As the war became increasingly unpopular, Friedrich Adler expressed his protest against the unconstitutional methods of the government by killing Prime Minister Count Stuergkh in 1916. He was condemned to death, but the government did not carry out the sentence so as not to antagonize the Social-Democratic workers— with whom the younger Adler was popular in spite of the disagreement with his father.

Two years after his conviction Friedrich Adler was freed as a result of the victory of the Allies. The Austro-Hungarian Empire was broken up and Austria—the purely German part of it—became a democratic republic. In the period between the two world wars (1919-39) Friedrich Adler was at first active in the "Two-And-A-Half International," which took an intermediate position between the Second (Socialist) and

Third (Communist) International. In 1923, the "Two-And-A-Half" and the Second Internationals merged and Friedrich Adler became one of the two secretaries of the Labor and Socialist International which took the place of the two merged bodies. Throughout the 1930's his attitude was one of extreme hostility toward the Stalin regime, whose persecution of political dissenters he attacked. When, however, after the conclusion of World War II, he saw that the problems of world politics had narrowed down to a conflict between the U.S.A. and the U.S.S.R., his anticapitalist radicalism made him adopt a somewhat conciliatory attitude with regard to the Soviet regime. In a choice between totalitarian socialism and democratic capitalism, he decided to give his preference to the former. By taking this attitude of complete disregard of the question of personal liberty, Friedrich Adler found himself quite isolated in the democratic socialist camp.

While, after his father's death, Friedrich Adler was active chiefly in behalf of the Socialist International, the leadership of the Austrian Social-Democratic party was largely in the hands of Otto Bauer (1881-1938). A Marxist scholar of note, as a very young man, long before Victor Adler's death, he had gained a reputation as the actual author of speeches delivered in the Vienna parliament by various deputies of his party.

Captured by the Russians during the World War, he returned to his country in 1918, where upon Victor Adler's death he became minister of foreign affairs after the Austrian revolution. He was until 1934 the chief spokesman of the powerful Social-Democratic party in the Vienna parliament.

During the February 1934 uprising of the Vienna socialist workers against the attempt of the Dollfuss regime to inaugurate an Austrian brand of Fascist totalitarianism, Otto Bauer took a leading part in the armed struggle. After the suppression of the revolt Bauer went to Czechoslovakia, where he remained until 1938, when he was forced to flee to France. During his stay in Czechoslovakia, he was editor of the theoretical socialist monthly *Der Kampf*, a publication which he later continued in Paris under the title of *Der sozialistische Kampf*.

Bauer was the author of a large number of books and pamphlets on socialist theory, political and economic problems, and foreign affairs. Best known, and of more than local or temporary importance, are *Bolschewismus oder Sozialdemokratie?* ("Bolshevism or Social-Democracy?", 1920), in which Bauer takes the position that while a revolution, Bolshevik-style, is possible in a backward agrarian country like Russia, it has no chance of success in Middle or Western Europe, where the economic fabric is much more sensitive, where property is more diffused, and the entire process of production depends upon imports of important raw materials from overseas. For this reason, according to Bauer, the change of the political and economic system in the West would have to be effected gradually, by democratic methods and through compensation of the owners of the nationalized enterprises, otherwise "we would be starved to death during the process of destruction." In 1923 Bauer published *Die oesterreichische Revolution* ("The Austrian Revolution"). Eight years later, in 1931, appeared the first part of what was to be his magnum opus in four volumes, *Kapitalismus und Sozialismus nach dem Weltkrieg* ("Capitalism and Socialism After the World War"). The materials, outlines, drafts, and manuscripts of the subsequent volumes were seized by the Vienna police in 1934. In 1936 Bauer published in Bratislava (Czechoslovakia) a sort of condensation (355 pages) of these intended three volumes, entitled *Zwischen zwei Weltkriegen?* ("Between

Two World Wars?"). Its subtitle, "The Crisis of World Economy, of Democracy and of Socialism" indicated the contents of the book.

Bauer's last book, published posthumously, is entitled *Die illegale Partei* ("The Illegal Party," Paris, 1939). It deals with the problems of revolutionary underground activities under Fascism and under nineteenth-century absolutism.

Within the Socialist International, in which he was one of the outstanding figures, Bauer represented the Marxist Left wing. He differed from many traditional representatives of international socialism in his appreciation of the Bolshevik Revolution. While condemning its methods and rejecting them for the rest of the world, he believed Bolshevism nevertheless played a progressive role in Russia and represented a step toward the realization of socialism.

The death of Otto Bauer shortly before the outbreak of World War II symbolized the end of an epoch of intransigent Austrian socialism. Since the liberation of Austria from the Fascist grip as a result of Germany's defeat in 1945, the socialists and their erstwhile Catholic clerical opponents (the former supporters of Dollfuss' clerico-Fascist dictatorship) have been ruling Austria jointly through the instrumentality of a coalition government, because each of the two parties was invariably supported by approximately half of the electorate, the industrial centers voting consistently socialist, while the peasant population just as consistently stuck to the clerical People's party.

SOCIALISM IN FRANCE

Outside Germany, the democratic socialist movement underwent an evolution from initial verbal intransigency to respectability or a sort of left-wing New Deal party. Only the points of departure were different, depending upon the history of the respective countries.

While in Germany during the 1860's two democratic socialist parties, the Lassalleans and the Marxist "Eisenachers," were competing for the allegiance of the workers, the French opponents of capitalism were at that time split between the mild, nonpolitical anarchism of Proudhon and the "putschism" of Blanqui. The regime they established during the Paris Commune of March-May 1871, though called by Marx a "dictatorship of the proletariat," was nothing of the kind. That uprising was a spontaneous democratic protest against a reactionary attempt to disarm Paris, and against the election of a monarchist majority to the National Assembly. None of the various reforms adopted by the socialist regime during the seventy-one days of its existence represented a serious infringement upon the rights of property.

For almost a decade after the suppression of the Commune there was in France practically no radical movement, its leaders having been killed in battle, executed, imprisoned, deported to penal colonies, or settled as refugees in England and Switzerland. By the end of the 1870's socialist ideas again began to stir the minds of young intellectuals and of the more alert workers. But the movement was disunited and sect-ridden. The alignment, however, was different from that existing before the Commune. The followers of Proudhon, those pacific anarchists who believed in mutual credit societies and co-operative organizations, had gradually disappeared. Their views had become obsolete with growing industrialism and the workers' interest in trade unions and strikes, in which Proudhon did not believe. Some adopted the revolutionary gospel of Bakunin, who tried to combine elements of Proudhon and Marx to form a higher revolutionary unity; others went over to Marx. The Blanquists, whose master died in 1881, after having spent half his long life in prison, gradually waned away or became gradualist socialists while paying lip service to the insurrectionary dreams of their past. The monarchy, the chief target of their attacks, was no more, and the democratic republic offered greater opportunities for talent than were available under previous regimes. As hope for a seizure of power by a sudden coup was growing fainter and fainter, many of the educated malcontents began to turn elsewhere for their inspiration. Karl Marx, long ignored in France, found invaluable apostles in two French intellectuals who had once been followers of Michael Bakunin: Jules Guesde and Paul Lafargue.

FREE-FOR-ALL

Guesde (1845-1923), French socialist orator and journalist, was jointly with Lafargue, a theorist and son-in-law of Karl Marx, the founder and leader of the Marxist *Parti Ouvrier* ("Workers party"), one of the largest and best organized socialist parties prior to the unification of the various socialist factions in 1905. He was repeatedly elected to parliament. In the Chamber of Deputies, he and his followers—they were usually called "Guesdists" after their leader—represented the intransigent, revolutionary branch of the socialist movement, as opposed to those socialists who under the leadership of Jaurès believed in co-operation with the bourgeois parties of the Left and in participation in liberal-democratic governments. He was just as implacably opposed to the anarchists and syndicalists and their propaganda for the general strike as a substitute for the ballot in bringing about the downfall of the capitalist system. During World War I Guesde joined the Cabinet of national defense headed by the former socialists Viviani and Briand, an act for which he was branded as a "renegade" by Leon Trotsky, then at the extreme Left of Russian socialism.

Guesde's *Parti Ouvrier* professed the tenets of orthodox Marxism and combined revolutionary verbiage concerning the future with law-abiding propaganda for the election of its leaders to Parliament and the organization of trade unions. The "Guesdists" were not the only socialist party active on the French political scene. The Blanquists followed a pseudo-revolutionary policy similar to that of the Guesdists in that they were radical politicians without a policy for immediate revolution but used the great name of Blanqui as a drawing card. There were the so-called "Possibilists," also called the "Broussists" after their leader Brousse, who, at first a "propagandist by the deed"—terrorist anarchist—had once played an important part in Guesde's party. They had concluded that to attract the masses it was necessary to fight for immediately realizable reforms and not merely to feed them the nebulous hope of revolution. They were bitterly opposed not only by the Guesdists but also by a dissident group that split off from their own ranks. These were the ultra-radical "Allemanists," after the name of their leader Jean Allemane, who advocated the general strike and opposed the admission of intellectuals and professionals into the Party.[5]

Outside of these four parties, each of which had a certain unifying set of principles or traditions, there was a loose Federation of Independent Socialists, who were not interested in theoretical hairsplittings and had neither a strict program nor rigid party discipline. The word "independent" in their name signified their independence from the Marxist Guesdists and other revolutionists. They were at the extreme right of the socialist rainbow, many of their leaders were always ready to join any of the progressive middle-class parties that held out hope of a cabinet career. Belief in "collectivism," meaning government ownership of industries and public utilities, was their only bond. According to a manifesto published by the federation, its object was "to rally the socialists who do not want to embody their theoretical conceptions in a formula whose narrowness cannot embrace the multiple aspirations of the modern world, now in the full upswing of economic, political, mental and moral development." In due time the "Independents" were destined to give to their country a president in the person of Alexandre Millerand; at least two prime ministers, Viviani and Briand; and one of the greatest orators of all time—Jean Jaurès.

Jaurès (1859-1914), a philosopher and historian, had begun his political career in 1885 when he was elected to the Chamber of Deputies as a conservative, or as it is called in France, a moderate republican. Moving to the Left, he became in the early 1890's the spokesman of the "Independent Socialists," one of the competing socialist parties prior to their unification in 1905. Jaurès and his fellow Independents rejected the Marxist view of the inevitability of a violent revolution which would bring down the capitalist system. In his opinion a peaceful transition from capitalism to socialism was possible through the instrumentality of gradual socialization of various industries, the extension of political democracy, and the adoption of laws for the protection of labor. During the Dreyfus Affair, he championed the cause of the innocent Jewish captain, and his efforts contributed to the defeat of the reactionaries. A champion of peace and Franco-German rapprochement, he was assassinated on the eve of World War I by a monarchist fanatic who believed the reactionary slanders that Jaurès was an agent of Germany.

The internecine struggles of the competing socialist parties and the careerism of some of their leaders were grist to the mill of those ultraradicals who were known either as anarchists or as syndicalists. The competition of these groups, as well as the general political situation of France and the example of most of the other European countries, each of which had only one socialist party, led to attempts to unify the split forces of French democratic socialism and to form a unified party. The first attempt of this kind was made in 1899. But the general socialist convention called that year failed to bring about the hoped-for result.

At that time the French Left was sorely split on the question which was agitating the entire socialist world. It was the question as to whether a member of a socialist party should be permitted to join a cabinet of representatives of nonsocialist parties. Before them was the example of Alexandre Millerand, one of the leaders of the "Independent Socialists," who joined a moderately liberal cabinet which, to sweeten the socialist pill for the somewhat perplexed bourgeoisie, included General Galliffet, the military commander who nearly three decades before had put down the Paris Commune. No agreement was reached at that convention—except that the split was somewhat simplified, the Guesdists (Marxists) and Blanquists forming a left-wing bloc called the Socialist party of France, while the moderate Independents and what was left of the "Possibilists" formed the right-wing French Socialist party. (The ultraradical, horny-handed Allemanists remained outside both groups.) Five years later the two blocs made peace, with the left bloc imposing on the other group the obligation not to vote for the government budget and to withdraw its representatives from the parliamentary committee of the "Republican Left"—that is, of the liberal middle-class parties. The adoption of this radical program appeared as a necessary measure to stave off the danger threatening the socialist movement. The party was disintegrating; revolt was brewing within the various sections, and over both factions hovered the threat of syndicalism, which was making heavy inroads in socialist ranks. The united party adopted the name of "Socialist Party, French Section of the Workers' International" (S.F.I.O.)—usually called "Unified Socialist Party."

The unification of the various socialist groups greatly added to the prestige and influence of the socialists. The struggle between the Left and the Right within the party gradually abated, as did the antagonism of the trade unions to the party, for, as they grew in membership, the trade unions gradually shelved their ultrarevolutionary, syndicalist opposition to parliamentary politics. There was a rapprochement between the no longer revolutionary trade union leaders and the "politicians"—as the syndicalists would say—of the Socialist party. When in 1914 France was invaded by the Germans, both the Marxists within the Socialist party and the erstwhile syndicalists within the trade union movement forgot the classical revolutionary slogan that "the workers have no country" and rallied to the defense of France. With the consent of the party, two of its prominent leaders, both of the left wing, the Marxist Guesde and the Blanquist Sembat, entered the government and became members of a cabinet of national defense. (During the 1900's, the followers of the "antipatriot" and "insurrectionist" Gustave Hervé constituted the extreme left-wing faction of the party. It disappeared when during World War I Hervé turned superpatriot, and, later, Fascist.)

After the conclusion of World War I, the Socialist party was confronted by the fact that the majority of its membership was under the spell of the growing prestige of the Soviet regime which had emerged victorious from the civil war. That mood was reflected at the party convention held in 1920, at which those favoring joining the Communist International carried the majority. There was a split; most of the Marxist and near-Marxist elements within the party formed the Communist party and took over the party's daily *l'Humanité*. The democratic socialists, under the leadership of Léon Blum, re-established the old Socialist party with its frank acceptance of gradualist, democratic methods within the framework of a democratic state.[6]

Blum (1872-1949) was the son of a wealthy merchant of Alsatian origin. His maternal grandmother had been an ardent republican at the time of Napoleon III. After having achieved academic distinction both in letters and in law he was admitted to a career at the Conseil d'Etat, a body whose functions included the settlement of jurisdictional conflicts between administrative and judicial authorities. There he rose to the rank of *maître des requêtes* ("reporter on petitions").

At twenty-two he was a recognized poet and a literary and dramatic critic. A contributor to various literary magazines, his name was associated with those of the most outstanding literary celebrities of his time. He wrote a book about Stendhal, entitled *Stendhal et le Beylisme* (Paris, 1914). His views on literature and the theatre are reflected in the books *En Lisant* (Paris, 1906) and *Au Theatre* (4 vols.; Paris, 1905, 1907, 1909, 1911). His *Du Mariage* (Paris, 1907), dealing with the problem of woman's rights, created a sensation because of the boldness of its ideas.

In 1896, during the campaign for the liberation of Dreyfus, he met Jean Jaurès, the famous orator and leader of the French socialists. Under the influence of the great tribune he joined the socialist movement in 1899 and contributed to the daily *Petite République* and later, beginning in 1904, to *l'Humanité*. His *Nouvelles conversations avec Eckermann* (Paris, 1901), presenting imaginary conversations betwen Goethe and Eckermann, reflect his keen interest in public affairs. However, politically he remained in the background until the outbreak of the war in 1914, when he was called upon by the minister of public works, the socialist Marcel Sembat, to become the executive secretary of the ministry.

At the conclusion of World War I, Léon Blum became the outstanding representative of his party in the Chamber of Deputies. When, after the split, the communists took over the old socialist daily *l'Humanité*, Blum's efforts were largely responsible for the foundation of the daily *Populaire*, which has since remained the chief organ of the Socialist party.

Throughout the 1920's the socialists, though in a minority at the convention which led to the split of 1920 and to the formation of the Communist party, succeeded in building up their strength; in the elections of 1928 the socialists obtained 1,700,000 votes as compared to 1,100,000 for the communists. At the same time the system of run-off elections, with the second balloting permitting the conclusion of alliances between various middle-class parties of the Left, enabled the socialists to obtain a very large representation in the Chamber of Deputies. These electoral successes became a source of friction within the Socialist party. The party had its left, center, and right wing. The left wing, afraid of the potentialities of communist competition, played with ultrarevolutionary slogans in order to keep the more radical following of the party. The right wing favored party participation in a progressive government coalition. But the most important section was the center, headed by the generally respected and admired party chief Léon Blum who—while opposing any concession to the ultraradical verbiage of the communists —was at the same time opposed to collaboration with any government, fearful lest the responsibilities thus assumed and the ensuing disappointment of the masses, be grist to the mill of the communists.

THE "NEO-SOCIALIST" INTERLUDE

Early in the 1930's the right-wing socialists, eager for a short cut to cabinet posts and afraid of the spectacular success of Fascism in Europe, developed a theory of their own which they called "neo-socialism." That new departure was to instill new blood into the socialist movement and stem the rising wave of Fascism by the simple device of stealing the Fascist thunder and substituting the slogans of "Order, Authority, and Nation" for the traditional slogans of freedom, democracy, and internationalism. They calculated that if the Fascists could be successful in winning both workers and the lower middle classes by adding socialist slogans to nationalist propaganda, the socialists could outbid Fascist competition by supplementing socialist propaganda with slogans borrowed from the arsenal of Fascism. They did not succeed in convincing the bulk of the party, and as a result, about forty right-wing members of parliament constituted a new party called the Neo-Socialist party. However, the events which took place between 1934 and 1936 did not give the leaders of that party a chance to evolve into a full-fledged Fascist organization. Except for Marcel Deat, leader of the Neo-Socialists, who had ambitions of becoming the French Hitler, most of the Neo-Socialist members of the Chamber joined various groups of the Left Republican Bloc, while those right-wingers who had never been full-fledged Neo-Socialists eventually returned to the Socialist party.

THE UNITED FRONT

The events of February 1934, which frustrated the hopes of the Neo-Socialists, had their origin in a scandal connected with the financial exploits of a swindler by the name of Stavisky. Many politicians of the Republican Left were involved, and this gave an opportunity to Fascists, neo-Fascists and royalists to arouse large crowds and to stage a violent demonstration which succeeded in overthrowing the cabinet and in nearly wrecking the republican regime. Realizing the danger threatening the republic, the pro-socialist General Confederation of Labor (C.G.T.) supported by the Socialist party, decided to call a twenty-four-hour general strike to show that organized labor was ready to defend the republic. This was also the sentiment dominant among the communist-influenced workers who forced their own trade union organization, the Unitary Confederation of Labor (C.G.T.U.), and the Communist party to join forces with the socialist workers and to participate in the general strike. This was the beginning of what was to be called the United Front, a collaboration of the socialists and communists against the common danger. It was a collaboration which the Communist party as such entered only half-heartedly. The communists—though they later tried to deny all the documentary evidence against them—had themselves participated in the Fascist demonstration of February 6, 1934, and attacked the Cabinet as a government of murderers because it had sent the armed forces against the demonstration. Moreover, their official "line," which they had from Moscow, had told them to attack the socialists and to insult them as "Social Fascists." They had not yet received any new instructions as to whether they should change their tactics. But they could not risk losing their working-class following, and so they also gave their blessing to the unification of the two trade union organizations (C.G.T. and C.G.T.U.), which henceforth went under the old name C.G.T., with the old C.G.T. president, Leon Jouhaux, as its head.

As time went by, Moscow officially gave its blessing to the United Front of the two parties and was even anxious to extend the United Front to a Popular Front that would embrace the more or less progressive middle-class parties as well. By that time the Soviet regime had given up all hope of coming to an understanding with Hitler, and as a result it was eagerly trying to make friends with Western governments with a view to an alliance against the aggressive intentions of the Nazis.

POPULAR FRONT

The elections of 1936 resulted in a victory of the Popular Front; the Socialists with 146 deputies, the Communists with 72, and the so-called Radicals or Radical Socialists[7] with 116 seats, holding jointly a majority in the Chamber of Deputies. Léon Blum, the leader of the Socialists, became prime minister, and the other cabinet posts were filled by Socialists and Radical Socialists. The communists took no part in the government, but supported it with their votes. During Blum's tenure of office, 1936 to 1937, a good many measures benefiting the workers were enacted—among them the establishment of the forty-four-hour week, paid vacations, recognition of the trade unions as bargaining agencies. They greatly enhanced the prestige of the Socialist party among the workers, but in the same proportion they contributed to Blum's becoming unpopular with the rightist circles. A flight of capital, through the withdrawal of gold from the Bank of France, threatened to undermine the stability of the currency. Blum's attempts to counteract this stratagem of what in France was popularly called the "two hundred families," through his proposed measures, were vetoed by the Senate, thus forcing him to resign.

The socialist successes on the domestic front were dimmed by the humiliations the Blum regime had to suffer in the field of foreign affairs. The revolt of Spain's reactionary and Fascist generals against the republic had found support from Nazi Germany and Fascist Italy, and it was natural that democratic opinion in France was in favor of supporting the cause of the democratic republic, particularly as Nazi Germany and Fascist Italy openly supported General Franco with men and supplies. However, the pressure of the British Conservative government forced the Blum administration to accede to a policy of "nonintervention." France was threatened by Britain with diplomatic isolation in case of a conflict with Germany and Italy.

After the fall of the Blum cabinet, the socialists continued to give their support to the Popular Front cabinet headed by the Radical party. In March 1938, Blum became prime minister for the second time, but he had to resign after four weeks, because the financial reforms, including a graduated capital levy, proposed by him, though supported by the majority of the Chamber, were opposed by the Senate.

The events leading up to the Munich Agreement (September 30, 1938), under which Germany annexed the Sudeten section of Czechoslovakia, found the socialists divided in their opinion as to how France should have reacted to Hitler's demands. A large minority, and possibly even a majority, headed by the secretary of the party, Paul Faure, wanted to avoid war at any price, claiming that this was the classical socialist attitude of opposition to all wars. The right-wing-and-center group was supported in its pacifist attitude by a left-wing group, headed by Marceau Pivert, who believed in what was called "revolutionary defeatism"— that is, Pivert based his revolutionary hopes upon the defeat of his own country. These pacifist positions were opposed by the pro-communist group, headed by Jean Zyromski, according to which France should have gone to war to defend Czechoslovakia. Blum fully realized the tragic implication of appeasing Hitler, yet he felt powerless to go against the pacifist attitude both within the party and the trade unions. He admitted that, although he had for many years dedicated his life to peace, he could not feel any joy over the fact that war was averted, adding that he was "merely filled with mixed feelings of cowardly relief and shame." About two months later, Italian threats against and territorial demands upon France made the majority of the party realize that the threat of war was still in the air and that appeasement was no way out of the situation. As a result, Blum's championship of collective security rallied the enormous majority of the party, leaving only

Paul Faure, the secretary of the party, and his comparatively small following as representatives of a peace-at-any-price policy.

Throughout this period, until the conclusion of the Nazi-Soviet Pact, the communists were interested chiefly in the maintenance of friendly relations between France and the Soviet Union for the purpose of warding off the Nazi menace. As a result, they carried on an ultra-patriotic masquerade, launching nationalist slogans such as "France aux Français" ("France to the Frenchmen"), displaying the national tricolor instead of the red flag, and singing the "Marseillaise" instead of the "Internationale."

The conclusion of the Soviet-Nazi Pact of August 23, 1939, and the ensuing war between France and Nazi Germany forced the French communists to show their true colors. They justified the conclusion of the pact and opposed France's entrance into the war. The communist leader, Maurice Thorez, on being called to the colors, deserted to Russia. Outlawed, the Communist party went underground. Its leaflets attacked the "imperialist war" and insulted the socialist leaders as "traitors" because they supported their country in the war against the Nazis. They violently attacked Great Britain as the real ruler of France, but were silent about the Nazis. Their followers in arms factories committed acts of sabotage, damaging airplane motors and causing the death of many fliers. Some of the communist saboteurs were apprehended and condemned to death.

Having contributed their share to France's defeat, the communists took up a new "line": They accused all the other parties of "treason," of having delivered France to the Nazis, and made a bid for power by insisting upon the necessity of a "popular government." At the same time, they took up negotiations with the Nazi embassy and the Gestapo in Paris to get permission for the legal publication of their daily *l'Humanité*, suppressed at the outset of the war. In their pleas for legalization, the communists reminded the Nazi authorities that they had defended the Soviet-Nazi Pact, while the French Fascists, whom the Nazis now favored, had attacked it. The communists went to great lengths to curry the favor of the German conquerors. In their secret leaflets they encouraged French workers to fraternize with the German soldiers. They appealed to workers to take up production, and denounced those who "sabotaged the country's economic revival." In the July 1, 1940, issue of their secretly published central organ, *l'Humanité*, there was mention of the Nazis who had just occupied France, but the most violent attacks were directed against the leaders of all political parties, and particularly of the socialists, who were declared to be responsible for the war. The attempt to organize resistance to the Nazis was dealt with as follows: "General de Gaulle and other agents of British financial interests would like the French to fight for the City [the financial center of London]." It was only after the Nazi attack upon Russia in June 1941 that the French communists departed from their neutral attitude and became active in the Resistance movement—evidence that the communists considered themselves bound by ties of loyalty to the U.S.S.R. and not to France.

In 1940 a military-Fascist dictatorship, headed by Marshal Pétain, was established in the nonoccupied section of France. Most socialist members of the Parliament capitulated to the new masters, while a minority of the socialist leadership, headed by Léon Blum, opposed the regime and was arrested.

After the expulsion of the Nazis in 1944, France was for a short time dominated by a coalition of communists, Popular Republicans (a progressive Catholic party), and socialists. In the elections to the Constituent Assembly held in 1946, the communists obtained 151 seats out of a total of 586, the socialists obtained 139, and the leftist Popular Republicans won 150. These were the three largest parties in the Assembly. The courageous record of the communist resistance fighters (for the sake of Russia and not of France, to be sure) made the voters forget their attitude during the first two years of the war. At the subsequent election to the National Assembly held in November 1948, the communists (with their affiliated groups) obtained 182 seats (out of a total of 618), while the number of socialist deputies was reduced to 102. This showed that the trend was in favor of the communists. The first regular government, established early in 1947, was headed by socialist President Vincent Auriol, and socialist Premier Paul Ramadier. His cabinet consisted of nine socialists, five communists, and twelve members of other parties. The communists insisted upon key positions in the government which would correspond to their strength as the largest party in the Assembly. Their demand was ignored, for either the ministry of National Defense or Interior (National Police) would have enabled them to attempt a *coup d'état* as did their comrades in Czechoslovakia. Eventually, the cabinet was reorganized without the communists, the government consisting of Socialists, Popular Republicans and Radicals. It was called the Third Force government, because it was opposed to the two dictatorial tendencies, that of De Gaulle and that of the communists.

The elections to the Chamber of Deputies, held in 1951 under a new voting system which to a large extent eliminated the system of proportional representation, reduced the number of communist seats from 182 to 140, while the number of socialist seats remained approximately the same. The changed political constellation in the Chamber, the rise of an extremely conservative nondictatorial "fourth force," and the conflict with the newly strengthened Radical party which was opposed to social reforms benefiting the workers, and with the Popular Republicans who insisted upon concessions to parochial schools, caused the socialists to leave the government coalition and join the opposition.

GUY MOLLET

During the turbulent 1950's, prior to the seizure of power by De Gaulle, when cabinets changed with greater frequency than some old-time Latin American revolutionary regimes, a right-wing Socialist, Guy Mollet, a former school teacher, became prime minister at the time when the Moslem revolt in Algeria was in full swing. In this capacity his attitude and that of the majority of his party became undistinguishable from that of all traditional parties which refused to grant independence to colonial peoples. The Socialist party had simply become a political machine of ambitious, slightly leftist antimonarchists and anticlericals with a following consisting largely of white collar workers and lower rank government functionaries, ready to serve the interests of French imperialism, just as the Communist party, with its working class following, is ready to serve those of Russian imperialism.

At the time of the *coup d'état* of 1958 which overthrew the Fourth Republic, Guy Mollet and his party supported De Gaulle. A section of the party refused to follow that course and formed a dissident socialist organization headed by former Prime Minister Mendès-France, who had left the mildly liberal Radical party.

At variance with most of the countries of the Western world, democratic socialism now plays a minor role in Italy, even though it had been an important political factor prior to the rise of Fascism in the early 1920's. Founded in 1892, the Socialist party of Italy took over the inheritance of the once influential insurrectionist movement inspired by Michael Bakunin. The famous Russian anarchist's following consisted chiefly of educated déclassés, intellectuals, and semi-intellectuals who saw in an *immediate* social revolution the only way out of a hopeless personal situation in a politically and economically backward country. In proportion as they lost hope in the imminence of Revolution and as the economic situation of the country began to show some improvement, many of the erstwhile Bakuninists abandoned their intransigent position and embraced the evolutionary vistas of Marxism. One of the first champions of Marxism in Italy was the Russian ex-terrorist Anna Kulishov (spelled in Italian, Kuliscioff), who is believed to have converted Andrea Costa, the outstanding leader of the anarchists, and, later, her husband, Filippo Turati, who was to become the leader of the Italian Socialist party.

A member of the upper middle classes and active in the democratic movement, Turati (1857-1932) became interested in socialist ideas during the 1880's, when, because of Italy's backward economic condition, Bakunin's ideas still found a fertile ground among the starving workers and déclassé intellectuals. Within the Italian Socialist party, which officially had accepted the theories of Marxism, he represented the "right" or "reformist" wing that was opposed to the revolutionary tactics and slogans of the left wing. He advocated a policy of gradual reforms and improvements to be obtained by legal parliamentary methods and insisted that the party should help in the organization of trade unions, co-operatives, and educational institutions. In the legislative bodies the party was to try to obtain a majority, while collaborating with the progressive middle-class parties, to institute social reforms benefiting the masses. After the uprising of workers in Milan in 1898, Turati was sentenced to sixteen years' imprisonment, but was released the following year due to the pressure of public opinion, expressed in the election of socialist candidates. He was a pacifist in matters of international policy and opposed both Italy's war against Turkey (1911) for the conquest of Libya and her intervention in World War I. After the conclusion of the war, Turati tried to counteract the influence of those within his party who, impressed by the Bolshevik Revolution, had caused the Socialist party to join the Communist International and had tried to parallel the Bolshevik experience. With the rise of Fascism in the 1920's, even before Mussolini's seizure of power in 1922, Turati witnessed the gradual destruction of the many trade unions, co-operatives, and educational institutions created with the assistance of his party, and which had secured its great influence. When in 1926 Mussolini dealt the last blow against the Socialist party by declaring it illegal and by suppressing *La Critica sociale*, the theoretical organ edited by Turati since 1890, the aged leader fled to France, where he died a few years later.

After Turati's death, one of the party's most influential leaders was Pietro Nenni, who returned from exile after the downfall of Mussolini. Under Nenni's leadership the party, which has a large number of representatives in the Chamber of Deputies, has consistently taken a position much closer to that of the Communist party than to that of his own party's former right wing which, under the leadership of Giuseppe Saragat, has formed the Social Democratic party. This gradualist socialist organization has a few representatives in Parliament who usually lend their support to left-of-center cabinets as against the right wing of the Christian Democratic party and its neo-Fascist and monarchist allies. During the early 1960's there have been frequent reports about a forthcoming break between Nenni's strong Socialist party and the powerful Communist party and about the prospects of the former taking a position similar to that of the Social Democratic party.

THE SPANISH SOCIALISTS

From the outset of the modern radical movement the Spanish democratic socialists—they were all followers of Marx—had to wage an uphill struggle against the anarchists who had won influence among the workers as the first champions of labor unions and of their bread-and-butter struggles. Under the leadership of Pablo Iglesias (1850-1925), a self-educated worker, the Marxists formed the Socialist Labor party in 1879, and in 1888 the General Union of Workers, a federation of trade unions professing their views. Both organizations were headed by Iglesias.

While the anarchists attracted the most temperamental and the most desperate elements among the underprivileged, the socialists bent over backwards in trying to prove their "reasonableness." An incident that happened in 1912 may serve as an illustration. In that year, Prime Minister Canalejas was killed by an anarchist in protest against the bloody suppression of the general strike in 1911, directed against the Moroccan war. The Cortes, in retaliation, decided to confer the hereditary ducal title upon the dead statesman's widow and his children. Pablo Iglesias, Marxist leader of the Spanish proletariat, and a pillar of the Socialist International, voted for the measure—an act that scandalized many of his fellow socialists outside Spain.

In August 1917, the impact of the Russian Revolution and the general revolutionary atmosphere caused the Socialist party to depart from its moderation and to participate in an antimonarchist uprising. The action misfired and some of the leaders of the party, including Francisco Largo Caballero—who succeeded Iglesias as the strong man of the party—were given life terms.

A few years later, Largo Caballero, who had been amnestied in the meantime, reverted to the traditional opportunism of his party by participating in the dictatorial regime established in 1923 by General Primo de Rivera. Another turn of events, and at the downfall of the monarchy in 1931, Largo Caballero became the leader of the revolutionary wing of the Socialist party. When the civil war broke out in 1936, he became the head of a Popular Front government in which all Leftist and autonomist parties were represented. After a few months his government was replaced by that of another socialist, Juan Negrin, who was generally believed to have been a captive of Stalin's agents. Throughout the civil war, the socialists, while at the helm of the republican government, were split into various cliques fighting each other for predominance. Since Franco's victory in 1939 they have been either in exile or in the Spanish underground.

Unlike the Italian socialists, those of Belgium, Holland, and the Scandinavian countries have followed the general pattern of their moderate namesakes in Germany, France, and England in that they either supported or participated in or headed various nonsocialist governments. However, each of these parties has, in the course of its history, displayed certain features of its own. In highly industrialized Belgium the party succeeded in establishing a close union of the strictly political with the trade union and co-operative organizations. In 1893 it turned a new leaf in socialist history in organizing a general strike in support of its demand for equal suffrage as against the "plural" vote favoring the privileged and property-owning classes. This gave a great spurt to the propaganda of the general strike idea by the extreme Left elements within the democratic socialist parties. For years "to talk Belgian" was a favorite threat uttered by socialists of those countries whose franchise was not equal, direct, or universal.

The Dutch socialists, whose country depended for much of its wealth on the possession of Indonesia, created an international scandal within the radical movement when in 1904, at the International Socialist Congress held in Amsterdam, one of their best-known representatives, Van Kol, came out frankly in defense of colonialism, which was violently opposed by the socialist parties of those countries which had no colonies.

Most successful of all socialist parties were those of Denmark, Norway, and Sweden, which ever since the 1930's have been at the helm of their respective governments, having polled either the majority or the plurality of votes at the many consecutive elections.

Their success in winning the electorate has been explained by the fact that they did not have to contend with the "red herrings" of nationalism, religious conflicts, and anti-Semitism, which in most other countries served the propaganda of reactionary rabble-rousers. Their countries were homogeneously Protestant, there were no scars of national defeats or humiliations to feed a chauvinistic lunatic fringe, and the Jews are just as scarce there as they are in India or China.

As distinguished from the British Labor party, the Scandinavian socialist parties did not engage in large-scale nationalization schemes—particularly as the railways and all the other public utilities had been run by the government ever since the inception of the industrial age. Instead, they applied a radical method of taxation that enabled them to evolve a vast system of social security which in turn won for them the allegiance of the majority of the electorate.

THE CZECHS AND THE POLES

A place apart within the anticapitalist orbit was held by the democratic socialists of two Slavic nationalities, the Czechs and the Poles. They subscribed to all the internationalist and class struggle tenets of pre-Leninist Marxism; but their antagonism to capitalism was largely overshadowed by nationalist resentment against the masters of the Habsburg and the Romanov empires whose unwilling subjects they were.

As a result, the Czech socialist-controlled trade unions insisted upon complete separation and independence from the general federation of Austrian trade unions, largely controlled by German-speaking socialists. And it was the Czech socialists who, having voluntarily merged with the communists after World War II, fully approved of the expulsion of the entire Sudeten German population.

Most Polish socialists were primarily left-wing anti-Russian nationalists whom the Marxist theoretician Rosa Luxemburg, who was the leader of a small Polish group of internationalist socialists, dubbed as Social-Patriots. The first plank of the program of the Polish Socialist party postulated the establishment of an independent democratic Polish Republic. Under the leadership of Joseph Pilsudski, who later became the near-Fascist dictator of Poland, the party carried on for years a terrorist struggle against the tsarist authorities. Upon the establishment of Poland's independence after the conclusion of World War I, the socialists fought, jointly with the other Polish nationalists, against those Ukrainians who demanded the independence of eastern Galicia which, though "historically" a Polish possession, was predominantly Ukrainian. However, the Polish socialists opposed the dictatorial tendencies of their renegade ex-leader Pilsudski. After the establishment of a communist regime at the conclusion of World War II, some of the Polish socialists joined the ruling party

Part II
The Anglo-Saxon and the Asian Orbits

SOCIALISM IN ENGLAND

From its very inception the democratic socialist movement in England followed a course that disregarded the ideas which put their stamp on the radical movements in the rest of Europe. A bird's-eye glance at the history of British radicalism may supply an understanding of this phenomenon.

British radicalism in a modern sense—that is, free of elements of religious sectarianism—goes back to the time of Cromwell's dictatorship, when the Levellers, headed by John Lilburne, raised their voice in behalf of political democracy. The social stratum they championed was the lower middle class, and their demand for a popular franchise did not extend to those who were too poor to be "housekeepers" and to pay assessments for the support of the poor. Socialist, communist, or equalitarian concepts formed no part of their practical demands or of their philosophical outlook. They are not to be confused with the "True Levellers" or "Diggers" who were active during the same period and were truly the champions of the "have-nots." It was their attempt to dig up some unused land that earned them the name under which they are known. Their ideas, as expressed in the writings of Gerrard Winstanley, represented a sort of near-anarchist form of communism. Like the Tolstoyan anarchists of two and a half centuries later, they were opposed to violence, and like the anarchists of Kropotkin's school, they believed that work should be done in common, with the products placed in storehouses at the free disposal of those in need. It is likely that, aside from religious mysticism, certain aspects of their creed contributed to the views of both the eighteenth-century anarchism of William Godwin and of the early nineteenth-century philanthropical socialism of Robert Owen.

These two aspects of early British radicalism—the purely political postulates aiming at the democratization and liberalization of the existing system without affecting its economic structure, and the basic economic changes involving some kind of public ownership—were to reappear under different forms and names both at the time of the French Revolution and throughout the nineteenth century.

The French Revolution evoked a powerful echo in England. The politically articulate section of those excluded from the banquet of the aristocratic and plutocratic oligarchy enthroned since the "glorious Revolution" of 1689 began to stir. It included the most alert among the skilled workers and large numbers of equally disfranchised intellectuals who saw in the "rotten borough" system of British parliamentarism a "stinking sewer of corruption." The London Corresponding Society, founded in 1792, became the rallying point of the "Jacobins" and the "Levellers," as all those were called who clamored for a reform of the parliamentary system then prevailing in England. Those radicals drew their inspiration to a large extent from Thomas Paine's *Rights of Man*. Persecutions were not slow in coming; the society was forced underground, and many of its leaders drew long terms of imprisonment. By 1799 the organization ceased to exist. But the movement for parliamentary reform was not dead. It was to revive a few years later, assuming in the 1830's and 1840's the character of a mass movement, known under the name of Chartism.

WILLIAM GODWIN AND THOMAS SPENCE

In the meantime, however, other ideas came to the fore which went beyond the simple demand for parliamentary reform. In 1793, less than one year after the founding of the London Corresponding Society, William Godwin's *Enquiry Concerning Political Justice*—as a rule called *Political Justice*—found an enthusiastic reception among many malcontents. It was no call to action, for what those two volumes advocated was a nebulous ideal of equalitarian anarchism. But it was a protest against all the sacred institutions of the past—government, laws, clergy, aristocracy, family. It did not preach violence; in fact, it was even opposed to any *organized* political activity, admitting only the method of individual persuasion; yet the boldness of its ideas was to put its stamp on the minds of many of his contemporaries and particularly on the growing younger generation of poets, such as Byron, Shelley, and others.

While Godwin's practical contribution to the struggle against the oligarchy was very slight—for his was a gospel for dreamers and poets—the ideas of another man were to become a revolutionary factor during the years to come, after they had been largely ignored during the lifetime of their originator. These were the ideas of Thomas Spence who, in 1793, republished, under the title *The Real Rights of Man*, a lecture he had delivered as far back as 1775 (it was also republished under the title of *The Meridian Sun of Liberty*). Spence advocated nationalization of the land, the parishes to become the owners of the land, leasing it to the farmers at a moderate rental. That rental was to be the only tax the government was to levy. To be sure, while eliminating absentee landowners, the scheme did not altogether do away with class distinctions, for not everybody could rent land, and the small tenant farmers would become a sort of privileged group as compared with the farm laborers in their employ.

Thomas Spence combined the advocacy of his land reform ideas with the political propaganda started by the London Corresponding Society. Gradually, he succeeded in winning a small but very vocal following which, in 1812, was organized in a society called the "Spencean Philanthropists." They constituted a very active element within the general democratic movement for parliamentary reform. The government, seriously disturbed by their propaganda, suppressed their organization in 1817.

This measure, joined with the brutality with which the authorities countered mass demonstrations against the Corn Laws and for parliamentary reform—the historical massacre of "Peterloo" (Saint Petersfield near Manchester in 1819)—made some of the Spenceans despair of the practicability of open propaganda. One of their leaders, Arthur Thistlewood, conceived the idea of using the weapon of terrorism against the leading members of the government. The result was the Cato Street Conspiracy and the gallows on which Thistlewood and his friends lost their lives.

MACHINE WRECKERS AND TRADE UNIONS

While the most energetic elements among the lower middle-class intelligentsia, supported by the most intelligent skilled workers, were campaigning for parliamentary and land reform the changes brought about by the industrial revolution called forth a reaction of another kind. The introduction of machinery had caused a lowering of the standard of living and unemployment among large sections of the working class. In desperation the workers had resorted to machine-wrecking as far back as the 1760's. That form of protest of the helpless underdog became a mass phenomenon between 1811 and 1818, when the rebels against early industrialism were called "Luddites," after a mythical Ned Ludd who was believed to have started the campaign of destruction. Gibbets and atrocious prison sentences were the government's reply to this elemental revolt of the first victims of the machine age. Byron's speech in the House of Lords in defense of the Luddites and his moving poem in which he glorified their martyrs testify to the reaction of the best minds of the time to the first steps in the triumphant march of modern industrialism.

Luddite violence was only the most spectacular aspect of the nascent spontaneous *labor* movement, as distinguished from political radicalism, whose driving force has always been the malcontent, déclassé intelligentsia. Another aspect of the rising labor movement was the formation of secret trade unions, for there were heavy penalties—prison and deportation to Australia—for any attempt to organize workers' resistance against their employers. The workers' persistence in their attempts to organize and to strike eventually led to the repeal of the "Combination Acts"—the laws which prohibited their "combinations." After 1824 it was no longer a crime to organize, though it was still a grave offense to administer a trade union oath or to break a contract of service.

OWENISM AND PROTO-SYNDICALISM

Encouraged by the abolition of the "Combination Acts," many workers took part in the democratic movement for the extension of the franchise. There were also those among the trade union members who lent an ear to the socialist propaganda of Robert Owen, dreamer, successful manufacturer, and philanthropist. Owen thought little of political activity and the struggle for the extension of the franchise. He gave his support to the labor unions and hoped that the latter, by organizing producers' co-operatives, would eventually effect the transition of the industries into the hands of the workers. He also believed that he would succeed in converting the privileged classes to his gospel and was hence opposed not only to any sort of violence but also to the very idea of the class struggle.

For a while Owen's propaganda was enhanced by the disappointment which seized many workers after the adoption of the Reform Bill in 1832. For the extension of the franchise for which they had fought, and which they expected from the adoption of that bill, turned out to be an extension in behalf of the middle classes only; the workers, the farm laborers, the lower middle-class intellectuals, and the white-collar employees had all been excluded from the benefits of that reform. But once they began to turn away from politics which had deceived their hopes, many workers began to listen to an "anti-political" gospel, which, though proceeding from Owenism, was more radical and appeared to be more realistic than the class-harmony pipe dream of the great philanthropist. It was a gospel preached by two of Owen's former followers, James Morrison, a self-educated construction worker, and James E. Smith, a lecturer and journalist. The theory which they elaborated anticipated by nearly seventy years the ideas of the French syndicalists. They deprecated the parliamentary-political struggle and put forward direct action and the general strike as the most effective weapons of the working class.

The Grand National Consolidated Trades Union, which was formed in 1834 as a central body embracing all trade unions, was for a short time the rallying point and the battlefield of three tendencies within the labor movement: trade unionism, pure and simple, which was interested only in higher wages and shorter hours; Owenism, which wanted to use the trade unions for the formation of producers' co-operatives aiming at the gradual establishment of socialism; and the syndicalism (the term was nonexistent as yet) of Morrison and Smith, which contemplated the violent overthrow of the capitalist system by the method of the general strike and the reconstruction of society on the basis of the trade unions. The "Consolidated" was not equal to the great difficulties it encountered from the start. The fierce opposition of the employers and of the government, the dishonesty of some of its officials who often stole the funds, and the internecine conflict between Owen and the syndicalists who, upon the urging of the grand old man, were removed from the organization, all contributed to the disintegration of the organization less than a year after it was formed.

CHARTISM

In their disappointment over the failure of the various aspects of trade union activity, many workers, eager for action, turned to radical politics or political radicalism, as embodied in the Chartist movement (1837-54). The "Charter," from which the movement got its name, was a succinct, six-point demand for political equality to be achieved by universal suffrage, equal electoral districts, abolition of property qualifications for candidates, annual elections, secret ballot, and payment to members of Parliament. For all the mass following they commanded, the Chartists never constituted a regular political organization, for the laws prevailing in England at that time forbade the formation of a national organization with local branches. The various local organizations differed from each other as to the character of their aims and the method which, in their belief, would lead to victory. The leadership was sorely split, and one could speak of the existence of two parties within the Chartist movement: the "moral force" party led by William Lovett, who believed only in peaceful methods, and the "physical force" party led by Feargus O'Connor. The movement was not committed to any specific social theories; it included champions of various schools of socialism, land reformers, and ordinary radical democrats.

The eventual defeat and disintegration of Chartism in the early 1850's is attributed to various causes: lack of unity within the movement, indifference of the trade unions, the erratic character of the most popular leader, Feargus O'Connor, and the passing of various liberal laws for the protection of labor as well as the repeal of the Corn Laws, which removed many grievances. And last but not least, the poor showing the Chartist party made during the "mad year" of 1848, when, continental fashion, it attempted a revolutionary uprising in London and gave up the attempt due to an acute attack of cold feet.

The final disappearance of Chartism and the total eclipse of all aspects of radicalism for nearly three decades may be explained by the prosperity which during that period was enjoyed by practically all sections of the population. It was the period when England's industry controlled the world market, when manufacturers could raise wages without being forced to do so by strikes, and when—as a cynic or a realist might put it—there was a good desk job for every potentially radical malcontent intellectual worker. It was the period when the British trade unions were in the tow of the Liberal party, the party of the manufacturers, and when Marx, in his exasperation, could say that "it was not an honor, but rather the opposite, to be a trade union leader because they are all sold to the Liberals." It was also the period when even harmless radicalism such as the Christian socialism of Maurice, Kingsley, and Ludlow, with its panacea of producers' co-operatives, could make no headway.

Even during the period when the British trade

unions adhered to the First International (1864-76), the real reason for that gesture was no spurt of radicalism or of international working-class solidarity, but the very practical consideration that the International might be helpful in stopping the immigration of potentially strikebreaking cheap labor from the European continent.

The depression starting in 1875 and lasting several years was largely responsible for a new spurt of radicalism in England. It was at that time—in the early 1880's—that a number of intellectuals began to show interest in the ideas of Karl Marx.

BRITISH MARXISM

The interest in the ideas of Marx was largely due to the repercussions of the depression upon the educated classes. Increased facilities for higher education had begun to produce an excess of young people of middle-class or lower middle-class origin who faced an uncertain future. Various schemes of social reform involving some public control of industries as against private monopoly were taken up with ardor not only by impecunious malcontents but also by a number of upper middle-class intellectuals. Some of the latter saw in socialism either a philanthropic protest against the growing misery of large sections of the laboring masses, or a peaceful means of averting the cataclysm that seemed to them inevitable, unless certain reforms were effected. Others came in the spirit of dilettantism or ambition, ready to play with, or to direct, the potential forces of a history-making upheaval. One of these was Henry M. Hyndman, who had studied the works of Marx and had many personal conversations with him. The result of these studies was Hyndman's *England for*

All (1881). It was the first book in which the economic ideas of Marx were presented by one of his followers.

In the same year Hyndman organized the first political group which professed these ideas. It was called Democratic Federation, a name changed three years later to Social Democratic Federation. Its membership consisted largely of professionals and other intellectual workers with a smattering of educated manual workers. The organization could boast of some outstanding names, such as Belfort Bax, a famous barrister and sociologist, William Morris, the poet and artist, Walter Crane, a painter of the Pre-Raphaelite school, very well-known in those years, Eleanor Marx, the brilliant daughter of her famous father, and her husband, Dr. Edward Aveling, a translator of Marx's *Das Kapital*. Bernard Shaw also considered entering the organization.

It was the ambition of its founder to create a socialist mass party after the German model. His hopes were never realized because the conditions in England were different from those on the European continent. In Germany and other European countries the socialists had been able to win the masses because they had helped them in the organization of their unions and in their struggles for better conditions. It was different in England, where industrial development had begun much earlier and where workers were organized in trade unions before the rise of the socialist movement. Hence, the indifference of the British workers when the Social Democratic Federation made its appearance and tried to win them over. The S.D.F., which in 1908 changed its name to Social Democratic party, never became a mass organization and its membership never exceeded 12,000. The situation did not change when, in 1911, the S.D.P. joined forces with a few other socialist groups, and formed the British Socialist party. There was a split in the British Socialist party in 1915, during World War I, when the majority took an internationalist attitude by endorsing the Zimmerwald Conference —called in an attempt to revive the internationalist spirit within the radical movement—while the minority, including Hyndman, the founder of the S.D.F., formed the National Socialist party.

The National Socialist party of England, founded many years before Hitler adopted the same name for his organization, at first differed from the British Socialist party chiefly in its attitude toward national defense by insisting that England had to be defended to the bitter end. After the Bolshevik Revolution in 1917 the British Socialist party left the Socialist International and jointly with a few other revolutionary groups formed the Communist party of Great Britain. The group which remained loyal to Hyndman—the National Socialist party—evolved in the very opposite direction by taking a strictly anticommunist attitude after the seizure of power by Lenin. It joined the Labour party and was absorbed by it.

THE SOCIALIST LEAGUE OF ENGLAND

During the early years of its existence the Social Democratic Federation became the involuntary sire of another socialist group. Rigid adherence to a definite set of principles was not insisted upon by Hyndman, the founder of the organization, as long as its members were willing to accept his authority. As a result, the S.D.F. included heterogenous elements—from orthodox Marxists, German-style, to antiparliamentarian socialists deprecating the use of the ballot and anarchists rejecting the very idea of any government authority. The exponents of these ideas were united only by their bitter opposition to the existing system. They were soon to be bitterly arrayed against each other in a struggle of personal ambitions and diverging conceptions. In the split that ensued many of the most outstanding personalities, such as William Morris, Belfort Bax, Walter Crane, and the Avelings, parted with Hyndman and founded the Socialist League of England.

The unifying idea of the Socialist League of England was its dislike and distrust of Hyndman, whose dictatorial propensities they denounced. The League published a weekly entitled *Commonweal*, which was edited by William Morris. By the end of the 1880's the anarchists won the upper hand in the League. This caused the withdrawal of most of the nonanarchists, including William Morris, who thereupon cut off his financial support. The organization ceased to exist soon after.

THE FABIAN SOCIETY

While the S.D.F. and the S.L.E. represented the more revolutionary aspects of the anticapitalist protest, another socialist organization, founded in 1883 and called the Fabian Society, took a somewhat different position. It was a position akin to the strategy of its patron saint, the Roman General Fabius Maximus, who avoided decisive battles and tried to weaken the enemy by cautious, dilatory actions. The Fabians were opposed to Marxism, particularly to that aspect of it which is called the theory of the increasing misery of the working class, a theory which implied the inevitability of a violent overthrow of the capitalist system. According to the Fabians, the economic situation of the workers had improved and would improve further: in this process, supported by the various social reforms adopted for the protection of labor, lay, in their opinion, the possibility of a gradual transition from capitalism to socialism. The Fabians did not intend to form a political party of their own; their ambition was to permeate other parties with their socialist ideas, which they expected to triumph without the unpleasantnesses of the class struggle through the orderly method of a parliamentary majority adhering to their ideas. Representatives of the most advanced wing of the liberal upper middle classes, the Fabians understood that government ownership, the panacea of nineteenth-century democratic socialism, was perfectly compatible with the preservation of economic inequality. High salaries in the administration and management of the nationalized industries, or compensation in the form of life annuities, would be substituted for the profits formerly derived by owners or stockholders from the privately owned industries; and these substitutes, as well as increased security and safety, would be sufficient compensation for the loss of private ownership rights. Shaw, however, advocated equality of income, except, possibly, for outstanding men such as he.

The outstanding spokesmen of the Fabians included Sidney Webb, his wife Beatrice Potter Webb, Bernard Shaw, and Graham Wallas. The Webbs and Shaw lived long enough to see certain ideas under the name of socialism realized in Russia and in England; and ironically, they were to become the apologists of the Russian brand of socialism—apparently because the complete abolition of private capitalism and the enthronement of a managerial and bureaucratic hierarchy meant more to them than considerations of personal liberty or cultural freedom.

A new departure of British radicalism during the late 1880's was a trend within the trade union movement which became known as New Unionism. Its impulse came from the London dockers' strike of 1889, which had become famous because of the mass demonstrations accompanying it. The economic stagnation caused by growing German and American competition on the world market inclined the British organized workers to listen to radical speakers who, like John Burns and Tom Mann, had gone through the school of the Social Democratic Federation. The agitation among the unemployed, the political mass protests sponsored by that group during 1886 and 1887 and the victorious dockers' strike of 1889 with its famous mass demonstrations led to the organization of unskilled workers—that section of the working class that had hitherto been ignored by the trade unions.

THE INDEPENDENT LABOUR PARTY

That turmoil prepared the ground for a new socialist party that was closer to the working masses. In the opinion of many educated workers and ex-workers who had gotten their political training in the Social Democratic Federation, the organization had become a group of sectarians using a Marxian vocabulary which the British workers were unwilling to learn. What the country needed, in the opinion of those socialists who were dissatisfied with the sectarianism of the S.D.F. was an independent labor party speaking a language understood by the rank and file, a party supported by the trade unions and able to exert pressure for the introduction of important social reforms including municipal or government ownership of public utilities.

The outstanding personality in the movement for an independent labor party was the Scottish miner Keir Hardie. He had arrived at socialism without going through the Marxist school; his first concern was to help organized labor become an independent political force, no longer the tail to the Liberal party. In his efforts he was supported by Tom Mann, who later became a syndicalist and still later a communist. Through the efforts of these men and others sharing their views the Independent Labour Party was formed in 1893. In time it was also joined by some intellectual workers who were repelled by the personality of the Marxist leader H. M. Hyndman—he was also disliked by Marx and Engels—or by the ineffectual methods of his organization.

The new party did not call itself "socialist," lest it frighten away the many working-class elements which had been prejudiced against that word by the daily press. Neither did its speakers and its publications use the vocabulary of Marxian socialism, which had become generally current in the labor movement of the European continent. The British trade unionism of the past generation had developed under the tutelage of former workers, and these had taken their political and intellectual inspiration from liberal employers with whom a certain harmony had been established at the time when British industry dominated the world market.

The Independent Labour party won a membership of 6,000 soon after its organization. Its first attempt to send representatives to Parliament failed. Not one of its twenty-eight candidates was elected in 1895 and its total vote did not exceed 44,000—a small figure as com-

pared with 1,500,000 votes polled by the German Social-Democratic party in 1893. Attempts to join forces
with the S.D.F. in a loose alliance came to nought. The
Marxist party insisted upon a complete merger which,
the leaders of the I.L.P. feared, would have amounted
to their being forced to recognize the domination of
Hyndman and his fellow intellectuals.

One of the outstanding personalities of the Independent Labour party was Ramsay MacDonald, later
head of the Labour party and of the first two Labour
party governments (1924 and 1929-31). It was under
his leadership that the I.L.P. contributed to the organization of the Labour party of which it was to become
an affiliate.

THE LABOUR PARTY

During the last few years of the nineteenth century
British labor engaged in a number of conflicts with employers. British industry no longer dominated the world
market and was trying to safeguard its interests either
by reducing wages or by refusing to grant increases.
Major strikes of machinists and miners took place in
1896 and 1897 and were lost after several months. Encroachments were made upon the hitherto recognized
rights of the labor unions. Picketing was forbidden in
1896, and the courts declared that trade unions were
responsible for the illegal actions of individual strikers.
In 1900 the trade union of the railway workers was
sentenced to pay damages to the Taff-Vale Railway
Company as a result of a strike directed against that
company.

The trade unions saw their existence threatened,
and they began to look for allies. Expecting no help
from either the Liberals or Conservatives, the Trade

Union Congress held in 1899 adopted a proposal submitted by members of the Independent Labour party, which advocated the calling of a special congress of cooperative and socialist organizations as well as of trade unions. That congress was to discuss methods of securing a large labor representation in Parliament, in order to defend the menaced rights of labor. A committee composed of representatives of the Parliamentary Committee of the trade unions (lobby committee), of the Independent Labour party, of the Social Democratic Federation, and of the Fabian Society was entrusted with the arrangements for the special congress which was held in 1900. At that congress the Labour Representation Committee—for the next six years the official name of the Labour party—was established. It was not a party in the usual meaning of the word, since it did not admit individuals. Only organized bodies as a whole could be affiliated with it. Individual membership was rendered possible only eighteen years later.

During the year 1900, forty-one trade unions and three socialist organizations joined the new party. They brought in a total membership of 380,000 trade unionists and socialists, including about 13,000 members of the Independent Labour party, 9,000 members of the Social Democratic Federation, and 861 Fabians. At the general elections held the same year only two Labour candidates were elected, Keir Hardie being one of them. It was a poor showing, caused by the fact that the workers had been carried away by the wave of jingoism which swept the country because of the war in South Africa.

In 1906 the Labour Representation Committee took the name Labour party—by then it had 900,000 members. The trade unions, aroused by the Taff-Vale sentence as well as similar judgments following that precedent, had begun to come over in increasing numbers. At the elections held in that year twenty-nine of fifty candidates of the Labour party were returned to Parliament. In addition, fourteen Labour members from the mining districts, who had been returned as Liberals, joined a few years later. The Labour party grew visibly and was on the way to power.

During the first period of its activities the Labour party was not committed to any socialist theories. The principle of nationalization of industries was not adopted by the party until 1917. Nor would the leaders of the party, particularly such men as Ramsay Mac-Donald, make any concessions to Marxist terminology and speak of the class struggle. According to them the conflict between labor and those who opposed it was one of principles and not of interests.

THE LABOUR PARTY BETWEEN TWO WORLD WARS

During the first World War (1914-18) the British Labour party took the position of full support of the government's war effort. As a result, it disowned its own chairman Ramsay MacDonald, who had taken a pacifist antiwar attitude during the days immediately preceding the beginning of hostilities. His views were shared by the Independent Labour party, then part of the Labour party.

As the war dragged on and the Russian Revolution entered its Bolshevik stage, the temper and behavior of the British working masses began to change. A growing labor unrest began to manifest itself in a number of strikes. The cry for peace was growing louder and the Labour party, which hitherto had not been officially committed to socialism, adopted public ownership of industries as part of its platform. Thousands of professionals and intellectuals perhaps felt that, at bottom, socialism meant the substitution of their rule for that of the capitalists. They accordingly began to stream into the Labour Party, which now changed its constitution and opened its doors to individual membership.

After the conclusion of the war British workers, who had been promised so much as a result of victory, saw that in 1919 their standard of living was actually lower than it was in 1913. They gave vent to their dissatisfaction in many strikes and in increasing sympathy for the communists, who had formed a party by merging two Marxist groups, one of which was the successor of the old Social Democratic Federation. The Independent Labour party, which had become a rallying point of many middle-class intellectuals who had become disappointed with the Liberal party, left the Socialist International and opened negotiations with the Communist International. (Five years later, when the revolutionary wave had abated, the Independent Labour party concurred in excluding the Communist party from the Labour party. As time went by, the I.L.P., after many vacillations—to the Right and Left— shrank to the size of an unimportant political sect.)

One of the effects of the militant mood of the workers, and particularly of those who had just returned from the trenches, was the granting of unemployment insurance. It was the greatest single reform directly affecting the status of all workers in England which had yet been achieved. As the British statesman Lloyd George declared, it was granted as an alternative to a revolution which, after the conclusion of the war, was nearer than at any other time.

In 1920 the threat of British and French intervention against Soviet Russia—as a result of the war between Poland and Russia—caused large sections of British labor to align with a "Committee of Action" opposed to intervention. It was not affection for Bolshevism, but fear lest a successful intervention give more power to the Tory elements and result in a general attack against all the concessions achieved by the workers.

The 1920's were characterized by two unsuccessful attempts of the British miners to prevent a reduction of their wages. Their defeats in 1921 and again in 1926, were compensated—in the opinion of some British Labour party leaders—by the fact that, during four successive elections, in 1922, 1923, 1924, and 1929, the Labour vote showed a continuous growth (4,236,733 in 1922, 4,348,379 in 1923, 5,487,620 in 1924, and 8,362,594 in 1929).

Twice during that decade the Labour party was entrusted with forming the government, with Ramsay MacDonald as prime minister, even though it did not command an absolute majority of seats. As a result, the Labour party was able in both cases to maintain itself in power only with the support of the Liberal party, a circumstance which prevented it from carrying out any socialist reforms such as it put in effect in 1945. At the height of the depression in 1931 the party suffered a severe setback by the defection of its leader, Ramsay MacDonald. The Labour party would not agree to have the workers bear the brunt of the depression by a reduction of social services. Prime Minister MacDonald joined two other prominent Cabinet members in deserting his party and forming a "National Government" with the Conservatives. The new elections, which took place the same year, cost the Labour party the loss of about two million votes (6,500,000 as against 8,360,000 in 1929) and of 236 seats in Parliament (52 as against 288). As time went by the shock of MacDonald's desertion wore off and in the elections of 1935 the Labour party obtained 8,300,000 votes— almost the same number as in 1929—carrying 154 seats.

World War II (1939-45) brought the Labour party back into the government in 1940 as partner in Churchill's coalition cabinet, with two members in the five-man War Cabinet.

IN POWER

The elections held in 1945, after the conclusion of the War, gave the Labour party an absolute majority of seats in the House of Commons with a popular vote of 11,992,292—48 per cent of the total cast. The reforms introduced by the Labour government during its tenure from 1945 to 1950 included both the extension of social services through the "Welfare State" and the nationalization of the Bank of England, the coal mines, communications system, electric power supply, inland transport, and civil aviation. The elections of 1950 returned the Labour party to power with a greatly reduced number of seats (315 as against 393 at the previous elections); its popular vote likewise decreased from 48 per cent in 1945 to 46 per cent in 1950, although its popular vote increased in absolute numbers—13,331,682, as compared with 11,992,292. The most important step adopted by the Labour government during its second term was the nationalization of the steel industry.

There was not always full harmony within the Labour party ranks during the six years it was in power. Deliberations at conventions of the party and of the trade unions, which were the backbone of the party, showed that there was antagonism between the leaders directly responsible for the conduct of the government, who had to face the financial difficulties of the regime, and the trade union leaders in direct contact with a rank and file affected by high prices and lagging wages. There was also left-wing opposition, led by Aneurin

Bevan, which opposed retrenchments with regard to social services and demanded instead a reduction of armament expenditures. That group mustered great strength at the Labour party convention of 1951, but the hopes of those who expected a split within the Labour camp were not realized.

The increasing domestic and foreign difficulties caused the Attlee Cabinet to call new elections in 1951. This time the Labour party lost by a small margin to the Conservatives (295 to 321 seats), even though its popular vote (13,911,582 or 48.74 per cent of the total) was larger than its vote at the 1950 elections and also larger than that of the victorious Conservatives, who obtained 13,721,346 votes (48.03 of the total).

There were two more general elections during the 1950's whose outcome was more disastrous than in 1951. Out of power, the Labour party was racked by internecine struggles for predominance between the radicals and the moderates. The main points at issue were disarmament and nationalization of industries. The radicals, supported by some powerful trade unions, were in favor of what has come to be called "unilateralism," meaning abandonment of nuclear weapons regardless of whether the communist bloc acted the same way. At one of the party conventions they even carried the majority. They were, however, defeated at the subsequent convention at which the right-wing leader, Gaitskell, succeeded in convincing the delegates of the irrationality of this defeatist attitude. He was, however, somewhat less successful with his suggestion that the party would have greater chances to win the majority of the electorate if it scrapped the idea of full nationalization of industries.

After the defection of Ramsay MacDonald, the Labour party's leading spokesman during the first decades of this century, the roster of the party's outstanding men included such names as Sir Stafford Cripps, Ernest Bevin, Clement Attlee, Aneurin Bevan, and Hugh Gaitskell. Of the five, Cripps, Attlee, and Gaitskell came from the middle classes, the former as a left-winger sympathizing with the communists, while the latter two have often been designated as left-wing liberals rather than as socialists intent upon the elimination of the capitalist system. It was, however, left to the two former workers, the ex-truck driver Bevin (1884-1951) and the ex-miner Bevan (1898-1960) to represent the two conflicting tendencies within the party. Bevin, the minister of foreign affairs in Attlee's Labour Cabinet (1945-51) and the strong man of the regime, was firmly opposed to the policies of the Soviet Union and a staunch supporter of collaboration with the Western powers. He did not insist on a further extension of his party's nationalization policy, and he did not object to the reduction of expenditures on certain social services.

The very opposite stand was taken by Aneurin Bevan, the most eloquent speaker of the party, who was minister of health in the Attlee-Bevin Cabinet. He resigned his post in protest against possible retrenchments of the free social services; he believed in nationalizing more and more branches of the nation's social and economic fabric and refused to take the threat of Soviet expansionism seriously. It was on this platform that he and his followers hoped both to win the election against the Conservatives who had come to power in 1951 and to displace the right-wing leadership of the party which, after Bevin's death, was dominated by Hugh Gaitskell.

When shortly before his own death in 1960, Bevan realized that on his own platform he had no chance of becoming either prime minister or minister of foreign affairs, he simply dropped his "Bevanite" point of view and aligned himself with the right wing in exchange for the promise of the number two post (minister of foreign affairs) in case of the party's victory at the forthcoming elections. His defection greatly affected his followers, who had to stick to the guns abandoned by their leader, for there were apparently not enough top posts in prospect for the leaders of both factions. There is now a new crop of Bevanites, recruited largely from among the graduate students and young instructors of the "red brick" universities.

A place apart from the common run of Labour party champions belongs to Harold Laski (1893-1950), who in 1945 served as chairman of the party's executive committee. A political scientist and writer rather than a politician, he exerted a major influence among students who attended his classes at the London School of Economics, where he was a teacher for many years. Although he was a prolific writer and popularizer of political concepts, he developed few original ideas, being primarily an exponent of the ideas of his predecessors and contemporaries. In his books and numerous essays, he set forth a series of concepts, some of which contradicted each other. His earliest works, including such books as *Authority in the Modern State*, and *The Foundations of Sovereignty*, asserted the claims of the community against the state and defended a "pluralistic conception of society." In his *Grammar of Politics* (1925), Laski noted the obligation of the state to provide services to the community, but insisted too on the duty of the individual to resist statist encroachments. Five years later, in *Democracy in Crisis*, and then in *The State in Theory and Practice* (1934), Laski accepted almost completely the Marxist-Leninist view of the state, although he did not credit it with having influenced his views. Although at various times critical of the Soviet Union and of the British Communist party, Laski in his two final works, *Reflections on the Revolution of Our Time* (1943) and *Faith, Reason and Civilization* (1944) asserted that in the Russian Revolution there had been generated a faith which could move men as had Christianity in its day. Critics of Laski's views held that his support of the Soviet Union, even while admitting its nondemocratic aspects, was based on an awe of the massive power wielded by the Communist party rulers of Russia, and on his desire not to be "anti-historical," for he apparently assumed that, for better or worse, the future belongs to the negators of capitalism. Moreover, his own deep-seated rejection of the status quo led him to accept even a totalitarian form of collectivism as the lesser evil.

THE DOMINIONS

The democratic socialist movements in the Dominions (Australia, Canada, New Zealand, and the Union of South Africa) have to a large extent been patterned on the British model. They are generally based on labor unions, and except for the Canadian party, the political organizations embodying their tendencies are as a rule called Labor parties. Very moderate, both in their programs and their tactical methods, they are vaguely socialist in their outlook but not sold on any specific philosophy. Marxism, for instance, never has played any part in the intellectual make-up of their leadership. Except in the case of Canada, they reject any ideas of internationalism, opposing as they do in Australia and New Zealand the immigration of persons of non-Nordic stock, and accepting their government's anti-Negro policy in South Africa. In Australia the Labor party has repeatedly been at the helm of the federal and of the various state governments, but it was rarely able to maintain its power for more than one term. The nature of the Australian Labor party, in particular, is best characterized by the fact that former Labor politicians, such as Cook, Hughes, and Lyons, ended their careers as anti-Labor prime ministers. A phenomenon which may apparently be explained by the fact that in a country like Australia which is not racked by very profound contrasts between the very rich, the educated déclassés, and the very poor, and in which opportunities open to talent are apparently very great, political radicalism very often assumes the aspects of ordinary politics.

THE UNITED STATES

Socialist ideas and activities in the United States can be classified under the following headings: (1) Settlements of a religious-communist nature, such as Amana, Aurora, Bethel, Ephrata, Harmony, Oneida, Shakers, Zoar; (2) experiments inspired by ideas of various utopian socialists, including Brook Farm, the Fourierists, the Icarians, and Weitling; (3) modern democratic-socialist, anarchist, syndicalist, and communist movements.

The impetus to democratic socialism in America came from the German revolutionists who migrated to the United States after the Revolution of 1848, among whom were Joseph Weydemeyer and F. A. Sorge, friends of Karl Marx. Both came in the early 1850's and made attempts to win the German workers to the idea of an independent labor party. In the late 1860's German immigrant socialists of the Lassallean school united with the German followers of Marx to form the General German Workingmen's Association, which joined the First International. Branches of the International were likewise formed by French and Czech (called "Bohemians" at the time) immigrants in New York, Chicago, and San Francisco. In the 1870's German socialist immigrants formed local labor parties in Illinois and in the East. In 1876 these parties united to launch the Workingmen's party of the United States.

Two tendencies struggled within that party for predominance. One of them put all the emphasis upon political propaganda and political action, while the other insisted on the paramount importance of working within the trade union movement. At a convention held in 1877 the "political faction" got the upper hand and changed the name of the party to Socialist Labor party. The party had about 7,000 members, the native American element constituting about one-tenth of that number. The new party was rent by internal conflicts. One of them was caused by the organization of "Societies for Study and Resistance" (*Lehr- und Wehr-Vereine*) formed by German immigrants in 1875 to repel police attacks against striking workers. The Socialist Labor party officially repudiated this organization, fearing lest "a recognition of the military organization would drive the law-abiding voters away from the party." However, those socialists who were active in the trade unions were in favor of this armed organization, which, as a result, continued in existence for many years.

There were also other circumstances which arrested the growth of the Socialist Labor party. With a view to immediate political success at the polls, the S.L.P. had begun to dicker with the Greenback party, a lower middle-class group which demanded monetary reform and had nothing in common with socialism. This stimulated the growth of a radical opposition within the S.L.P.—which eventually resulted in many workers turning their backs on socialist politics and joining the ranks of the anarchists. A new phase in the history of the S.L.P. began in 1890, when Daniel De Leon joined the party.

DANIEL DE LEON

Born in the Dutch West Indies (Curaçao) Daniel De Leon (1852-1914) came to the United States in 1872 after having studied at German and Dutch universities. He continued his studies at Columbia University, at which he later lectured on international law. His first fling at political activity was as a supporter of Henry George's mayoralty campaign in 1886. The Single Tax commanded his allegiance for a short time only, and after the appearance of Edward Bellamy's *Looking Backward* (1887), he joined the "Nationalists," the name given to the movement which sprang up under the impact of the impression made by that best-selling novel about socialist America in the year 2000.

In 1890 he joined the Socialist Labor party, of which he soon became the undisputed leader, a position he held until his death. De Leon's philosophy was a peculiar sort of orthodox Marxism, a Marxism which, to a certain extent, harked back to those ideas of the *Communist Manifesto* which neither the Marx of later years, nor his disciples in most countries after their parties had grown out of the pupal stage of revolutionary sects, still accepted. De Leon believed in the class struggle and in trade unions, but strikes for better conditions played no part in his concept of the socialist strategy for the abolition of capitalism. He did not believe that improvements in the standard of living of the workers were possible under capitalism and emphasized the importance of the propaganda of socialist ideas and participation in elections for the purpose of spreading these ideas. He saw in the trade unions a good medium for bringing the masses to accept his ideas, but he turned against both the American Federation of Labor and the Knights of Labor when he realized that he could not capture those organizations for his purposes.

As a result, De Leon founded his own trade union organization, the Socialist Trade and Labor Alliance (1895), a body in which the workers were united not according to crafts, as they were in the American Federation of Labor, but according to industries. His underlying idea was that as soon as the socialists had obtained a majority in Congress a socialist commonwealth was to be organized on the basis of those industrial organizations. Until that moment arrived, however, the role of these organizations was to be the voting agencies for his party—even though he did not put it as frankly as that.

De Leon's violent attacks against the existing trade unions, his domineering manner, and his intolerance toward any dissenting opinion within his organization eventually resulted in a split within his party, in a gradual loss of influence, and in the formation of a new party, the Socialist party of America, whose ensuing growth gradually reduced De Leon's influence to that of the uncontested chief of a dwindling sect claiming to be in possession of the only true brand of Marxism.

That split occurred within the Socialist Labor party in 1900. It was preceded by the organization of the Social Democratic party in 1898, whose foremost leaders were Eugene V. Debs and Victor Berger. It was out of the fusion of this new organization with the anti-De Leon faction within the Socialist Labor party that the Socialist party was formed in 1901. Since that time the S.L.P. has ceased to play any role in the history of American radicalism.

Ever since the foundation of the Socialist party, one man towered over all other leaders of that organization—even though he was by no means the brains of the party. A man of extraordinary oratorical gifts, Debs (1855-1926) was at first a trade union leader, having risen from the ranks to the post of national secretary of the Brotherhood of Locomotive Firemen. Convinced that craft unionism was unable to oppose the power of the railway companies, he left his union to form the American Railway Union, an organization that was to include all railway employees, skilled and unskilled alike. Politically, he was then active in the Democratic party. His political outlook was influenced by the attitude of the federal government which, over the objection of the liberal Governor John P. Altgeld, sent troops to Illinois to break the "Pullman strike" of 1894. Debs was arrested; while he was in prison Victor L. Berger, prominent American socialist, who visited him, introduced Debs to the ideas of socialism. Debs became convinced that trade unionism alone was not sufficient to advance the cause of labor and that independent political action by workers was necessary. At the time the American socialist movement was torn by internal dissensions due to the dissatisfaction with the ideas and the personality of Daniel De Leon, leader of the Socialist Labor party.

When in 1901 the Socialist party of America was

created, Debs was among its founders, and became the most popular speaker of the party. He was five times the candidate of his party for the presidency of the United States. When he ran for the last time, in 1920, he polled over 900,000 votes. Debs was in sympathy with the Industrial Workers of the World, a quasi-syndicalist organization which advocated industrial unionism (organization of skilled and unskilled alike), as against the craft unionism of the American Federation of Labor. But he opposed its leaders on the subject of sabotage, which he rejected, and on the subject of the political struggle (participation in elections and in representative bodies), which he considered necessary but which they rejected. During World War I Debs took the same position as most of his party's leadership and in 1918 was sentenced to ten years' imprisonment because of a speech against the war. The Russian November Revolution aroused his enthusiasm, and as a result he declared himself a "Bolshevik." However, he never joined the communists in the United States, remaining instead as a left-winger in the Socialist party, criticizing his more moderate fellow socialists for their lack of revolutionary spirit.

Debs made no contribution to socialist theory, his approach being emotional rather than what the Marxists call "scientific." This emotionalism, his overflowing altruism in personal relations, his overpowering eloquence, and the fact that he was one of the few native Americans among the socialist top leadership made him a legend while he was still alive. He is also the only figure in the American radical movement whose memory is cherished by socialists and communists alike.

For eleven years in succession (1901-12) the Socialist party grew without interruption, as shown by its
membership figures, which rose from 15,075 in 1903 to
118,045 in 1912. During that period the party's presidential vote likewise showed a consistent growth,
rising from 87,814 votes which Eugene V. Debs received in 1900 to 897,011 in 1912. During that year the
party had one spokesman in Congress, Victor Berger,
fifty-six mayors, several representatives in state legisla-
tures, and over 300 aldermen. From an organization
which at its foundation had to contend with an ultraradical wing that opposed the inclusion of so-called
"immediate demands" in its platform, the party gradually developed into a full-fledged party of reforms with
a strong appeal not only to workers but also to the
middle class. The list of contributors to its publications
included some outstanding American intellectuals of
the time, such as Leonard D. Abbott, Sherwood Ander-
son, Charles A. Beard, George Bellows, Floyd Dell,
John Dewey, Abraham Cahan, Max Eastman, Char-
lotte Perkins Gilman, Arturo Giovannitti, Robert
Hunter, George D. Herron, Frederick C. Howe, William Dean Howells, Helen Keller, George R. Kirk-
patrick, Harry W. Laidler, Algernon Lee, Vachel
Lindsay, Walter Lippmann, Jack London, John Macy,
Edwin Markham, Gustavus Myers, Scott Nearing, James
Oneal, James Oppenheim, David Graham Phillips, Er-
nest Poole, Walter Rauschenbush, Boardman Robinson,
I. M. Rubinow, Charles Edward Russell, Carl Sand-
burg, A. M. Simons, Upton Sinclair, John Sloan, Bishop
J. L. Spaulding, Lincoln Steffens, Charles P. Steinmetz,
Horace Traubel, Thorstein Veblen, Louis Untermeyer,
William English Walling, Lester F. Ward, Clement

Wood, Walter E. Weyl, and Art Young. The influence wielded at that time by the Socialist party within the labor movement is best measured by the fact that at the election for president of the American Federation of Labor the socialist candidate Max Hayes, who ran against Samuel Gompers, the founder and grand old man of the organization, polled one-third of the total vote. The party had also many adherents within the more radical labor element, as represented by the near-syndicalist I.W.W. (Industrial Workers of the World.)

It was its attitude towards the I.W.W. that caused the first break in the growth of the Socialist party. The I.W.W., taking its inspiration from the French syndicalists, advocated sabotage and direct action—methods generally repudiated by the socialist parties the world over. In an amendment to the party constitution adopted in 1912, these methods were condemned by the Socialist party, and in the following year William D. Haywood, leader of the I.W.W., was expelled from the Executive Committee of the party. The loss in the party's membership—from 118,045 in 1912 to 95,957 in 1913—was the result of the alienation of the more radical working-class groups caused by this measure and by the apprehension the discussion of this subject may have aroused among its more moderate middle-class following.

World War I caused a deep rift within the ranks and the leadership of the party. Sympathies for the Western democracies, England and France, fighting against German militarism and semiabsolutism, were very strong among a large section of the native-born American intellectuals. Internationalist sentiment among radical groups, admiration for the German Social-Democratic party, the model socialist party of the world, and hostility to the tsarist regime allied with the Western democracies caused the majority of the party to adopt a neutral attitude which was interpreted as pro-Germanism. The presidential elections of 1916, in which the Socialist party lost one-third of the vote received in 1912, showed the effect of this rift on the electorate. Another cause of this weakening of the party's attractive power was the domestic policy of President Woodrow Wilson who, to a certain extent, stole the radical thunder of the Socialists, both by his policies friendly to labor and by his claim that he "kept us out of war." (The United States did not enter the war until a few months after the election.)

America's entrance into the war in April 1917 brought the rift within the Socialist party to an open split, when the majority of the party leadership, headed by Morris Hillquit, came out squarely against America's participation in the conflict and urged its followers to protest against all the measures which it expected the government to take in the pursuance of the war. A number of prominent intellectuals left the party to form what they called the Social Democratic League of America—an organization which soon disappeared. More serious than this defection were the measures adopted by the government in retaliation for the party's antiwar stand. Many socialist papers were suppressed, and many of the party's speakers, among them Eugene Debs, were arrested and convicted. The membership, which had reached its peak in 1912, dropped to 80,379 in 1917.

MORRIS HILLQUIT

Morris Hillquit (1870-1933), who since the turn of the century was considered the brains of the party, was a Marxist of the "Centrist" brand, as represented by Karl Kautsky, the outstanding theorist of the German Social-Democratic party. Born in Russia in 1870, Hillquit immigrated to the United States during the 1880's. He was a successful lawyer and a prolific writer about the history of the radical movement in America (*History of Socialism in the United States*) and the theoretical problems of socialism (*Socialism Summed Up* and *From Marx to Lenin*).

The Russian Revolution of 1917, particularly in its second phase—the seizure of power by the Bolsheviks in November of the same year—had a favorable effect upon the growth of the party at first. Its membership rose to 82,344 in 1918 and to 108,504 in 1919. The immigrant workers, organized in foreign-language federations, supplied most of that increase. However, that growth contained the germ of the party's eventual decline. For the foreign-language federations of the Socialist party were to form the bulk of the so-called left wing of the party, which in 1919 broke with the parent body to become part of the international communist movement.

As a result of the defection of its pro-Bolshevik elements, the Socialist party lost over three-fourths of its membership, declining from 108,504 in 1919 to 26,766 in 1920. It was to decline still further during subsequent years.

During the early 1920's the Socialist party became interested in the movement initiated by a number of labor unions and Western farm organizations aiming at exerting pressure upon the two major parties. As a result, some of the outstanding leaders of the Socialist party participated in the Conference for Progressive Political Action called by some of the country's largest trade unions within and outside the American Federation of Labor. Morris Hillquit, the party's major strategist, became a member of the permanent committee of the C. for P.P.A. The activities of that

organization resulted in the support given by the
Socialist party in 1924 to the third-party presidential
candidacy of Robert LaFollette, who was a progressive
Republican. The Socialists fully endorsed that candidacy by abstaining from nominating a candidate of
their own. However, nothing came of its hopes that the
campaign would be followed by the organization of a
permanent labor or farmer-labor party. The leaders
of the large trade unions, who had initiated that movement, were not prepared for a definite and permanent
break with the Democrats and Republicans.

Its hopes for an independent labor party frustrated,
the Socialist party entered upon the subsequent presidential campaign (1928) with a candidate of its own.
He was Norman Thomas who, after Debs's death in
1926, became the party's most eloquent speaker and
after Hillquit's death in 1933 its dominant personality.

NORMAN THOMAS

Six times the party's candidate for the presidency,
Norman Thomas (born in 1884) holds an unusual
place on the American political scene. Although never
successful in achieving office, he succeeded in becoming one of the most respected public personalities in
America. As spokesman for the Socialist party (now
the Socialist Party-Social Democratic Federation), he
has appeared for years on forums and nation-wide
broadcasts. He was active throughout in aiding the
trade union movement, fighting for civil rights, and
exposing the threat of totalitarian groups, including
Nazis, Fascists, and communists. In the textile strike
in Passaic, New Jersey, he defied a "riot law," and was
arrested by local authorities, but his action resulted in
the repeal of the law. Similar actions on his part in

behalf of strikers in Vigo County, Indiana, and Jersey City, resulted in the exposure and subsequent repeal of antidemocratic laws. One of the first to call attention to the plight of the Southern sharecroppers, Thomas helped organize the Southern Tenant Farmers Union in the face of police hounding and threats of violence. The author of a number of books on socialism, including *A Socialist's Faith*, Thomas has presented an undogmatic and fluid version of socialism in terms which might be acceptable to the pragmatic outlook of the American populace. His socialism has been influenced particularly by a humanitarian approach, possibly deriving in part from the fact that, for a period of ten years before World War I, he was a pastor at an East Harlem church in New York.

A graduate of Princeton, where he was valedictorian of his graduating class, Thomas joined the staff of a New York settlement house soon after leaving college, simultaneously attending Union Theological Seminary. Active in the antiwar movement, he was forced to leave his parish because of his support for the American Union Against Militarism and his campaign on behalf of Morris Hillquit, Socialist candidate for mayor of New York in 1917. In his first presidential campaign (1928), Thomas obtained only 267,420 votes, as compared with 915,302 votes which Debs had gathered eight years before. The decline can be explained by the fact that 1920 was a year of postwar excitement and uncertainty, with Debs enjoying great popularity among both Socialists and Communists, while 1928 was the pre-crash year of full prosperity when, additionally, a deep rift separated the Socialists from the Communists. Four years later, in the depths of the depression, Thomas' vote rose to 884,781. But it dropped to 187,720 in 1936 because those dissatisfied with the existing conditions apparently voted for the

New Deal, which had borrowed much of the Socialist thunder.

"MILITANTS" VS "OLD GUARD"

The misfortunes of the Socialist party were increased by an internal rift between the radical-minded "Militants," whose views were accepted by Norman Thomas, and what was called the "Old Guard" of the party, which held the traditional moderate views of gradualist socialism. Following the radical trend of the 1930's, the Socialist "Militants" were ready to engage in joint actions such as May First celebrations and the like with the Communists who at that time offered a "united front" to the Socialists. Moreover, at the Socialist party convention held in 1934, the "Militants" succeeded in having a resolution adopted which, in the opinion of the "Old Guard," could be interpreted as a concession to the Communist viewpoint favoring a minority dictatorship. That resolution, or declaration of principles, read as follows:

"Capitalism is doomed. If it can be superseded by majority vote, the Socialist party will rejoice. If the crisis comes through the denial of majority rights after the electorate has given us a mandate we shall not hesitate to crush by our labor solidarity the reckless forces of reaction and to consolidate the Socialist state. If the capitalist system should collapse in a general chaos and confusion, which cannot permit of orderly procedure, the Socialist party, whether or not in such a case it is a majority, will not shrink from the responsibility of organizing and maintaining a government under the workers' rule. True democracy is a worthy means to progress; but true democracy must be created by the workers of the world."

The "Militant" majority was also ready to take a somewhat charitable view of the operations of the Soviet regime which, in its opinion, was a "workers' state"—all its faults and shortcomings notwithstanding. To emphasize its radicalism, the Socialist party in 1936 opened its ranks to the Trotskyists whom, however, it expelled a year later, when the newcomers persisted in their attempt to win the party over to their brand of communism.

The "Old Guard," which would have no dealings whatsoever with the Communists nor make any concessions to their viewpoints, and who apparently resented Norman Thomas' dominant position within the party, bolted from the party in 1936 and founded the Social Democratic Federation, an organization representing the extreme right wing of democratic socialism. The Social Democratic Federation did not intend to run its own candidates to federal, state, and municipal offices. It favored the foundation of a progressive third party and encouraged its members to vote for the New Deal administration and to support such organizations as the American Labor party (before it was captured by the Communists) and the Liberal party in New York.

WORLD WAR II AND AFTER

At the outset of World War II the Socialist party took a pacifist and neutralist position. The leaders of the party were afraid lest America's participation in the war against the Fascist powers result in the militarization of America's public life, with the ensuing danger of totalitarianism. In view of the mounting Nazi danger, this led to a vote of only 100,264 for Norman Thomas in the presidential election of 1940. That attitude also stood in the way of a reconciliation with the Old Guard of the Social Democratic Federation, which favored America's intervention in the war.

When the United States entered the war, the Socialist party, which in the meantime had shed all its illusions about the "working class character" of the Soviet regime and about the desirability of collaborating with the communists, opposed the demand for "unconditional surrender" as likely to continue the war.

The 1950's and early 1960's witnessed the shrinking of the Socialist party to the size of a well-nigh insignificant group despite its unification in 1957 with an important part of the "Old Guard" Social Democratic Federation.

The failure of democratic socialism to acquire a permanent and prominent place in America's political setup has been attributed to various causes. Foremost among them is the middle-class mentality of the skilled and semiskilled workers whose comparatively high standard of living has made them impervious to denunciations of the capitalist system and to any advocacy of a thorough change of the status quo, as embodied in what is called the socialist ideal or "maximum program." And as to its minimum program—reforms to be obtained within the capitalist system—most of them have been realized by the New Deal and the Welfare State, thus securing the permanent allegiance of the wage workers to the party of Franklin Roosevelt and his Democratic successors.

There has also been a basic, historical reason for the native American workers' "sales resistance" to radical ideas. American capitalism grew up under conditions different from those of its European counterpart. It had no masses of paupers to draw on for its industrial army—the demand for labor being often larger than the offer—and was therefore compelled to grant its workers a higher standard of living than they could get in Europe. This was possible without any serious curtailment of capitalist profits, since the natural resources of the country were practically unlimited. The early possibilities of obtaining free land and the fascinating example of so many have-nots who rose to wealth and power created among workers individualistic tendencies and democratic delusions of "equal opportunity." At the same time the division of the laboring class into three racially and culturally distinct and antagonistic groups, the "aristocratic" natives, the non-English-speaking white immigrants, and, after the Civil War, the colored pariahs prevented the development of anything like the class solidarity that, to a certain extent, exists in Europe. In addition to this, owing to the rapid growth and development of industry and commerce, as well as to the democratic organization of the governmental machinery, there was at the outset no class of hungry and dissatisfied intellectuals such as formed the revolutionary leaven in Western Europe and especially in Russia. The absence of these déclassés and of their revolutionary activity at the founding of the labor movement in America therefore meant an absence of socialist tradition and ideology within the ranks of the native American workers whose unions and wage struggles preceded the appearance of preachers of radical ideas—mostly lower middle-class intellectuals.

JAPAN

Highly industrialized Japan is the only Asian country with a well-organized socialist mass movement. That trend started at the turn of the century when malcontent college students, familiar with conditions

in Western Europe, engaged in a propaganda of socialist ideas and in helping the industrial workers in organizing trade unions. The immediate aim of these
activities was the democratization of Japan's political
structure. Frightened by the growth of the movement,
the police suppressed the Socialist party which was
formed in 1901, prohibited the organization of strikes,
and crushed the labor unions. Shortly after that, at the
end of the first decade of this century, it turned upon
the radical elements among the intelligentsia, and,
anticipating by twenty years Stalin's methods, sentenced twenty-four of the outstanding socialists and
anarchists either to death or to life imprisonment.

Silenced for a while, radical activities revived under
the impact of World War I and of the Russian Revolution of 1917. The nationwide uprising known under
the name of "Rice Riots of 1918," provoked by the
profiteers who had driven up the price of the most
important food item of the poorer population—though
in no way connected with the socialist or labor movement—taught the government that a more lenient
policy was the only way of preventing a real revolution.
The franchise was extended, and the organization of
labor unions and the activities of competing democratic socialist parties were not interfered with. By
1936 a trend towards unity led to the formation of the
Social Mass party, which included radicals of various
schools, except communists. In its general character it
was very much akin to the British Labour party. It
polled over 900,000 votes at the elections of 1937 and
sent thirty-seven members to the House of Representatives.

The year of its triumph was also the year of its
moral downfall. In 1937 the military-Fascist regime
of Japan started its "total" war for the conquest of
China. Unlike the Fascists in other countries, those of

the Japanese variety were outspoken in their hostility to capitalism. They demanded that the nation's wealth should be taken away from the few privileged families and given to the government. They called their aim either "state socialism" or "imperial communism." This anticapitalist attitude impressed some socialist leaders who forsook their old ideas about democracy, political liberty and the independence of labor. They joined the Fascists. They argued that the conquest of rich chunks of the Asian continent would further the development of Japan's industries and thus benefit the workers as well. At the October 1937 meeting of the Japan Labor Union Conference, a body embracing all the labor organizations of the country, a resolution was adopted for "reorganization on a totalitarian basis." The All-Japan Federation of Labor shortly afterwards decided to oppose all strikes for the duration of the war and to support the government's war policy. The Social Mass party decided to follow the policy of the labor unions. In November of the same year (1937) it adopted a resolution which abandoned the traditional socialist point of view concerning the class struggle. Instead, it "associated itself with nationalist activities," as one of its leaders stated in a report published in 1938—it jumped on the militarist bandwagon. There was, however, a minority which opposed the move. In July 1940, the Social Mass party followed the example of all the other political parties which dissolved voluntarily without waiting for their official suppression, for a month earlier the Japanese prime minister had announced that the structure of the state would be totalitarian.

Japan's defeat put an end to the military-Fascist interlude. The country was reorganized on a Western democratic basis with the radical movement split between democratic socialists on the one hand and communists on the other. The socialists were by far the stronger—apparently because the frankly pro-Russian reputation of the communists was not particularly helpful in getting popular support in a country in which there still lingered an aversion to the "hereditary enemy," as it were.

Until 1955, the democratic socialists were split into two parties running separate candidate lists at the elections. They were of about equal strength, the left-wing Socialists polling 4,506,469 votes at the 1953 election, as against 4,679,687 votes obtained by the right-wing Socialists. What divided them was chiefly the attitude towards the communist bloc and the United States. On reunification, the party largely inclined toward the policy of the pro-communists, chiefly because for its votes it was largely dependent upon the powerful General Council of Japanese Trade Unions *(Sohyo)*, which is pro-Soviet. As a result it insists upon the abolition of American military bases, the cancellation of the Japan-U.S. Security Treaty and a rapprochement between Japan and Communist China. On the domestic front, however, the party, with an eye toward winning the majority of the electorate, was inclined to adopt a rather right-wing attitude of toning down the class struggle and of championing the interests of the nation as a whole.

However, there was a new split in 1959, as a result of which the right wing seceded from the party. The platform of the new party, whose followers call themselves Democratic Socialists, came out against the class struggle and against the domination of the movement by the pro-communist General Council of Japanese Trade Unions. Nor do they accept the foreign policy of the Socialist party, which differs little from that of the communists.

Conditions in China were not conducive to the creation of a socialist movement. To be sure, a socialist organization was formed immediately after the Revolution of 1911 overthrew the old absolutist regime. And the Kuomintang, the nationalist party, incorporated many vague socialist concepts held by its founder Sun Yat-sen, the Father of the Revolution. But both the Socialist party and the democratic socialist ideas professed by the Kuomintang became casualties of the civil war and the chaos following the revolution. In order to survive, the partisans of the republic had to rely upon military and political assistance of the Soviet Union. As a result large sections of the intelligentsia—particularly those of its members who were *not*, one way or another, connected with the rising capitalist interests of the new regime—embraced the gospel of communism which held out to them the hope of immediate seizure of power at the end of the civil war. The communists thus becoming the militant champions of those opposed to the property-owning interests, there was no occasion for the formation of a moderate or middle-of-the-road socialist party, particularly in view of Chiang Kai-shek's unwillingness to make any concessions to the peasants at the expense of the financial interests to whom most of them were indebted.

THE EX-COLONIES

Anticapitalist protest in the former colonial possessions, such as the Middle East, India, and Indonesia, to mention only the largest territorial complexes, has always been combined with a strong dose of nationalism, considering that capitalist profitmaking in those countries was almost exclusively a function of foreign enterprises. Obversely, it could also be said that in those countries nationalism was characterized by a strong dose of socialist verbiage. An outstanding instance of this kind of democratic socialism is the ruling Congress party of India, whose leader, Prime Minister Jawaharlal Nehru, calls himself a socialist, even though his regime has hardly carried out any substantial reforms which would warrant classifying his party as socialist.

Some outright socialist organizations in India during the 1950's merged to form the Praja Socialist party. Most of its members had originally belonged to Nehru's Congress party, and their most influential leader, Jayaprakash Narayan, was for many years, with Nehru's approval, considered as the prime minister's potential successor in case of his death or retirement.

Having become independent, India's democratic socialists, who faced strong communist competition, have leaned backwards to win those elements opposed to violence. While on the one hand, they advocate, like the socialists of the West, the nationalization of key industries and public utilities, they have also made concessions to Gandhi's ideas. As a result many of their leaders have endorsed Vinoba Bhave's "Bhoodan" campaign which presumes to solve the agrarian problem not by a government-enforced distribution of the big estates among the landless, but by futile attempts to persuade the big land owners to *donate* as much land as possible to those in need of it. Needless to say that, so far, the results of this propaganda have been very unimpressive.

As an organization, the democratic socialists are almost nonexistent in Indonesia, which freed itself from Holland's colonial tutelage after World War II. The Dutch masters having consistently maintained their colony in the backward state of producer of raw materials while at the same time withholding all opportunities for higher education, the archipelago found itself, at the time of its liberation, both without any numerous industrial working class and with a very sparse stratum of intellectuals with European education. Most of these were absorbed either by the bureaucratic apparatus of the government or by the political machines of the regular political parties defending the new status quo. Those of the educated who were left holding the bag sought, and are seeking, a short cut to power by hitching their wagon to the rising star of Chinese communism, and trying to win the masses by a gospel of violence which, in countries with a very low standard of living, has a better chance of success than the advocacy of democratic methods. As a result, the few intellectuals who profess the ideas of Western socialism remained without a following and formed a mere tail to the regular middle-class parties. More recently, the "guided democracy" of Prime Minister Sukarno has suppressed the publications of the gifted socialist leader and former Prime Minister Sutan Sjahrir, who was one of the organizers of the struggle for independence.

BURMA AND ISRAEL

With the end of World War II, the socialists of two countries which became independent immediately assumed the leadership of their countries' governments. They were the Burma Socialist party and MAPAI, the Jewish Labor party of Israel. Both had engaged in a revolutionary struggle against the British, and in the end, it was the British Labour government which yielded to their demands for national independence.

The Burma Socialist party arose out of the Burmese Revolutionary party and the All-Burma Peasants Organization which co-operated with the Japanese during the war and helped drive the British out of Burma. The educated young men of Burma had been drawn to these groups throughout the thirties, leading peasant revolts and strikes of oil workers in opposition to the British and their upper-strata Burmese retainers. With the onset of the war, they saw an opportunity to throw off British control, even at the cost of collaboration with the militarists of Japan. "Thirty comrades" were dispatched to Japan for military training, and they subsequently organized a Burmese Independence Army, which fought side by side with the Japanese. (In 1948, the socialist leader of the Army, Aung San, then prime minister, and the peasant leader, Thakin Mya, were assassinated.)

In March 1945, the Anti-Fascist People's Freedom League, organized by the socialists (at that time including the Communist party), turned on its erstwhile collaborators, the Imperial Army of Fascist Japan, and helped the British turn out the Japanese invaders. The Burma Revolutionary Army then urged the continuation of the war by an attack on the British. However, the communists, then under Moscow orders to support British imperialism on behalf of Soviet foreign policy, betrayed the secret plans to the British. As a result of this betrayal, the Revolutionary Army was dissolved. The Burma Socialist party then openly appeared on the political scene, organizing trade unions, peasant organizations, women's groups, and cultural sections through the Anti-Fascist People's Freedom League. In October 1946 the British requested the AFPFL to form a government, which the Socialist party did after expelling the communists from the coalition. By 1946 the Soviet line had changed, and it was now incumbent on communists throughout the world to struggle against the British rather than co-operate with them. From 1948, when Burma obtained its independence, the AFPFL governed Burma without interruption. In 1958, however, a split in the socialist ranks over the prerogatives of office led U Nu, leader of the AFPFL, to retire from office, although he returned in 1960. U Nu, a socialist although he is not a member of the Socialist party, reflects the basic ideas of Burmese socialism, which accepts as equally valid the spiritual assumptions of Buddhism, the philosophy of Marxism, and political democracy. Burma is one of the so-called "neutral" countries, although a good part of the government's efforts in the early days after independence were devoted to fighting off communist guerrilla forces, organized as White Flag and Red Flag insurgents. In 1962 U Nu's regime was overthrown by a military dictatorship, but the situation seems to be in a flux.

MAPAI

The Jewish Labor Party of Israel (MAPAI) is even more strongly nationalist than the Burma Socialist party. MAPAI, one of whose organizers was Prime Minister David Ben Gurion, has been one of the driving forces of political Zionism, which aimed at resettlement of Jews in Israel. Simultaneously, through Histadrut, the General Federation of Labor, MAPAI has become a state within a state, since Histadrut is not only a trade union but also the basic economic force of the country.

MAPAI was organized in January 1930 as a result of the merger of the two active socialist parties then in Palestine—Poale Zion and Hapoel Hatzair. Histadrut had been organized in 1921 by the two organizations before their merger. After the achievement of statehood, MAPAI, with over 160,000 members, has governed Israel through coalition regimes. It remains the single largest party in Israel, holding one-third of the seats in the Knesset (Parliament).

MAPAI has been dominated since its formation by the personality of David Ben Gurion, who has been prime minister of Israel during most of the period since independence. An intense Zionist, he has on occasion announced that every Jew outside Israel has a primary obligation to migrate to that country. The Israeli Army fought off the invasion of Arab states in 1947–48, and in 1956 Ben Gurion ordered the Israeli Army to join the British and French in the occupation of the Suez Canal zone, an invasion which was called off at the behest of the United Nations.

With the emergence of independent states in Africa and Asia, Israel, through the facilities of Histadrut, has offered its services and technical knowledge to various African and Asian countries. The Burmese have been particularly impressed by the *kibbutzim*, the co-operative agricultural communities. These, organized to settle the dangerous desert areas, have begun to lose their importance as the country becomes more urbanized, and as Histadrut, with a membership of nearly 600,000, has taken on the direction of the Israeli economy through its control of industry, co-operatives, and trade unions.

Chapter V

THE ULTRAS

Long before international Leninist "communism" declared war on the democratic socialists, the theory and
practice of Marx's followers had been under attack by
radicals of other schools. Foremost among such critics
were the followers of Proudhon and of Bakunin, who,
at a whimsical suggestion of the former, called themselves anarchists.

During the 1860's and 1870's, the anarchists,
whether Proudhonists or Bakuninists, were members of
the International Workingmens' Association (the First
International). After their expulsion from that body in
1872, those branches of the I.W.A. which professed the
ideas of Bakunin continued to consider themselves as
constituting the original International, and for several
years the revolutionary movements of the Latin countries were completely under their sway. However, most
of these sections, with the exception of the Spanish
organizations, disappeared by the end of the seventies.
Their militants, having lost their faith in the possibility
of an immediate social revolution, accepted the "revolutionary" gradualism of the Marxists. There remained,
however, a hard core of dreamers and irreconcilables
who would not give up. They made a fetish of the term
"anarchy" as the incarnation of the ideal of a stateless
and classless society; and they continued the veneration

of Bakunin as the great prophet of their Allah—anarchy
—even though the initiated few now realized that,
despite his superhuman heroism, Bakunin was a false
prophet, for he too actually strove for power. Such
power was to be only a "transition," to be sure, but it
was not designed to produce the immediate abolition
of all government as he claimed in his public pronouncements. Aside from his scandalous "invisible
dictatorship" idea, ignored by most rank and file anarchists, they found some nonanarchistic flaws in his ideal
of a "collectivist anarchism." In Proudhon's and Bakunin's time the term "communism" usually denoted the
Marxist and pre-Marxist concept of government ownership. Bakunin, therefore, chose the term "collectivism,"
which meant that the land and the means of production were to become the collective property of voluntary producers' and consumers' associations and not of
the state.

PETER KROPOTKIN

Bakunin's admirers, particularly Peter Kropotkin
(1842-1921), realized that if their hero's principle of
reward according to accomplishment was to be applied,
then statistical or similar controlling or computing
commissions or committees would have to be established—bodies which smelled of state authority. They
thereupon substituted "to everybody according to his
needs" for the principle of "according to his works."
This improvement of Bakunin's "collectivism" they
called "communist anarchism" or "anarchist communism." The possibility of such an ideal sort of ideal
under which there would be *no obligation to work* if
one wants to consume, they based upon two very
optimistic assumptions: That man was essentially good

and honest by nature and that all, or at least an enormous majority, would *voluntarily* contribute to society their share of work; that capitalist society has accumulated such enormous surpluses of goods that it would not matter if during the first turbulent years after the victorious social revolution there was a great deal of loafing. In time the loafing consumers would come to their senses and do their share of work voluntarily.

This idea was completely in keeping with the noble character of Peter Kropotkin, an authentic Russian prince, descendant in direct line from Russia's first ruling dynasty established by the Scandinavian conqueror Rurik a thousand years ago. Kropotkin had never met Bakunin, for he was in prison during the last years of his great predecessor's life. A former army officer, like Bakunin, he was by temperament a dreamer and a scholar—he was a geographer and a naturalist—rather than a man of action, such as Bakunin. But, once converted to the cause of the Revolution, he acted courageously, spending six years in Russian and French prisons for his beliefs.

After his flight from a Russian prison, where he was confined (1873-76) because of his participation in the Populist "going into the people" movement, he spent the rest of his life in Switzerland, France, and England, where he became the author of many books which became the bible of post-Bakunin anarchism, notably his *Words of a Rebel (Paroles d'un révolté)* and *Conquest of Bread*. His *Memoirs of a Revolutionist* was translated into many languages and so was also his *Mutual Aid, a Factor of Evolution*, a work in which, apparently with an eye to supporting his thesis of altruistic anarchism, he tried to prove that the principle of mutual aid was just as dominating in animal and primitive human life as that of the struggle for existence. His history of the French Revolution *(La*

Grande Revolution 1789-1793) was generally acclaimed as a serious historical contribution.

For all his extreme "communist anarchism" Kropotkin was what one might call—paradoxical as it may sound—a "gradualist" like most Western Marxists. Kropotkin's anarchism was *not* aimed at overthrowing the existing system *immediately*, for he apparently realized that this would result not in the abolition of the state but in the rise to power of the socialist politicians whom he despised, and also because *he* personally was *not* (in contradistinction to Bakunin) hungry for power. After purifying Bakunin's anarchism of its remnants of "statism," Kropokin and his friends conceived of anarchist revolutionary activity not as a *conspiracy* for *immediate* revolutions, but as a permanent *protest* against capital and the state. But it was not to be a mere *theoretical* protest in behalf of a better blueprint for the future society. It was to take a form that was to put fear into the hearts of the beneficiaries of the status quo and thus give hope and courage to the masses in their struggle for a better world.

"PROPAGANDA BY THE DEED"

In 1881 an attempt was made by the anarchists to revive the old International—without the Marxists and the other "parliamentary" socialists, of course. A convention held that year in London showed that the conceptions of the anarchists had changed since the death of Bakunin. The idea of *immediate* revolution resulting from mass movements, which was one of the main strategic tenets of Bakuninism, went into discard under the impact of the failure of the inherent revolutionary readiness of the masses to reveal itself. Many anarchists became convinced that it was necessary to revolutionize the masses by acts of individual terrorism, a tactic to which they gave the name of "propaganda by the deed." That tactic consisted in individual acts of violence directed against representatives of the existing system. The anarchists attributed to these acts a propagandistic value in arousing the masses against capitalism and the authority of the state. These acts are not to be confused with the terrorism of the so-called "Nihilists" of the "People's Will" party of Russia, of the later 1870's and early 1880's, and of their successors, the Social-Revolutionaries, of the early 1900's, whose terrorism was directed exclusively against tsarist absolutism, and who rejected acts of violence under a system of political democracy. In contradistinction to these Russian "Liberals with a bomb," as they were sometimes called, the anarchist terrorists nearly always worked without any prearranged plan. Their activities—whether it was the killing of the head of a government, a government official, an employer of labor, or the throwing of a bomb into a theater or a restaurant patronized by the rich—were either individual acts of protest, or indirect suicides prompted by misery, personal disappointment, or thirst for glory.

The socialists, while sympathetic toward acts of terrorism directed against despotic regimes—witness Karl Marx's approval of attempts upon the lives of Napoleon III and Tsar Alexander II—always opposed anarchist "propaganda by the deed" which, in their opinion, very often became grist to the mill of the reactionaries. The only socialist of note who ever glorified such acts—for instance, the throwing of a bomb into a theater in Buenos Aires—was Benito Mussolini about ten years before he entered upon his career as the founder of Fascism.

The original champion of this method of "propaganda" was Paul Brousee (1844-1912), a French follower of Michael Bakunin, who, with Kropotkin, was among the first champions of this new religion of violent protest. His enthusiam did not last long; in the early 1880's he joined the French Marxists ("Guesdists") and after a short stay with them became the leader of the "Possibilists," the most moderate group of French socialists. The leap from extreme impossibilism to its very opposite is not very difficult.

Kropotkin's revolutionary "gradualism" showed in his attitude toward the problems confronting his followers—there were not very many—in Russia. He did not believe that tsarist Russia was ripe for a social revolution, and, around the turn of the century, assigned to the coming upheaval in his country the role of the great French Revolution of 1789. This earned him the accusation, on the part of some ultraradicals, of being at bottom a liberal. So did his attitude during World War I, when he declared that the democratic countries of the West, such as France, would have to be defended against the semiabsolutism of Germany.

Upon his return to Russia, after the downfall of tsarism in 1917, Kropotkin was anything but elated about the activities of Lenin and rejected the latter's offer—after the Bolshevik seizure of power—to have all his works published by the government. He would have no dealings with any government. He was not molested, and after his death in 1921 the house in which he was born was officially converted into the Kropotkin Museum. Such was the respect his great idealism inspired even in his worst enemies.

ENRICO MALATESTA

A close friend and comrade of Kropotkin's for many years was the Italian anarchist Enrico Malatesta

(1853-1932), a romantic rebel of the classical mold, who took part in revolutionary activities in all the countries speaking the Romance languages. The author of many pamphlets and a man of action at the same time, Malatesta gradually moved away from many of Kropotkin's ultranaive and ultramoderate concepts. His own view and that of some of his friends was to the effect that the anarchists should help the revolutionary socialists in overthrowing the capitalist system, whereupon, once a democratic socialist system was established, the anarchists would endeavor, through their example and experimentation, to convince the majority of the superiority of voluntary associations to government-controlled economy. Nothing came of this plan, of course. For the democratic socialists, for all their Marxist verbiage, had no intention of engaging in any really revolutionary activities in the more or less democratic West; while the Leninists had no intention of granting any rights of social experimentation. When, during the Italian near-revolution of 1920, Malatesta was urged by his still numerous followers to become the leader of the uprising, he refused, for he realized that a victorious revolution led by anarchists who, after all, were a small minority, would result in a Bolshevik-like dictatorship by anarchists using a different vocabulary. It would have been a too ridiculous conclusion of his life-long apostolate of "no-government." Like Kropotkin, he preferred democratic liberty to a dictatorial revolution.

Such was the prestige he enjoyed that during the last ten years of his long life, from 1922 to 1932, he was not molested by Mussolini, who possibly was grateful to him for refusing to become an anarchist dictator in 1920, and thus unwittingly opening the way for Mussolini's dictatorship two years later.

(Less philosophical or consistent than Malatesta

were the Spanish anarchists who in 1933, one year after his death, made a vain attempt at the seizure of power by their own group, and who three years later, during the Spanish civil war, participated in the loyalist governments established in the various provinces.)

REVOLUTIONARY SYNDICALISM

At the time (1920) when Malatesta *deliberately* "missed the bus" that *might* have bestowed upon him the glory of being the Italian Lenin, anarchism was no longer what it had been two or three decades earlier. Twenty-six years after the London convention of 1881, another attempt was made to form an international organization. An international convention was held in Amsterdam in 1907, at which the ticklish subject of *individual* acts of revolt was practically ignored. In a declaration adopted on that subject it is said (on p. 7 of *Resolutions approuvées par le Congrès Anarchiste tenu à Amsterdam 1907*) that "such acts, with their causes and motives, should be understood rather than praised or condemned." This was to be a sop for those few still extant anarchists whom one of their critics once called *"les maniaques de la dynamite."* The majority of the delegates had in the meantime realized, without admitting it openly, that the alleged "propaganda" value of terrorist acts of protest was more than offset by the persecutions following in their wake.

What really interested the majority of the delegates was the attitude they would have to take with regard to a new revolutionary phenomenon that in the meantime had made its appearance. That new phenomenon was called "revolutionary syndicalism." It had its inception as far back as 1895. Its origin is to be ascribed to Fernand Pelloutier (1867-1901), a former Marxist turned anarchist. Discouraged by the bad aftereffects of the terrorist phase of French anarchism (1892-94), he was groping for an efficient method of establishing contact between the revolutionists and the masses. The formula he found and which was henceforth called "revolutionary syndicalism" consisted of two ideas: The labor union (*syndicat* in French) was to be the instrument of the workers' class struggle for better living conditions, and the weapons of that struggle were to be sabotage, direct action (i.e., violence), and the general strike. The latter was to be both a weapon of protest within the capitalist system and, at a propitious moment, the final blow resulting in the expropriation of the capitalists. That final general strike was called "the expropriatory general strike." Pelloutier was not very explicit about the actual turn such a strike would take. Some of his naive followers imagined that capitalism would just collapse after a few days or weeks of a peaceful "folded arms" (*mains croisées*) strike. Those who were not so naive realized that it was the "folded arms" strike that was bound to collapse if the peaceful workers were out to *starve out* the capitalists. So they explained—not in print, of course—that, after a short peaceful prelude, the hungry workers would resort to requisitioning foodstuffs, in short, to a violent attack upon capitalist private property. And that would be the beginning of the social revolution.

The second basic tenet of the theory dealt with reconstruction after the victorious general strike. The solution of that question was easy: the general federation of the labor unions became the owner of all means of production and took care of building up a co-operative, nonexploitative, stateless commonwealth.

The idea of the general strike was not invented by Pelloutier. It had been advocated in England during the 1830's by early precursors of syndicalism (see p. 156); it had been known during the early 1870's to the anarchists of Bakunin's school and had been preached in the United States during the eight-hour day movement of the middle 1880's. But Pelloutier made that idea the central point of a fundamental revision of all the previous conceptions held by the various socialist and anarchist schools.

Pelloutier and his closest collaborators in the task of launching the syndicalist movement did not attach the anarchist label to the new theory. That label, in their opinion, was anything but an asset in view of the many crackpots and unsavory characters which the "broadness" of the anarchist philosophy had attracted.

An organizer and not only a theorist, Pelloutier successfully undertook the task of unifying in one single national body all the French labor unions which hitherto had been just vote-getting appendages to the various mutually competing socialist parties. In this task he was supported not only by a number of anarchists who were tired of the "propaganda by the deed," but by some socialists whose ideas were not unsimilar to his. These were the so-called "Allemanists," named after their leader Jean Allemane, a printer who had participated in the uprising of the Paris Commune of 1871. He had a socialist party of his own called *Parti Ouvrier Socialiste Révolutionnaire* ("Socialist Revolutionary Workers Party"). What distinguished the Allemanists from the other socialist parties in France was its advocacy of the general strike as a method of overthrowing the capitalist system. However, their acceptance of this revolutionary method did not imply their repudiation of parliamentarism; they had their representatives in the Chamber of Deputies. Another distinctive feature of their organization was hostility to intellectuals and professionals: only persons engaged in manual labor (workers or small independent artisans) were admitted to membership. With their general strike plank and their hostility to intellectuals and professional men, the Allemanists contributed an important share to the formation of the theory and practice of syndicalism, some of whose first militants came from their ranks.

GEORGES SOREL

It is customary to speak of Georges Sorel (1846-1922) as the father of syndicalism. He never claimed to be the originator of that revolutionary philosophy and frankly gave credit for it to Fernand Pelloutier. Also, his *Reflections on Violence* (1907) and his other volumes were never accepted by the syndicalist militants as their credo, and practically all of them insisted that they never read him. He also discredited himself by his inconsistencies, such as his flirtation with the reactionaries and later by his glorification of Lenin.[1] The "violence" which he glorified—it was to this glorification that his book owed its phenomenal success among the intelligentsia—was at bottom only a sensational synonym for the "direct action" advocated and practiced during a certain period by the French syndicalist militants who ignored Sorel and his writings. And as for the general strike to which Sorel devoted so many pages, that idea had been in vogue in the French labor movement since the early nineties of the last century. His only "original" contribution—that the general strike was merely a courage-inspiring *myth*, but not something that was actually to be expected to occur—was rejected by the syndicalists.

One of the outstanding militants of French syndicalism, whose long life epitomizes the history of that movement, was Pierre Monatte (1881-1960). A graduate of a lycée (combination of high school and junior college) and thus an intellectual rather than a manual worker, he was, in his capacity as proofreader since 1902, a member of the union embracing all employees of the printing trades. At first a prosyndicalist anarchist, he eventually became the most articulate exponent of revolutionary syndicalism, pure and simple. For "syndicalism"—he and his friends in the General Confederation of Labor argued—was "sufficient unto itself" without either an anarchist or socialist qualification.

A member of the ruling body (*Comité Confédéral*) of the General Confederation of Labor, but a theorist rather than a leader, he never held an executive position comparable to that of either Samuel Gompers or Walter Reuther. Yet his counsel was always highly valued during the heyday of that movement. The semimonthly *La Vie ouvrière*, founded by him in 1909, became the theoretical mouthpiece of the movement and was read by all syndicalist militants the world over. One of its eager students was William Z. Foster, who got from it his inspiration for his "single-union" French-style syndicalism, as against the dual unionism of the American I.W.W. (That was before he joined the communists.)

World War I interrupted its publication for the four years which the editor spent in the trenches. Monatte survived the war, but syndicalism, as originally conceived, did not. As the syndicalist-inspired and led labor unions grew, both their members and leaders gradually swung away from the illegal tactics of sabotage and violent direct action and from the early Marxist "the-workers-have-no-country" ideology. For these were the methods and concepts adopted at a time when, the unions being mere skeletons, workers and leaders had literally "nothing to lose but their chains," as Marx's *Communist Manifesto* had it in 1848. By moving away from their ultraradical past, the French syndicalists adopted the ways of all European labor unions with their close affinity to the socialist parties, an attitude which during the war resulted in the adoption of the *union sacrée* of all classes bent upon the defense of the fatherland.

Out of the trenches in 1918, Monatte, who had resigned from the Comité Confédéral when the Confederation of Labor abandoned its hitherto "anti-patriotic" attitude, saw the French labor union leadership divided into two camps: the moderates of the better-paid trades were in close contact with the right-wing socialists, while the more radical elements sympathized with the Bolsheviks (the future French communists were in the Socialist party until 1920). That was one of the consequences of the impact of the November Revolution of 1917. The other consequence was that even the consistent syndicalists who, like Monatte, had remained true to their old philosophy, threw overboard their rejection of all "political action" and joined the Communist party.

However, they were not to stay there more than a couple of years. Soon enough the masters of the Kremlin began to suspect, not without reason, that Monatte and his friends were not of the same stripe as the other leaders of the French Communist party. They did not intend to be mere flunkeys taking orders from Moscow, but instead, they wanted to use the prestige of the Russian Revolution for the purpose of furthering their own cause: that of a social revolution carried out by the labor unions officered by syndicalists posing as communists. Monatte and his friends were expelled from the Communist party in 1924. Since Monatte's revived *La Vie ouvrière* had been taken over by the Communist party, he founded (in 1925) *Le Révolution prolétarienne*, a theoretical organ which continued under the sponsorship and later editorship of Robert Louzon, a wealthy idealist who had come to syndicalism from the Marxist camp.

Once more on his own, Monatte did not revert to the original quasi-anarchist syndicalism that ignored the question of power. A new slogan was added to the vocabulary of syndicalism, one modeled on the Bolshevik "all power to the Soviets." It read "all power to the labor unions" (*au syndicat le pouvoir*).

Neither Monatte nor his friends liked to be told that in case of a victorious social revolution to which they aspired "all power to the unions" would actually come to mean "all power to the syndicalist union leaders" whose rule would differ only in its slogans and its personnel, but not in its essence, from that of socialist or communist officeholders.

The adoption of the new slogan did not help Monatte and his friends regain the popularity which their gospel had achieved at the turn of the century. Monatte died a disappointed man, a forgotten prophet in a land where the sons and grandsons of his former followers would lynch his few surviving friends should the *"révolution prolétarienne"* convert France into a satellite of the Kremlin.

Altogether different from the labor-union career of the obscure Monatte was that of the Nobel peace prize winner Léon Jouhaux (1879-1954). A worker in a government match factory, he joined the Confédération Générale du Travail at the turn of the century to become its general secretary in 1908. Originally an anarchist and later a revolutionary syndicalist, he gradually moved toward the moderate wing of French labor unionism and toward collaboration with the Socialist party. During World War I he headed those former syndicalists who became advocates of national defense as against those old-time syndicalists who stuck to their "anti-patriotic" guns. He maintained his position as head of the C.G.T. throughout the two world wars and the period between them. When after World War II communists captured the C.G.T. he remained one of the general secretaries of the organization—a concession which the communists made to the noncommunist minority. In 1947 the minority, consisting largely of socialists and syndicalists, left the C.G.T. to form an organization called *Force Ouvrière* ("Labor Force") with Jouhaux as president.

ANARCHO-SYNDICALISM

During the first years after their appearance the basic concepts of revolutionary syndicalism infused fresh blood in the anarchist movement which, outside Spain, seemed to be doomed to the stagnation of a sterile sect. For all the admiration the anarchists felt for Kropotkin, to most of them his "anarchist-communist" idea of "free groups" undertaking the reconstruction of society after the faraway social revolution seemed somewhat nebulous, if not altogether unrealistic. Pelloutier's concept of the labor unions slated to become the basis of a "stateless" ideal society gave them pause. To be sure— prompted either by word-fetishism or bravado—they were unwilling to drop the word "anarchism" from the vocabulary of their credo. But more and more of them began to substitute "syndicalism" for "communism" and to call themselves "anarchist-(or anarcho-) syndicalists"—with the understanding that syndicalist methods were to serve as an instrument for attaining their anarchist ideal.

Malatesta, who approved of participation by the anarchists in the labor movement, was not enthusiastic about those of his comrades who were ready to swallow syndicalism hook, line, and sinker. He did not believe in the anarchists merging themselves completely with the labor movement. He saw in the labor movement a propitious arena for the propaganda of the anarchist ideal and was afraid that, left to itself, the syndicalist movement (which, as its theorists claimed, "sufficed unto itself") would eventually bog down in the morass of trade unionism, pure and simple. He foresaw that the very growth of the French syndicalist labor unions would spell the eventual decline of the revolutionary spirit animating its leaders. In short, that they would become "respectable." For growth was bound to bring in its wake the formation of a self-satisfied trade-union bureaucracy which eventually went the way of all trade unionist flesh. As a result, Malatesta declared at the Amsterdam Anarchist Conference (1907) that an anarchist who became a functionary in a labor union was lost to anarchism, for if he wanted to keep his job, he would have to bow to the mentality of the non-anarchist majority. Needless to add, the old romantic's analysis turned out to be prophetic.

That Amsterdam Conference (1907) failed to instill new life into a dying movement. Capitalism was still on the upgrade; the bulk of the workers were not interested in ultrarevolutionary protestations, and ultra-radical "protesters" of the anarchist brand would sooner or later either give up their apostolate or turn into gradualist Sancho Panzas. As a result, the International

Anarchist Bureau, which constituted itself with head-quarters in London, soon closed.

The last attempt to found an international anar-chist organization was made in 1922. In that year anarcho-syndicalists and syndicalists of various countries held a convention in Berlin (Dec. 25, 1922, to Jan. 2, 1923) whose outcome was the formation of an organiza-tion which reacquired the name of the First Interna-tional, International Workingmens' Association. During the 1920's the organization held a number of conven-tions; however, like its predecessors, it soon disap-peared from public view. The potential followers the new International might have attracted were all swallowed by the growing communist movement, the realism of whose revolutionary mystique was more than a match for anarchist utopianism.

SYNDICALISM OUTSIDE FRANCE

Shortly after its appearance as a new revolutionary current, French syndicalism began to spread to those countries in which, up to the turn of the century, ex-treme radicalism in the form of anarchism had never gone beyond the stage of a noisy sect. The way the converts began to apply the new gospel was not at all to the liking of its French originators. At the outset of their activities, the French syndicalists had the good luck to get control of the General Confederation of Labor that was *of their own creation*. The would-be emulators of French syndicalism in other countries were confronted by existing central trade-union bodies, whether controlled by the socialists as in Germany, Austria, and Italy, or leading an altogether independent existence as in England and in the United States. To permeate those unions with the revolutionary spirit of syndicalism was a difficult task. Those attempting to make propaganda for such views faced ostracism and expulsion. They thereupon formed their own syndicalist unions. This was entirely against the basic principle of syndicalism, which was dead set against the creation of competing or "dual" unions, particularly as these dual unions were bound to become sectarian propaganda societies stewing in their own juice, rather than mass organizations influenced by the new ideas.

I.W.W.

A case in point was the now defunct American variant of syndicalism once known as the Industrial Workers of the World (I.W.W.), which flourished between 1905 and 1920 and whose members were usually referred to as "Wobblies." The basic purpose of the I.W.W. was to organize the American workers along industrial lines, as distinguished from the system of craft unionism represented by the American Federation of Labor. Thus, to a certain extent, the I.W.W. anticipated by exactly three decades the basic idea of the Congress of Industrial Organizations (C.I.O.), which was founded in 1935. It appealed largely to the migratory, unskilled, and semiskilled workers ineligible to join the American Federation of Labor (A.F. of L.).

The I.W.W. owed its origin to a multiplicity of factors. At the turn of the century, many American radicals were dissatisfied with what they called the stagnation of the socialist and labor movement. Many socialists, both of the Socialist Labor party and of the Socialist party, were impatient with the American Federation of Labor because, under Gompers' leadership, it refused to commit itself to the cause of socialism, either ideologically, by accepting its aims, or practically, by enjoining its members to vote for the socialists. At the same time, many workers in the West, particularly in the ore-mining districts, became receptive to the idea of revolutionary trade unionism. Strikes developed into bloody fights between the troops and armed workers. And it was not the workers who provoked these violent clashes. This was grist to the mill of the anarchists, who believed neither in the ballot nor in peaceful trade-union methods and who began to accept the idea of French revolutionary syndicalism.

It was the syndicalist idea of emphasis upon the economic struggle for bread-and-butter, or wage-and-hours, objectives rather than upon the political struggle for votes, which eventually prevailed within the I.W.W., even though some of its leaders who believed in both methods, such as William ("Big Bill") D. Haywood were also members of the Socialist party. The open espousal of revolutionary slogans and methods by the I.W.W. brought it under constant attack. Refused permission to hold meetings in the West, the "Wobblies" staged "free speech" fights in many cities. Their spectacular methods and the persecution to which they were exposed attracted the adventurous and the more daring elements among the unskilled and semiskilled—the I.W.W. was often called the organization of the "wife-less, the homeless and the jobless"—but the masses stayed away, for the masses are not heroic. It is believed that the membership never exceeded 100,000. During World War I the organization's opposition to American participation in the conflict caused its leaders to be prosecuted for violation of the "Espionage Act." The sentences were heavy and sent the indicted men to the penitentiary for many years. Such prosecution, added to many personal frictions among the leaders, greatly contributed to the decline of the I.W.W. The main reason of its eventual eclipse, however, was the emergence of the communist movement as a result of the Bolshevik Revolution. Radical elements, hitherto "eligible" to the I.W.W., were attracted to communism. As time went by, many of the militant "Wobblies" such as Earl Browder, James P. Cannon, and Elizabeth Gurley Flynn joined the Communist party.[2] The I.W.W. gradually shrank to an insignificant sect, whose existence was indicated by the fact that it continued publishing its weekly *Industrial Worker* in Chicago.

HAYWOOD AND GIOVANNITTI

The outstanding and most glamorous personality among the "Wobblies" was William D. Haywood (1869-1928), the founder and leader of their organization. For many years a worker in the mines of Nevada, Utah and Idaho, he became secretary-treasurer of the Western Federation of Miners in 1901. In 1905 he took part in the founding of the I.W.W. Arrested in the same year on a trumped-up charge of having caused the murder of Governor Steunenberg, he was acquitted after fifteen months of imprisonment. A member of the Executive Committee of the Socialist party, he antagonized the official leadership of the party both by his hostility towards the American Federation of Labor and by his advocacy of sabotage. An amendment to the Socialist party's constitution, known as Article 2, Section 6, which condemned sabotage and violence, caused his expulsion in 1913 from the Executive Committee of the party. He was repeatedly arrested and convicted for his participation and leadership in various strikes throughout the United States. Because of his antiwar attitude during World War I, he was indicted under the Espionage Act. Released on bail in 1920, he escaped to Russia because, as he explained, a conviction which was a foregone conclusion at that time would have meant spending the rest of his life in prison. For a time he was in charge of the Kuzbas coal development in Siberia, supervising American workers. He died in Moscow, a broken and disappointed man, for he apparently never felt at home in the Russian Communist party, which he had joined—or had been forced to join.

Next to Haywood, one of the most colorful personalities of the I.W.W. movement was Arturo Giovannitti (1884-1960), a native of Italy. Born into a middle-class family, he came to the United States at the age of sixteen and was at first slated for the ministry. Having become interested in socialist ideas, he took an active part—as a fluent orator in both Italian and English—in the strikes conducted by the I.W.W., particularly where Italian workers were involved. In 1912, during the strike of the textile workers of Lawrence, Massachusetts, he was arrested and indicted as an accessory to murder, because a woman striker had been killed during a clash with the police. His case aroused protests and demonstrations on the part of radicals and trade unionists the world over. Acquitted and his ultra-radicalism somewhat cooled, he later became general secretary of the Italian Chamber of Labor of New York and an organizer for the International Ladies' Garment Workers Union. The poetry he wrote, both in English and Italian, reflected the social struggles of the period between 1910 and 1920. His volume of English verse *Arrows in the Gale* was in its time hailed as an outstanding poetical achievement.

Among the intellectuals who sympathized with the movement were Frank Bohn and William English Walling, both of whom could be called its unofficial philosophers. During World War I both were carried away by the wave of pro-Allied partisanship and turned their backs on all aspects of radicalism.

SAMUEL GOMPERS

Ironically, the most rabid adversary of both Haywood and Giovannitti was, at the outset of his career, himself a radical. Samuel Gompers (1850-1924), the founder of the American Federation of Labor, was born in London of Jewish parents and immigrated to the United States in 1863. A cigarmaker by trade, he came early under the influence of the First International and admired Karl Marx for his championship of the trade unions as a means of improving the workers' situation. He devoted his energy to building the cigarmakers union of which he became the president. During the 1880's he contributed more than anyone else to the formation of the American Federation of Labor, of which he was to hold the presidency with one interruption (1895) until his death. His early enthusiasm for socialist ideas was gradually replaced by hostility to all attempts made by radicals of all schools—socialists, anarchists, syndicalists, communists—to capture the trade unions. He believed that "the trade unions, pure and simple, are the natural organizations of the wage workers to secure their present material and practical improvement and to achieve their final emancipation." This, to a certain extent, was an idea closely akin to syndicalism. He was, however, officially opposed to the revolutionary tactics advocated by the syndicalists, though he often looked the other way when some of his own unions resorted to illegal methods. His hostility to socialist and communist attempts to win control over the trade union movement did not imply complete syndicalist-like aversion to all politics. He believed in what he called "rewarding friends and punishing enemies"—in giving the labor vote to those candidates whether Republicans or Democrats—who were more friendly or less hostile to the cause of labor.

In his later years Gompers epitomized his philosophy in the slogan of "more and always more." This apparently expressed his skepticism as to the possibility of achieving an ideal social system, or his renunciation of what in an earlier phase he called the "final emancipation." It also expressed his conviction that workers, regardless of changes in the social structure, would always have to wage an organized struggle for a better share in the good things of life. Gompers' activities were devoted largely to the cause of the skilled workers. Only shortly before his death did he become interested in the unskilled who in his time were considered as unorganizable.

AMERICAN ANARCHISTS

Gompers' most rabid opponents in the labor movement were the anarchists, even though they agreed with his bitter denunciation of the socialists.

In speaking about American anarchism, one has to keep in mind that the designation covers two separate categories: The followers of native American brands of anarchism representing extreme aspects of individualism and liberalism and having practically no point of contact with socialism, communism, or any other radical mass movements; and disciples of various European schools of anarchism, such as Bakuninism, Kropotkinism, anarcho-syndicalism, or their combinations or variants. The views of the former group are embodied in the writings of Josiah Warren, Stephen Pearl Andrews, and Benjamin Tucker. That group, now extinct, consisted exclusively of native American middle-class intellectuals of a philosophical rather than of a revolutionary bent. The other group, now likewise practically extinct, but very active during the 1880's and 1890's, consisted largely of German, Jewish, Russian, Italian, and Czech immigrants, with the German element predominating.

An ultraradical mood prevailed among the immigrant workers at the end of the 1870's due to the depression which held the United States in its grip for several years. The very moderate Socialist Labor party, whose composition was largely German, was gradually deserted by its more energetic members. These were absorbed by the Revolutionary Socialist party which was founded in 1881 and which was in favor of "armed workers organizations ready to repel, rifle in hand, any encroachments upon the rights of the workers." Albert Parsons and August Spies, the outstanding figures in the Chicago Haymarket tragedy of 1886-87, were among the first militants of the new organization.

JOHANN MOST

The propaganda of that group was stimulated by the arrival in 1882 of Johann Most (1846-1906), once an outstanding leader of the German socialists. He was born in Bavaria, where he learned the trade of bookbinder. At the age of seventeen he started out on the traditional *Wanderschaft* of the old-time German skilled workers, which brought him into most cities of Germany, Austria, Switzerland, and northern Italy. In Switzerland he came in contact with a branch of the First International. Converted to socialism—and a diligent reader—he soon became an effective public speaker. In 1870 he incurred a five-year sentence in Vienna because of "high treason" committed in one of his speeches. Released after one year, he rose quickly in the hierarchy of the socialist movement and in 1874, at the age of twenty-eight, he was elected to the German parliament. A speech delivered during the recess earned him a two-year sentence—in all, he was to spend ten years of his life in prison (counting his sentences in Austria, Germany, England, and the United States).

The antisocialist laws adopted in Germany in 1878 forced Most to emigrate to England, where he founded a revolutionary socialist weekly *Freiheit*. Expelled from the Social-Democratic party because of his violent criticism of the moderate tactics of its leaders, he gradually moved toward a position of ultraradicalism which was a hodgepodge of Marxism, Blanquism, Bakuninism, and Russian terrorism. In 1881 he was sentenced to eighteen months' imprisonment because of an article in which he glorified the assassination of Tsar Alexander II by the Russian terrorists. Unable to find a printer for his paper in England, he went to the United States, where he continued to publish *Freiheit*.

In the United States his own brand of anarchism found many followers among the numerous German workers who were swayed by his oratory. (It was an unorthodox, rather obsolete, brand of anarchism, harking back to Bakunin and not in conformity with the ideas of Kropotkin, then receiving general acceptance by the international anarchist movement.)

The main feature of his propaganda was the glorification of terrorist acts, or as it was called at the time, of "propaganda by the deed." The terrorism he preached was not meant for the United States; it was directed chiefly against the semiabsolutist regimes of Germany and Austria. As for America, he limited himself to a purely theoretical propaganda for the overthrow of the capitalist system. A believer in the "iron law of wages"—the inability of the workers to rise above the subsistence level within the capitalist system —he was not interested in strikes for higher wages. On this point his views differed from those of the Chicago anarchists who exerted a certain influence upon the labor movement and who were among the most active champions of the strike movement for the eight-hour day.

When by the middle of the 1890's French syndicalism made its appearance, Most showed great interest in the new movement and began to fill the columns of his paper with translations of pamphlets and articles published by the new school. Early in the 1890's, Most had anticipated one of the basic tenets of syndicalism by declaring that after the victory of the revolution, the trade unions would have the mission of reorganizing society. Ten years later he hailed the appearance of the I.W.W. But he showed no interest in the other basic idea of syndicalism—the immediate struggle for material improvement. Such indifference was largely the result of his desperate "all or nothing" outlook which he adopted after his break with the Social Democratic party.

EMMA GOLDMAN

American anarchism suffered a fatal blow as a result of the Haymarket bomb affair of Chicago (1886-87), which led to the conviction and the execution of the outstanding leaders of the Chicago anarchists. New York, the other center of American anarchism, which was the headquarters of Johann Most's propaganda, was at the same time the focal point of internecine quarrels within the movement. These greatly contributed to repel many followers and to weaken the movement. There was also the additional circumstance that the abrogation of the antisocialist laws in Germany (1890) and the general economic upswing in that country greatly reduced the flow of German immigrants to America. The new immigrants were not primarily interested in revolutionary ideas.

Next to Johann Most, the best known figure among the American anarchists was Emma Goldman (1869-1940). Born in Russia, she immigrated to the United States while in her teens. A factory girl, she came under the influence of anarchist propagandists who at that time were influential among immigrant workers. Johann Most discovered her budding oratorical talent and coached her for her future career as lecturer in the English language. The brand of anarchism she began to preach was contemptuous of the workers' struggles for immediate demands. In *Living My Life,* she records that she considered the struggles for an eight-hour day as a waste of energy and that she "scoffed at the stupidity of the workers who fought for such trifles" and were ready "to give up a great future for some small temporary gains." The only aim worth fighting for, in her opinion, was the abolition of the capitalist system. Her fiery eloquence, coupled with her close association with the terrorist Alexander Berkman, who in 1891, during a strike, made an attempt to kill the manager of the Homestead, Pennsylvania, steelworks, gave her name a renown that spread over both hemispheres. On the strength of her reputation she was often arrested and sentenced to prison terms. In 1901 her name was mentioned in connection with the assassination of President McKinley, although she had no connection whatsoever with the act of a halfwit who called himself an anarchist. Arrested and convicted for opposing America's participation in World War I, she was deported to Russia in 1920. Her initial enthusiasm for the Bolshevik Revolution evaporated upon close contact with the realities of the situation, particularly in view of the persecution of the anarchists by the Soviet regime. She contributed her share to dispelling procommunist illusions of many French and German syndicalists and some American "Wobblies," and left Russia in 1922, living in England, France, and Canada. During the 1930's she was permitted to visit the United States, where she delivered a number of lectures about anarcho-syndicalism to which she had become converted. Her most important works are *Anarchism and Other Essays* (1910) and *Living My Life* (1931).

ECLIPSE

Never strong among the American native workers, proanarchist sentiment among the foreign-born gradually disappeared for a variety of reasons—aside from the internecine struggles among the leaders and would-be leaders of various sects and subsects. The influx of immigrants whose initial struggles made them susceptible to ultraradical slogans and labels ended, and there was the growing prosperity of those becoming more or less "Americanized." The new, no less radical but less visionary, gospels of I.W.W.'ism and later Soviet communism supplied the desired psychological tonic to those in need of a violent gospel of salvation.

A few remnants of anarchist indoctrination still survive among some old-time Italian- and Yiddish-speaking immigrants. An Italian-language weekly, *Adunata dei Refrattari*, is published in New Jersey and a Yiddish biweekly, *Freie Arbeiter-Stimme*, in New

York. The Italian periodical is devoted to the ideas of a minor anarchist prophet by the name of Luigi Galleani, who, around the turn of the century, preached hostility to all forms of organization, seasoned with the gospel of "individual action." It looks down with contempt upon the everyday struggles for bread-and-butter demands and extolls the beauties of the anarchist ideal and of rebellious deeds against the status quo. The Yiddish periodical, which is closer to a very mild form of anarcho-syndicalism, has been largely devoted to the cult of the personality of another minor anarchist prophet by the name of Rudolf Rocker, a German "Aryan" who, having learned Yiddish, by his educational activities in the London ghetto raised an entire generation of well-indoctrinated Russian-Jewish workers. These, in turn, having migrated to the United States, as time went by, sufficiently watered down their erstwhile fiery philosophy of protest to qualify as leaders or functionaries of the needle-workers' unions.

THE SPANISH ANARCHISTS

While anarchism and syndicalism are dead in practically all countries, except for a few insignificant groups, a movement professing a combination of both philosophies is still very much alive in the Spanish-speaking countries. This is largely due to the fact that the first labor struggles in Spain were initiated and supported by Bakunin's followers, thus endowing anarchism with a prolabor tradition which even the fiercest attacks of the socialists and later of the communists were unable to destroy.

The history of Spanish anarchism is a long succession of savage persecution by the police, terrorist acts of retaliation, uprisings, and general strikes.

Ideologically, the movement was at first under the sway of Bakuninism with its "collectivist anarchism" (reward according to works) and a partly open, partly veiled striving for power on the crest of the hoped-for revolution. When that hope ended, the Spanish anarchists accepted the ideas of Kropotkin, which postponed the social revolution to the Greek calends, the loss of that hope to be compensated for by terrorist acts of revenge or protest. After that came the phase of anarcho-syndicalism, marked in 1911 by the organization of the C.N.T. (National Confederation of Labor). During World War I and shortly after the Bolshevik Revolution, the strike activities of the C.N.T. were partly supplemented and partly replaced by terrorist "groups of action," which engaged in killing employers or managers who refused to accede to the workers' demands. The employers retaliated with mass terror against union leaders and militants in the course of which hired gangsters succeeded in killing some of the outstanding leaders among Barcelona's anarcho-syndicalists. This period was concluded by the dictatorship of Primo de Rivera (1923-30) in the course of which all radical activities were suppressed.

The Spanish revolution and civil war of 1931-39 had a marked effect on the anarchist movement. The bloodless revolution of 1931, which ushered in an era of political democracy, resulted in the breaking away of a powerful wing of anarcho-syndicalist trade unionists, who decided to abandon the old revolutionary tradition and to pursue the gradualist tactics of typical trade unionism while retaining the old slogans of syndicalism, very much as the gradualist socialists retained the old slogans of revolutionary Marxism. On the other hand, the same event and the example of the Bolsheviks of 1917 led to the formation of a strong organization of insurrectionist anarchists called FAI

(*Federación Anarquista Iberica*) which was frankly out for an immediate anticapitalist revolution with a thinly veiled program of anarchist dictatorship, Bakunin style. These were the younger, more impulsive elements among the self-educated manual and white-collar workers who were just as hungry for power as were the corresponding elements which in other countries embraced the communist "line." The subsequent events in Spain (1936-39) led to the further abandonment by the Spanish anarchists of some of the traditional concepts of anarchist tactics; they voted for the democratic parties during the elections of 1936 (hitherto voting had been taboo among all anarchists); and after the Falangist military uprising they actively participated as cabinet members in the Loyalist government.

The victory of Generalissimo Franco drove the active anarchists either into exile or into the underground. In 1962, twenty-three years after the collapse of the democratic Republic, the Spanish anarcho-syndicalists gave up their intransigent organizational isolation when the National Confederation of Labor (CNT) controlled by them, concluded an alliance (*Alianza Sindical*) with the labor unions controlled by socialists and other groups for a joint struggle against Franco's dictatorship.

Spanish (and Portuguese) anarchists and anarcho-syndicalists were the first apostles of Western radical ideas in Latin America, and particularly in Argentina and Brazil. Hence the labor organizations in these countries were, before the turn of the century, largely under their influence. Internecine struggles within the movement (in Argentina), and the later arrival of German immigrants, enabled the Marxists to organize parties and labor unions professing the views of the European democratic socialists. In turn, the Bolshevik

Revolution led to the same splits and divisions as in all other countries. All of these tendencies suffered greatly during Perón's dictatorship, not only because of persecutions, but chiefly because the great concessions, in the matter of wages and other benefits, made to the workers under the dictatorial regime, won over to his cause the bulk of organized workers, regardless of their previous indoctrination. There was practically no trace of anarchist influence in the radical movements of Chile and Mexico, where the democratic socialists had been the first apostles of anticapitalist protest. As time went by, communist propaganda led to permanent dissensions and schisms within the political and trade union movements of the Left, with the communists—backed by Russia's prestige and financial support—as a rule getting the upper hand. Such was the pro-Stalinist fanaticism, or worse, of the Mexican communists that they repeatedly organized attempts to assassinate Leon Trotsky, to whom the Cárdenas administration had offered a haven.

ANARCHISM IN RUSSIA

Unlike the development of anarchism in Spain, its Russian counterpart, in spite of its glorious ancestry —Bakunin and Kropotkin—never became a mass movement. Spain, for all the reactionary character of its various nineteenth-century regimes, always had a modicum of political liberty. This enabled many malcontent elements among the intelligentsia to blow off rebellious steam without resorting to underground, illegal activities. It was "only" against striking workers that the regime was merciless and quick on the trigger. This added fuel to the irreconcilability of the self-educated worker-militants who had grown up in the anarchist tradition. It was different in absolutist tsarist Russia, where the entire radical intelligentsia, brought up either in the Marxist or the populist tradition, had to resort to illegal and often terrorist methods to vent its dissatisfaction. Hence, even the most radical elements, which in other countries were attracted by the intransigency of anarchism, could not complain about the lack of revolutionary fervor on the part of the old-established and powerful underground organizations of the democratic socialist parties. Moreover, it stands to reason that what irks an educated déclassé most under absolutism is the lack of political liberty rather than the oppressive character of the state qua state.

The few ultras who were attracted to anarchism were divided among various sects. Some fully accepted Kropotkin's view that Russia was ripe only for a democratic revolution; others put their emphasis on the philosophy of French syndicalism; these, in turn, were opposed by a group that insisted upon the propagandistic usefulness of killing members of the privileged classes indiscriminately—for the mere crime of being bourgeois. Throwing bombs into fashionable cafes and theaters patronized by the rich were to be the manifestations of this kind of social protest, which was called "unmotivated" (*bezmotivni*) terror because it was not provoked by any *special* motive, such as *excessive* brutality, or *excessive* exploitation. They also recommended the seizure of provincial towns for a few days, accompanied by the expropriation of the bourgeosie and the abolition of all authority—just for the sake of giving a heroic example. The champion of this school of anarchism, Judah Grossman-Roshchyn, was a brilliant young philosopher who never threw any bombs himself and who, after the Russian Revolution, joined the Bolsheviks. Other groups were even fiercer in their antibourgeois hatred. These were sometimes infested by plain bandits using anarchism as an ideological justification.

After the Bolshevik Revolution two novel forms of anarchism made their appearance. One of them was called "Makhnovism," after Nestor Makhno, a Ukrainian anarchist-terrorist of the pre-1917 period. After his liberation from prison he waged, for nearly two years, a guerrilla war of Ukrainian peasants both against the Whites and against the Reds, playing, for all practical purposes, the role of benevolent anarchist military dictator. There were also, during the early 1920's, pro-Bolshevik anarchists who were either unable or unwilling to throw overboard their anarchist pasts at one stroke. They found a sort of ideological refuge in a theory called "anarcho-bolshevism," which openly advocated a revolutionary dictatorship by anarchists during the transitional period from capitalism to anarchist communism. It was a frank reversion to the dictatorial aspect of Bakuninism which as a rule was ignored or denied by the later anarchists. In most cases, however, "anarcho-bolshevism" proved merely a short "transitional period" between anarchism and complete acceptance of official Russian "communism."

Equally unsuccessful as these Russians were the few English enthusiasts who attempted to start an anarchist movement in Great Britain. To be sure, there had been a pro-anarchist current among the avant-garde intellectuals during the 1880's. At that time they even succeeded in gaining control of the "Socialist League," an organization of radicals who, under the leadership of the poet and artist William Morris, had seceded from the Marxist Social Democratic Federation. By gaining control the anarchists killed the League and its publication *The Commonweal*, for it could not exist without the financial support of William Morris, who had resigned.

There had been a fresh spurt in the same direction during the subsequent decade when bombs were exploding in Paris, and almost the entire literary *bohème* of France was in sympathy with the dynamiters. A few anarchist or near-anarchist periodicals sprang up in London; there were highly publicized trials of men dabbling with explosives, as well as a number of frameups by the police, so that for a time the public was interested in the new revolutionary phenomenon. But after the echo of the French bombs had died away, nothing remained during the 1900's of the entire movement in England except a four-page periodical, *Freedom*, published monthly by a group of highly cultured English anarchists devoted to the ideas of Peter Kropotkin.

To be sure, there were many anarchists in London. But they were French, Italian, Spanish, German, Russian, and eastern European Jewish immigrants and refugees from the Continent. Anarchism, as the most violent expression of anticapitalist protest prior to the appearance of Leninist communism, had its chief appeal to the educated déclassés and to the more temperamental underpaid skilled workers in the economically backward countries. But the skilled workers were not underpaid in England, and the educated déclassés of that country could find their spiritual and emotional shelter in the Marxist Social Democratic Federation, which, for reasons already explained, never became an influential political party. Due to the liberty of the press existing in England, that party could indulge in verbal violence against the bourgeoisie exceeding even that offered by Continental anarchists. The British Marxists were thus able to attract most potential recruits of anarchism.

A few decades later, the same ultraradical elements were absorbed first by the syndicalists and later by communists, whose radicalism was just as violent, but considerably less chimerical than that of the anarchists. Syndicalism represented only a comparatively short phase in the history of British radicalism. It had, at the turn of the century, found an enthusiastic advocate in Tom Mann, a veteran of the socialist and trade-union movements since the 1880's. However, both Mann and his followers in the labor unions were soon to be swept off their feet by the powerful wave of communism coming from Russia. The intellectuals, in turn, who had become sympathetic to syndicalist ideas, soon evolved a theory of their own, which became known as guild socialism.

This new school of socialism owed its origin to the collective thought of three English political theorists, the medievalist and Christian socialist A. J. Penty, who revived the ancient idea of the guilds, and the Marxists S. G. Hobson and G. D. H. Cole. The theory represented a blend of syndicalism and democratic socialism. Its concept of a socialist system accepted both the syndicalist idea of the trade unions as the managers of the socialized industries, and the democratic-socialist idea of the democratic state which, however, is shorn of its "sovereign power." (In the original concept of syndicalism there is no place for the state.) The syndicalist ingredient of guild socialism is modified in that the trade unions are to evolve into "guilds," bodies which are to embrace "all the hand and brain workers employed in each industry" (G. D. H. Cole), that is, the clerical, technical, and managerial personnel, as well as the manual workers. It is to these "self-governing guilds or corporations" that, according to the guild socialists, "the administration of the socialized industries and services should be entrusted" rather than to the government departments. Guild socialism shared with syndicalism the emphasis upon the "economic" struggle—strikes for better conditions—rather than political action in support of socialist candidates. The emphasis on violence, so frequently encountered in syndicalist literature, is absent from the writings of the guild socialists.

There were considerable differences of opinion among the theoretical exponents of guild socialism concerning the role of the state. Some, accepting the orthodox Marxist vocabulary, spoke of the "withering away" of the state. Others gave the state the harmless name of "commune," which they entrusted with the "spiritual problems" of the nation. In view of the differences of opinion in the guild socialist camp, it is impossible to draw a sharp line between the powers of the guilds and those of the state (or the commune). However, it was generally assumed that while the central congress of the guilds was to represent the producers, Parliament, shorn of its old-time power, would represent the general interests of the nation at large.

The guild socialist movement disappeared in the course of the 1920's. Its protagonists have apparently been attracted either by the growing power of the British Labour party or by the growing revolutionary prestige of Russian "communism."

The emphasis upon the "economic" struggle for higher wages, which was one of the characteristics of syndicalism, was also the chief feature of another school of radical thought which is often designated either as anarchist or as syndicalist, although it rejected these labels, and actually represented a class by itself. That school or group called itself officially the "Workers' Conspiracy," but its followers were called "Makhayevtzy" after the name of its founder, the Polish-Russian revolutionist Waclaw Machajski[3] (1866-1926). The basic tenet of his theory was the idea that nineteenth-century socialism was not the expression of the interests of the manual workers but the ideology of the impecunious, malcontent, lower middle-class intellectual workers. These, according to Machajski, were dangling before the workers the socialist ideal of equality with a view to getting their support both in their political campaigns within the capitalist system and in their efforts to establish a new system of exploitation, a system of government ownership under which well-paid officeholders, managers, and technicians would take the place of the private owners. In short, he predicted what is now called the "managerial revolution" more than forty years before the appearance of the book of that title.

Writing in the peaceful days of capitalism's upward trend, Machajski saw this change coming as a result of the gradualist policy of the social-democratic (socialist) parties whose leadership in the Western democratic countries had become quite a respectable group of Leftist politicians averse to any revolutionary adventures. At that time the rebellious, declassed professional (or "intellectual") of the decades preceding and following 1848 was no longer a mass phenomenon outside of such politically and economically backward countries as Russia (including Russian Poland) and Spain. That phenomenon was to recur in the wake of World War I, when the hordes of unemployed or underpaid professional or white-collar workers began to embrace, en masse, the Bolshevist gospel of immediate anticapitalist revolution. Long before Lenin, Machajski, a conspirator by temperament, hoped to initiate an international, anti-capitalist revolution with the help of the then not very numerous déclassés who, in Russia, were not satisfied with a mere democratic, bourgeois revolution, and who, in the democratic West, wasted their anticapitalist intransigency in the utopian protest of various post-Bakuninist anarchist sects. With his criticism of socialist gradualism, whose champions postponed the abolition of capitalism to a distant future, he was trying to attract the radical elements dissatisfied with the slow tempo of the anticapitalist struggle.

Machajski's basic idea to the effect that the reality behind the socialist "ideal" was a new form of exploitation for the benefit of the officeholders and managers of the socialized state may have been inspired by a remark made by Bakunin in his *Statism and Anarchy* (in Russian) in which he accused the Marxists of aiming at such a new form of exploitation. The similarity of Machajski's views to those of Bakunin shows up in another respect as well. Bakunin operated with two contradictory theories, as it were: one for the general public, which advocated complete destruction of the state immediately after the victorious revolution, and another, expressed in confidential documents, in which he favored a revolutionary dictatorship by his own leading elite.

Machajski, who may or may not have been aware of this dualism of Bakunin's, likewise had two theories:

in one, somewhat related to syndicalism, he advocated an exclusively nonpolitical mass struggle for higher wages and for jobs for the unemployed—a sort of direct action movement against private employers and against the state; in his opinion this struggle, in its further development, would lead to the expropriation of the capitalists and to the complete equalization of incomes of manual and intellectual workers—thus bringing about the liquidation of the state by the disappearance of economic inequalities. The other theory, postulating the seizure of power in the form of a "revolutionary dictatorship," was hidden in passages of his earlier writings; in the opinion of most of his followers, it was considered abandoned by the teacher himself. But Machajski never explicitly repudiated that allegedly "outdated" view of his. (The idea of seizure of power in the wake of a revolutionary mass struggle for the workers' bread-and-butter demands was a carefully guarded "top secret"—lest his philosophy lose its appeal as a genuinely working-class tendency with no power strings attached to it. For the pure-in-heart ultra-revolutionary romantics among the anarchists whom he hoped to win over would have been repelled by *that* aspect of his theory.)

Thus, his nonpolitical, purely "economic," direct action egalitarianism, which had points of contact with both "pure-and-simple" trade unionism and anarcho-syndicalism, was allowed to exist side by side with a pre-Leninist form of neo-Blanquism advocating a "world conspiracy and dictatorship of the proletariat," which meant of course the seizure of power by his own group. In his later writings, he camouflaged this idea behind the cryptic phrase of the "working class dictating the law to the government." This implied that the intellectuals and self-educated former workers constituting Machajski's group of professional conspirators and claiming to speak in behalf of the "working class," would not take advantage of the opportunity of substituting themselves for a government to which they were strong enough to "dictate the law." This was, of course, in contradiction to his basic sociological thesis about the exploitative, unequalitarian tendencies animating the owners of higher education, that is, those able to seize power. It assumed that the educated men who were to constitute the officeholding setup of a Machajski-controlled revolutionary government would be exempt from those exploitative tendencies.

Thus, while giving the world an interesting and prophetic analysis of the cloven-hoof character of the allegedly disinterested proworkingclass idealism of the various anticapitalist tendencies, Machajski "forgot" to apply it to his own revolutionary passion for power.

Machajski's supersubtle plan was a dismal failure. The romantics and idealists who has joined him because they saw in his theory a realistic approach to the abolition of all power and privilege left him and withdrew from all revolutionary activities as soon as the Machiavellian, "two truths" character of their teacher's intentions became apparent to them. Those who had come to him from the various socialist parties and who saw in his purely economic bread-and-butter-struggle masquerade an excellent method of arousing the masses for the purpose of overthrowing capitalism and *seizing power* were not slow to join the Bolsheviks who were able to accomplish that aim without *that* masquerade.

Chapter VI

THE NEW MASTERS

The dream of a perfect society ushered in by the violent overthrow of the capitalist system—which inspired anarchists, syndicalists, and also some extreme left wing democratic socialists—began to take shape during the last two years of World War I. A group of Russian unorthodox Marxists, assisted by some anarchists and extreme left wingers of a non-Marxist socialist party, took power and then attached the label of communism to their party and to the system they promised to establish.

Communism, in the sense of economic equality, and communism as a term designating the social philosophy professed by those who came to power in the Soviet Union, are two different things. Even before it became identified with the policies symbolized by the names of Lenin and his successors, the term communism had begun to assume a variety of meanings. In the early part of the last century it was associated with revolutionary equalitarian groups, such as the "Babouvists" in France and the followers of Wilhelm Weitling in Germany, who believed in the immediate violent overthrow of the existing capitalist system. It also covered the ideas represented by Karl Marx, with his frankly skeptical attitude toward economic equalitarianism.

During the second half of the nineteenth century, with the socialist (or social-democratic) parties in control of the labor movement on the European continent, the word "communism" was relegated to the museum of historico-linguistic antiquities, if we disregard the revival of its use by the followers of Peter Kropotkin, who applied the adjective "communist" to their brand of anarchism. Marx and Engels alone insisted upon calling themselves "communists"—apparently as a gesture of radical anti-capitalist defiance.

In modern times the term "communist" has been connected almost exclusively with the party that has been ruling Russia ever since the Revolution of 1917, and with the movements in other countries which either sprung up spontaneously under the inspiration of that historical event or were organized with the active support of the Soviet regime.

LENIN OR TROTSKY?

The idea of abolishing capitalism "in our own lifetime"—as a British phrase has it—was not fathered by Lenin, as is generally assumed. It was Leon Trotsky (1878-1940), Lenin's lieutenant in preparing the victorious Bolshevik coup of November 1917, who during the abortive Russian Revolution of 1905 had first proffered this idea in what is called his theory of the "permanent revolution." Trotsky's theory held that the Russian revolution could not remain merely democratic in scope. The revolutionary government, Trotsky believed, would be obliged to make substantial concessions to the workers, such as providing for the unemployed and taking over those industries whose owners refused to satisfy the demands of the workers. He assumed that the capitalistically minded peasants would not agree to these reforms and thus come into conflict with the workers. Should the workers win in that conflict, the economic backwardness of the country would make it impossible to carry out the necessary socialist measures. The only way out of the impasse would be a revolution in Western Europe, which would join hands with the Russian proletariat in establishing socialism.

Thus, several years before the Revolution of 1917, Leon Trotsky envisaged the idea of a sort of international socialist revolution starting in Russia in the wake of a democratic anti-tsarist upheaval, and from there spreading over Western Europe. This was something new in the European socialism of that time—when "social revolution" had become a mere liturgical phrase and the realization of the "final aim" was visualized as a gradual transition to a democratic system of government ownership.

Lenin's views on the character of the Russian Revolution to come, as recorded in his writings since 1905, underwent many changes and eventually became practically identical with those of Trotsky. In his *Permanent Revolution*, a pamphlet written after his fall from power in the late 1920's, Trotsky boils down the difference between his opinion and Lenin's to the question whether "the participation of the representatives of the proletariat as a *minority* [emphasis added] in the democratic government"—expected to be established as a result of the Revolution of 1905—was "theoretically permissible." This question was answered in the affirmative by Lenin, who was ready to accept a peasant ("Social-Revolutionist") majority in the government, while Trotsky insisted upon a "proletarian" majority—that is, a majority composed of Marxian intellectuals, politicians, and ex-conspirators. The historical test of the Revolution of 1917 actually settled the controversy. "In November 1917," Trotsky wrote in his *Permanent Revolution*, "a struggle raged in the summits of the party around the question of a coalition government with the Social-Revolutionists and the Mensheviks. Lenin was not opposed in principle to a coalition on the basis of the Soviets, but he categorically demanded a firm safeguarding of the Bolshevik majority. I went along with him hand in hand." It was therefore Trotsky's point of view which actually became the basis of Bolshevik policy in the crucial months of the Revolution of 1917.

THE BOLSHEVIKS TAKE OVER

By the end of February 1917 the tsarist system broke down under the blows of the German military machine. The warweary soldiers stationed in Petrograd made common cause with the hungry protesting masses. No revolutionary party could claim exclusive credit for bringing about the liquidation of the hated regime. During eight months—between March and November 1917—the country was ruled by a provisional government. It was a coalition of progressive middle-class and moderate socialist parties among which the Social-Revolutionaries, the representatives of the Russian peasantry, were the most influential element.

In November of the same year, the followers of Lenin, who had been joined by Trotsky, taking advantage of the warweariness of the soldiers and of the land-hunger of the peasants, staged a successful coup against the Provisional Government. The communists have been in power ever since.

It was not the intention of the victorious Bolsheviks

—they began to call themselves communists only about a year later—to carry out an immediate socialization of Russia's economic fabric. The land was "nationalized," to be sure. But this meant only that the peasants, having seized the land of the big owners, had no right to sell their individual holdings. Beyond that the Bolsheviks proposed merely to nationalize the banking system and to establish government control—not ownership—of the industries.

Under normal conditions the process of transition from that system to full government ownership might have taken decades. Conditions in 1917 were however, not normal, and it took only ten months to bring about a complete nationalization of all industries. A multiplicity of causes led to this development. In many cases the workers were infuriated by the refusal of the manufacturers to comply with their demands. As a result, they simply drove out the owners and occupied the factories. The Soviet government, dependent as it was upon the support of the laboring masses, could not afford to lose face as a "proletarian regime" by restoring these plants to their legal owners. It therefore had no choice but to take them over, particularly as the workers themselves were not in a position to run those enterprises by their own efforts. In other cases factories were taken over to protect them against sabotage from their owners while the country was in the throes of civil war. There were also numerous instances in which the plants were seized by the government in order to prevent their being sold to German capital after the German-Soviet peace treaty of 1918. Thus, the Bolsheviks did not seize power in order to establish a system of government ownership. Rather they consented to the dispossession of the capitalists and to the establishment of government ownership in order to keep power.

The nationalization of industries was accompanied by a system of forcible seizures of foodstuffs from the peasantry. The cities produced exclusively for the needs of the army engaged in civil war and had nothing to offer the peasants in exchange. This resulted in what is usually termed "wartime communism"—a condition which lasted from the middle of 1919 to the end of the civil war, or more exactly, to the spring of 1921.

In reality it was not communism at all, if under communism one is to understand a system guaranteeing an equal share of the good things of life to every member of the community. It was a system of bureaucratic plundering of the peasantry for the purpose of feeding the army and providing starvation rations for the workers engaged in the war industries, while securing a fairly decent livelihood for the privileged members of the administrative machine—party leaders, bureaucrats, army officers, and the higher technical and managerial personnel.

"NEP" AND AFTER

The general dissatisfaction of the population, which manifested itself in numerous strikes, peasant uprisings, and the sailors' revolt at Kronstadt (March 1921), eventually led to the adoption of the so-called New Economic Policy (NEP). It was a sort of compromise between private capitalism and government ownership—with the state owning all key industries, while private enterprise was permitted in agriculture, trade, and the manufacture of consumers' goods. That system was maintained for about seven years—until 1928. At that time Stalin and his faction, having won in the struggle for power against the party elements opposing his personal ascendancy, adopted the program of his defeated opponents. The result was a policy of large-scale industrialization and agricultural collectivization which eventually did away with all vestiges of private enterprise. The entire country was converted into one great economic unit managed hierarchically by a bureaucratic apparatus that covers all aspects of industrial and agricultural production and distribution.

Through the years, that single economic unit evolved into the second largest industrial state of the world, surpassed only by the United States. There are no statistics concerning the cost in human lives of that imposing result. The goal was achieved by the starvation of millions—victims of initial inefficiency and of the export of foodstuffs, fibers, leather, and other materials indispensable for maintaining sheer life—in order to import industrial equipment and to produce military materiel—all for the benefit of a well-fed administrative and managerial bureaucracy.

The philosophy behind the new system established upon the ruins of the past was supplied by Marxist clichés, which in many instances were turned into their opposite by the "revisions" effected by Lenin. The mixture was called "Marxism-Leninism." Where Marx assumed that economic conditions and the laws of economic development were stronger than man's will or his desires, Lenin, though paying obeisance to the Teacher, asserted and proved the opposite. While, according to Marx, the economically advanced nation was the pattern of the future evolution for the undeveloped countries—implying that a socialized economy would appear first in the more industrialized sections of the world—Lenin demonstrated that politics—the will of a power-hungry minority—was stronger than the "laws of economic development." It was the very opposite of the Marxist thesis that economics determined politics.

In *State and Revolution,* a pamphlet written a few months before the seizure of power by his party, Lenin laid down the theoretical justification for his policy. His argument is largely based upon a famous passage from Karl Marx's *Critique of the Gotha Program.* That passage reads as follows: "Between the capitalist and the communist society lies the period of the revolutionary transformation of the former into the latter. To this also corresponds a political transition period in which the state can be no other than the revolutionary dictatorship of the proletariat." Lenin in his *State and Revolution,* and after him Stalin, in his *Foundations of Leninism,* interpreted this "revolutionary dictatorship of the proletariat" as a "state that is . . . democratic for the proletariat and the poor in general" (Lenin), or as a "proletarian democracy—the democracy of the exploited majority based upon the limitation of the rights of an exploiting minority and directed against this minority" (Stalin).

It would seem that with the complete elimination of all vestiges of capitalism in Russia there was no longer in existence any "exploiting minority" in the Marxist-Leninist-Stalinist sense against which that "limitation of rights" would have to be exercised. Yet as time went on those "limitations" grew to fantastic proportions both qualitatively and quantitatively. From 1928 the victims of such "limitations" were no longer capitalists but workers, peasants, or intellectuals holding nonconformist views, whose only "antiproletarian" crime was opposition to the autocratic methods of the regime.

In extolling the alleged democratic character of the coming "dictatorship of the proletariat" Lenin insisted that after the seizure of power the regime would be a "state of *armed workers*" [emphasis in the original] and not a "state of bureaucrats" (*State and Revolution*). The main attributes of that state would be the election of all officials without exception, their recall at any time, and their remuneration at salaries that have been reduced to the level of "workingmen's wages." Under modern capitalism, according to this classic of Lenin's (chapter 3, subdivision 2), "the great majority of functions of the old 'state power' have become so simplified and can be reduced to such simple operations of registration, filing, and checking that they will be quite within the reach of every literate person and it will be possible to perform them for 'workingmen's wages,' which circumstance can and must strip those functions of every shadow of privilege." In other words, there would be no bureaucracy, for everyone who could read and write would become a bureaucrat.

This regime, according to Lenin, was not meant to be the definitive form of a socialist society. With the development of technical resources society would gradually be enabled to dispense with compulsory measures necessary for maintaining certain inequalities inherent in the "first phase of communism." The process of gradually dispensing with governmental compulsion was called by Lenin "the withering away of the State," an expression coined by the founders of Marxism. Thus, the "dictatorship of the proletariat" would eventually evolve into that ideal system which the theorists of anarchism chose to call "anarchy"—an expression by which they understood a system of libertarian communism functioning on the basis of voluntary agreements.

It is beside the point whether Lenin had his tongue in his cheek when he argued that the main functions of government could be reduced to checking, filing, and registering. As time went on, with all the power in the hands of the "proletariat," all the main attributes of "proletarian dictatorship" as specified by Lenin went the way of all promises made by political parties. Soviet government officials are not elected but appointed from above; they are not subject to recall by their constituents, but are simply demoted, with or without lethal sequels; and their remuneration is as much above "workingmen's wages" as are the emoluments of a judge or factory manager above those of a mechanic or filing clerk in any capitalist country. And last but not least, the development of the technical resources of the Soviet Union has brought in its wake not a relaxation, but on the contrary a sharpening of the compulsory measures necessary for maintaining the ever-*growing* inequalities in the standard of living of the various groups of Russia's "classless" society. The "withering away of the state" was fated to become a mere liturgical phrase devoid of any practical significance.

For the interim period preceding the complete "withering away of the state," Lenin had launched the slogan that soon "every cook" would be able to attend to the affairs of the state. A new generation of those humble little ladies has grown up since that time, but they keep on cooking for the officeholders.

There are unorthodox partisans of the Bolshevik revolution who believe that the dictatorship of the Communist party, culminating in the personal dictatorship of its leader, are deviations from the original concept of the proletarian dictatorship as advocated by Lenin. Unfortunately for them, there are "slips" by the founder of Bolshevism himself indicating that they are sadly mistaken. When during the months preceding the November uprising of 1917 the Soviets, at that time still controlled by the Mensheviks and Social-Revolutionists, showed no inclination to join the Bolsheviks, Lenin dropped the pretense of "all power to the Soviets" declaring openly that this slogan would have to be replaced by that of "all power to the party."[1] On another occasion he stated that "Soviet socialist democracy is not inconsistent with personal rule and dictatorship, for the will of a class is at times best carried out by a dictator who alone will accomplish more and who is often more needed" (Vol. 17, p. 89, Russian ed., 1925).

COMMUNISM AND EQUALITY OF INCOMES

While the question of power was of paramount importance to the Communist party during the preparations for the November 1917 coup, the question of the distribution of incomes after the Revolution was agitating the rank and file to such an extent that Lenin had to devote a special section to this matter in his *State and Revolution*, written in September of that year. The task which he set himself was delicate. He himself was of the opinion that no great importance was to be attached to that problem, for, once *power* was in the right hands, it was obvious—to his party, at least—that the distribution of the good things of life would be carried out on an equitable basis. However, the unsophisticated, and at the same time apparently suspicious, proletarian man in the street wanted to know what the Bolshevik attitude was with regard to the idea of economic equality allegedly implied in the concepts of socialism and communism.

The father of Bolshevism knew very well that he was on dangerous ground. He had to appear as an equalitarian in order not to step on the toes of the party's working-class element, which at that time was exposed to a barrage of anarchist propaganda. And he had to take care not to be too explicit about his equalitarianism, lest his utopianism or plain demagogy became too apparent as soon as the realization of the "first phase" was to be attempted. Thus, he followed in the footsteps of his teacher, Karl Marx, who dealt with the subject in a way that lent itself to the most contradictory interpretations. In a document called *Critique of the Gotha Program,* Marx had written that "the first phase of communism" represented a system that was still "in every respect tainted economically, morally and intellectually with the birthmarks of the old society from whose womb it is emerging." Hence the "equal right" of the new system was "still handicapped by bourgeois limitations. The right of the producers is proportional to the amount of labor they contribute; the equality consists in the fact that everything is measured by an equal measure, labor. But one man excels another physically or intellectually, and so contributes, in the same time, more labor, or can labor for a longer time; and the labor, to serve as a measure, must be defined by its duration or intensity, otherwise it ceases to be a standard of measure. This equal right is an unequal right for unequal work. It recognizes no class differences because every worker ranks as a worker like his fellows: but it tacitly recognizes unequal individual endowment, and thus capacities for production, as natural privileges."[2] In other words, there is "equality"—even though an engineer or manager, because of his intellectual superiority, is paid ten or fifty times as much as an unskilled worker. For, as Lenin—in commenting upon Marx's views expressed in the *Critique*—says in Chapter 5, subdivision 3, "every worker receives from society as much as he has given it."

In expanding upon these ideas of Marx, Lenin glosses over the unequalitarian aspects of this passage which, as a matter of fact, he does not quote. Instead, he uses such expressions as "equality of labor and equality in the distribution of products," "for an equal quantity of labor an equal quantity of products," "equality of labor and equality of wages," "the whole of society will have become one office and one factory, with equal work and equal pay."

In the minds of practically every reader, these phrases create the impression that in the "first phase of communism" equality of incomes was going to be established. The only drawback in this equality, as Lenin puts it, would seem to be that "different people are not alike: one is strong, another is weak; one is married, the other is not; one has more children, another has less, and so on." "With equal labor," Lenin quotes Marx to this effect, "and therefore an equal share in the social consumption fund, one man in fact receives more than the other, one is richer than the other, and so forth. In order to avoid all these defects, right, instead of equal, must be unequal." And he further paraphrases Marx's argument in the *Critique* by saying: " 'For an equal quantity of labor, an equal quantity of products'—this socialist principle is also *already* [emphasized by Lenin] realized. However, this is not yet communism, and this does not abolish 'bourgeois right' which gives to unequal individuals, in return for an unequal (in reality unequal) amount of work, an equal quantity of products." For all its obscurity, or because of its obscurity, this again creates the *impression* that there is to be equality of incomes, affected only by the size of the family, etc., and marred by the necessity of "distributing the articles of consumption 'according to work performed' (and not according to need)."

Thus, it would *seem* that the only difference between the "first phase of communism" and the "higher phase" was the circumstance that under the former there was equality of incomes enforced by the authority of the state, while under the "higher phase," to use

Marx's words quoted by Lenin, "it will be possible to pass completely beyond the narrow horizon of bourgeois rights, and for society to inscribe on its banners: from each according to his ability; to each according to his needs!"

It is hard to say whether Lenin misunderstood Marx's obvious plea for inequality of rewards for intellectual and skilled as against manual and unskilled labor (which is hard to assume in a man of Lenin's genius); or whether he thought it more expedient to disregard this fundamental aspect of Marx's views. At any rate, both in his "April theses" of 1917, and in *State and Revolution* published a few months later, Lenin demanded that government officeholders be paid no more than skilled manual workers. This was an open advocacy of equalitarianism, for it is hard to conceive that in speaking of government officials he should have meant only letter carriers and garbage removers.

The actual practice of the Soviet regime has made hash of all the equalitarian or near-equalitarian ideas—regardless of the question of whether Lenin's phrases were or were not deliberately concealing the very opposite they seemed to convey. To be sure, Lenin himself—who was hungry only for power but not for material comforts—personally never claimed for himself a share that could have placed him in any privileged category. But, to paraphrase the remark of a disgruntled ex-official of the Soviet regime, the important thing was not how Lenin lived, but how the good things of life were distributed among the various sections of the Russian people.

Fourteen years after the appearance of Lenin's pamphlet, Stalin, in his speech of June 23, 1931, solemnly proclaimed inequality as the guiding principle of a better world in the making. "It is unbearable," he said, "to see the locomotive driver receiving the same wages as a copyist." That sentence meant that from now on not only the unskilled manual workers, mostly raw peasants from the countryside, but also the lower white-collar employees, whose education did not go beyond spelling and figuring, would stay in the lowest income brackets. And that everything would be done to give satisfaction not only to the technical experts but also to the highly skilled workers.

In another speech, delivered at the seventeenth convention of the Communist party held in 1934, Stalin elaborated theoretically on the subject of inequality and ridiculed the concept of equality of incomes as being tantamount to the idea "that all humans were to wear the same clothes and to eat the same foodstuffs in the same quantities." (As if under any social system persons in the same income brackets had to submit to such a crazy rule.)

Stalin's proclamation of inequality as the basic tenet of socialism was the signal for a speedy abandonment of all egalitarian masquerades of the initial phase of the Revolution. The Russian cities eventually resumed the normal aspect of the prerevolutionary era with its external manifestations of wealth and poverty. In the December 25, 1935, issue of the *New York Times,* Walter Duranty, who had been consistently friendly to the Soviet regime, remarked that the "differentiation of wages. . . . must lead to a new class differentiation in what claims to be a classless society, a new class of bureaucrats and directors of state enterprises, a new class of high paid upper workers all of whom together will form, or are forming a new bourgeoisie." The hereditary character of this new setup is not affected by the fact that the *more gifted* children of the manual workers are eligible for university scholarships, for, as against this lucky *minority* rising from the lower strata, *all* children of the bureaucratic-managerial elite, regardless of their abilities, have the economic opportunity to enter higher educational institutions.

The frank admission that an increasing inequality of incomes was henceforth to be the chief feature of a system that claimed to represent socialism on its way toward "full communism" was the unheralded landmark of a departure in the history of "new Russia." It implied *conscious* realization by the Communist party of the accomplished consolidation of a new privileged class of political and administrative officeholders, technical experts, managers, and army officers. This class had arisen from the ranks of the lower middle-class professionals, declassed intellectuals, and self-taught white-collar and ex-manual workers. It no longer had to pay obeisance to the workers and peasants whose struggles and privations had raised it to power and affluence. The masses were now thoroughly cowed and disoriented. They had been gradually deprived of their most intelligent and militant elements who had either been absorbed by the new bureaucratic apparatus or liquidated by a most efficient secret police unhampered by any legal squeamishness.

Slowly but steadily the communist top layer of the new ruling class began to shed those modern ideas which in the course of the nineteenth century had become the common property of all liberals and radicals. Traditional bourgeois concepts on all aspects of life began to come back with a vengeance. True, there was no reversion to the racial and religious intolerance of the tsarist system. In a country consisting of nearly two hundred different races and tribes, and in which the Russians proper constituted hardly more than half of the population, this would not be practical, particularly as Stalin himself and Beria, his chief of police, were both of non-Slavic origin, and since such a policy would have hurt the regime's expansionist designs in Asia. (Discrimination against Jews and even outright Jew-baiting were eventually resumed as a method of pandering to the deep-rooted prejudices of the masses. It was only at the outset of the Revolution that anti-Semitism was fought fiercely by the Bolsheviks, for at that time the presence of many Jews in the front ranks of the party was often used as an argument by the monarchist counter-revolutionists. But as the latter have in the meantime disappeared, anti-Semitism can now be used as a prop for the regime. Such is the "dialectic" of history.)

But aside from racialism, the official propaganda agencies shelved once and for all the original cosmopolitanism of the bohemian days of the Bolshevik conspirators, which was coupled with a deep contempt for Russia's despotic past. The new ruling class began to wallow in an orgy of nationalist vanity. Russia's history was no longer a horrid nightmare of barbarism, feudalism, and serfdom. Its "glorious" aspects, as represented by the country's victorious struggles against all her neighbors, whether invaders or invaded, were again presented as an inspiration to old and young. Peter the Great was no longer the sadistic brute he had been in the descriptions of the early Soviet historians, when it was still necessary to combat all vestiges of tsarist ideology. Now that the tsarist peril was at rest, Peter became a symbol of Russia's grandeur, glorified in novels and heroic cinema serials. In the eyes of Russia's new nobility, Peter's military conquests, as well as those of Ivan the Terrible and Catherine the Great, outweigh all the crimes they committed against Russia's peasant masses whose burden became ever heavier under their glorious rule. It was in line with reversion to bourgeois type that during Russia's war with the Nazis the highest reward for military prowess was named after Suvorov, a great warrior, to be sure, but one who had won his laurels in the struggle of reactionary Europe against the French Revolution and who had earned the bitter hatred of all liberals and progressives by the suppression of Pugachev's peasant uprising, and by the Warsaw massacre perpetrated in the campaign in which he was instrumental in destroying Poland's independence.

Hand in hand with this reversion to fierce nationalism went a retreat in all other fields as well. Easy divorce and voluntary parenthood—birth control and abortion —extolled during the first decade as great contributions to individual freedom in personal relations became a matter of the past. Childbearing has been declared the chief duty of woman. The daily paper of the Communist Youth expounds Victorian notions with regard to chastity and woman's honor.

Having come to appreciate the conservative value of the once derided shibboleths of patriotism, family, marriage, chastity, etc., Russia's new ruling class of officeholders, technical experts, and army officers quite naturally reconsidered its previous iconoclastic attitude with regard to religion. Old Russia's conversion to Christianity was extolled as a great civilizing feat, and a musical comedy by the hitherto popular official poet Demian Byedny was taken off the stage because it had burlesqued that event. Antireligious propaganda was suspended and the Russian Orthodox hierarchy was accepted as part of the Soviet system provided it prayed for the regime. After the annexation of eastern Poland, as a result of World War II, the Ukrainian peasants inhabiting that region, who had hitherto professed an Eastern version of Roman Catholicism, were compelled to give up their allegiance to the Vatican and to join the Orthodox Church to which the Ukrainians of the Soviet Union belong. (It was in line with the same opportunist policy dictated by the desire to win the Catholic electorate that in April 1947 the Italian communists voted with the Rightist parties for the recognition of Catholicism as the country's state religion, a decision which implied the obligation of all non-Catholics to pay taxes for the support of the Church. That the Italian communist vote was no "deviation" is evidenced by the fact that at about the same time Roman Catholic services preceded the Warsaw funeral of General Karol Swierczewski, a Polish communist, who, under the name of "Walter," was one of the leaders of the "International Brigade" during the civil war in Spain. At the outset of the Revolution such services for a prominent Communist would have been unthinkable.[3]

Needless to say, the same retrogression has marked the attitude of the present rulers toward art as well. During the first years of the Revolution the Soviet authorities encouraged all sorts of modernistic trends in art, thus rallying to their cause all the younger elements which struggled against academism. But the years of "storm and stress" were over in the middle of the 1930's; the government then began to cater to the simple tastes of the country's none too cultured new nobility of officeholders. Artists blazing new paths fell into disfavor. Modern currents in art were officially condemned as "decadent modernistic influence," to borrow a phrase used by the Moscow *Izvestia*, official organ of the Soviet government, in its issue of September 2, 1938. The condemnation likewise included "French impressionism," "post-impressionism" and "bourgeois romanticism." As the Austrian Marxist Otto Bauer put it, in matters of art and literature

"Bolshevist Russia of today combats exactly the same thing that Fascism in the West is fighting as '*Kultur-Bolschewismus*.'" It goes without saying that only artists following the official government art "line" can expect to have their works presented to the public.

THE ETHICS OF POWER

Soviet Russia's backsliding to bourgeois respectability was accompanied by the abandonment of all ethical values which throughout the nineteenth century were cherished by liberals and radicals of all denominations. True, their moral standard was not always very high when an intraparty and interparty struggle for power would arouse all the evil passions such conflicts have been known to call forth since the beginning of time. With the communists in power, the gentle art of character assassination became one of the main weapons of propaganda and politics in general. It assumed proportions comparable only to those attained by the Nazis, whose Fuehrer acted on the principle, proclaimed by himself, that the bigger the lie the greater the probability that it would be believed. With the maintenance of power over one-sixth of the globe at stake the communists let go of all moral restraint, even as—according to a famous saying quoted by Marx—a capitalist would not refrain from any crime if a profit of 300 per cent would beckon to him. Leon Trotsky, in his heyday, had no compunctions in slandering the Leftist opponents of his dictatorship as agents of the monarchists, the capitalists, and the "kulaks." When he lost to another faction of his own party, he and his followers were eventually branded as "Nazi agents"; and after his assassination by a G.P.U. agent, *Pravda* (August 24, 1940), the largest newspaper of the Soviet Union, announced the news in a story headlined: "Death of an international spy."

The assassination of Trotsky on foreign soil was only one link in a series of similar assassinations committed with impunity in Switzerland, France, Spain, Mexico, the United States, and, after the termination of World War II, in the various countries and "zones" occupied by the Russian army. These murders were not acts of protest by self-sacrificing fanatics against their respective governments or ruling classes, acts which, in the opinion of radicals and liberals, were often surrounded with a halo of heroism and martyrdom. They were perpetrated in cold blood by professional killers entrusted by the Soviet government with the extermination of ex-communists or members of Leftist groups for whose sake the governments of the foreign territories concerned did not care to raise a diplomatic issue.

In still another respect did the communists recede behind the standards commonly observed by all progressive organizations. Nineteenth-century radicalism was republican and democratic at heart and as such vigorously opposed to excessive leader worship. Cheering of leaders on all occasions or, what the Germans called *"Personen-Kultus"* ("cult of leading personalities"), was condemned as one of the vestiges of reactionary, monarchist mentality. The communists resuscitated this ultrareactionary, authoritarian vice to an extent almost unthinkable in the bourgeois world. Lenin's body was embalmed and preserved as a sort of deity for the veneration of the masses. Stalin—before his de-deification in 1961—was celebrated in songs and stories in several scores of languages of the Soviet Union. Postal stamps during World War II bore the legend *Za Rodinu—za Stalina* (For Fatherland—for Stalin). For nearly two decades every speech, every article, every treatise published in Russia had to be studded with quotations from the *Vozhd*, the Russian equivalent of the *Fuehrer*, a title which was invariably applied to him. The top leaders of the communist parties outside Russia, Thaelmann in Germany, Thorez in France, Browder in the United States, Tito in Yugoslavia, Dimitrov in Bulgaria, became the object of similar servile veneration cleverly organized by the party and willingly submitted to by the recipient.

More telling still than the retrogression behind the generally accepted standards of radical and liberal conduct, more telling than the "framing" and the extermination of political dissenters, are certain stipulations of the criminal code referring to nonpolitical offences. Soviet Russia has the distinction of being the only country in which the capital penalty is applied for theft of state property—thus harking back to the most barbaric periods of European history, when similar punishment was meted out for stealing private property. According to the Act of April 7, 1935 (printed in *Pravda* of April 8, 1935): "Minors, twelve years of age and older, apprehended stealing, committing violence" etc., are to be "brought before the criminal court where all measures of criminal punishment may be applied to them." This obviously included the capital penalty—for twelve-year-olds.

Russia is likewise the only country in which under the law of June 8, 1934, a peacetime deserter, if apprehended, is condemned to death and where in case of his escape or failure to return from a journey abroad, all close relatives of the offender are subject to imprisonment.[4]

The seizure of power by the Bolshevik party was followed by the gradual disappearance of all political liberties, not only of those established during the short interval between the downfall of tsarism and the Bolshevik *coup d'état*, but also of those, restricted though they were, which had existed under the old regime since 1905, when both liberal-democratic and socialist publications, including those of the Leninist brand, were tolerated. Shortly after the inauguration of the new regime, the Communist party established a monopoly over all public activities—political and otherwise. There was to be only one political party, one editorial policy in all newspapers, one trade-union organization which thus became a company union of the Employer State, one association in every field of human endeavor—with all these bodies becoming mere subsidiaries of the ruling party. This policy has remained unchanged under Khrushchev's "liberal" policy as well.

To be sure, there were representative assemblies, called soviets, composed of delegates of workers and peasants; but it did not take long before these bodies were reduced to mere decorative institutions, bossed completely by the communists. Elections to these bodies were effected by a show of hands, and the list of candidates was always submitted by the communist caucus. No attempts at submitting other lists were made, for they meant a conflict with the "unsheathed sword of the Revolution," the dreaded secret police, known at different times as "Cheka," "G.P.U." (or O.G.P.U.), "N.K.V.D.," "MVD," etc.

In the early 1930's this totalitarian concept of politics found cynical expression in the notorious words of Michael Tomsky, then head of the Soviet trade unions: "Any number of political parties may exist in Russia, provided one of them is in power and the others in prison." (It is a grim commentary upon that system that Tomsky was one of the first to pay with his life when Stalin decided to extend that lofty principle to all those who within the party disagreed with him on one point or another.)

Russia's new "democracy" took final shape in the Soviet constitution of 1936, which remained in force after Stalin's death. For the benefit of those potential sympathizers who had as yet been unable to overcome their sentimental attachment to the concept of democracy, Lenin evolved the famous formula that "proletarian democracy is a million times more democratic than any bourgeois democracy and the Soviet regime is a million times more democratic than the most democratic regime in a bourgeois republic." The new constitution, which became officially known as the "Stalin Constitution," gave the franchise to all persons of both sexes, eighteen years or over. Nothing could be more democratic than that. A "franchise," of course, is granted for the purpose of elections. But there are no elections. The very word "election" presupposes a choice among various candidates. But there is no such choice because the constitution maintains the totalitarian one-party system. There is only one candidate or one set of candidates in each district. The selection of the candidates is effected by the Communist party machine, and confirmed by an *open* vote of party members, which renders impossible the putting up of a slate of candidates who are not agreeable to the party machine. For any one who would openly vote against the officially proposed set of candidates, would automatically set himself down as an "enemy of the people."

Despite the 146 articles of the constitution there

is no personal liberty in the Soviet Union in the sense in which it exists in all civilized countries. A Russian physicist, Professor Peter Kapitza, had made his home in England, where he had become director of the Royal Society's Mond Laboratory at Cambridge. When he came to Russia on a visit in 1935 he suddenly was deprived of his passport and forced to remain in a country from which he had expatriated himself many years before. He had never engaged in politics. But the Soviet authorities simply declared that they preferred him to do his scientific work in Russia rather than in England. It was as if Henry James, on a visit to his native country, had been told by the American authorities that he could not go back to England and that henceforth he would have to write his novels in the United States.[5]

Passports, though nominally in existence in Russia, are actually beyond the reach of the ordinary inhabitant. Applications for a passport are always rejected. That coveted document is given only to trusted supporters of the regime or to members of the bureaucracy sent abroad on an official mission. The actual reason for that refusal, though never admitted, is the same as that which had prompted the governments of Fascist Italy and Nazi Germany to take the same attitude. Neither of these regimes, in the opinion of a Paris correspondent of the *New York Times*, wanted its nationals to see for themselves the political and social conditions abroad.

On the other hand, there is a compulsory document in Russia which has the unassuming name of "work-book." That book lists every job its holder ever had and the exact reason why he left it in every case. This is to make it impossible for industrial workers to leave an establishment to seek better accommodations elsewhere. Such a "selfish" attitude is considered highly dishonorable and disqualifies the holder of the book from obtaining another job.

Such is the status of Russia's "free" workers. Yet it was enviable as compared with the situation of *millions* of recalcitrant "individualist" peasants and political dissenters enrolled in those branches of Soviet economy which employed forced labor, such as timber cutting and the building of canals, roads, and fortifications. These branches of slave economy were under the direct management of the secret police. For obvious reasons there were no statistical figures about these slave workers whose number has been estimated at between fourteen and twenty million. For disloyalty during World War II entire tribes of non-Slavic races, such as the Kalmucks, the Crimean Tartars, the Volga-Germans and various nationalities on both slopes of the Caucasus range, where they had lived since time immemorial, were transplanted to regions where forced labor and an unaccustomed climate doomed them to extinction. The same fate was also meted out to many Latvians and Estonians for the purpose of settling the formerly independent Baltic republics with Russians proper.[6]

The "purges" and the "trials" of the late thirties are still generally remembered. They were devices by which Stalin—aside from getting rid of some of his opponents —tried to placate the masses and thus to consolidate his own power. To the man in the street the liquidated Old Guard of the Communist party, including practically all the top figures in the various central and autonomous administrations, was the symbol of all his sufferings and privations during the first two decades of the Soviet republic. The "confessions," extorted under threat of torture or of extermination of the victims' families—those who refused to "confess" were shot without trial—have been justly compared with medieval witch trials at which the unfortunate women gave minute accounts of their traffic with the devil. These "confessions"—despite their obvious falsity—were stubbornly defended as genuine by communists and fellow travelers the world over. They only began to speak of Stalin's "mistakes"—"incorrect methods of work," as William Z. Foster of the American Communist party reluctantly admitted—after Khrushchev, for reasons of his own (he himself had apparently been slated for liquidation), gave his famous "secret" speech of 1956.

A state wielding such power over its subjects has also the authority of prescribing to them what they are to read or rather what they are not to read. The younger generation of officeholders cannot even conceive the idea that a newspaper should criticize the government. The same restrictions that hold for the press are applied to all other aspects of the country's cultural life. The theater, the cinema, radio, book publishing—are all co-ordinated according to the most rigid totalitarian principles. Authors who for years had enjoyed the greatest reputations, such as Pilniak, Panteleymon Romanov, Zoshchenko, Akhmatova, and Pasternak, are suddenly silenced or liquidated, if in their novels, short stories, satires, or poems they give expression to moods at variance with the official optimism and compulsory sycophancy required by the regime from its "artists in uniform"—to use a phrase coined by Max Eastman.

Science as well as literature has also felt the heavy hand of official inquisition. Certain branches of learning are lavishly subsidized if they promise to further the process of industrialization and thus aid the country's military preparedness. But whenever a scientific theory may lend itself to interpretation remotely conflicting with the political theology of the regime, official intolerance is even more outspoken than that of the fundamentalists who prohibited the teaching of evolution in Tennessee.

From the outset, it was the official policy of the Soviet government to treat all opponents—even those of the various democratic socialist schools—as a sort of fifth column. When the civil war and its after-effects could no longer serve as an excuse for the banning of all political activity outside the Communist party, another argument was advanced. In an interview given in 1936 to Roy Howard, the copublisher of the Scripps-Howard chain of papers in the United States, Stalin ventured a theoretical explanation as to why not more than one party was permitted to exist despite the pretended democracy of the new constitution. "As soon as there are no more classes," he said, "as soon as boundaries between classes are effaced . . . there can no longer be any nourishing ground for the formation of parties struggling among themselves. *Where there are not in existence several classes there cannot be several parties because a party is a part of a class.*"[7]

The idea that with the elimination of the propertied classes Russia has become a "classless" society is not only part of the official folklore of communism; it is a logical sequence of the Marxist doctrine which determines a person's class status not according to his income but according to his "relation to the process of production"; this deceptive half-truth by stressing merely the question of "owner or employee" places the high-class executive in the category of "workers" alongside the laborer who may earn less than one-fiftieth of his income. It is this Marxist fallacy which has furnished the ideological cloak for the unmitigated class rule of Russia's new aristocracy—or new bourgeoisie, if you will—over the enormous mass of workers and peasants. It is as the most militant "part" of this new nobility that the Communist party maintains its political domination.

One aspect of that "classless" myth is the constantly repeated claim that, as Stalin put it (*Daily Worker*, New York, Nov. 27, 1936), the workers "possessed the industries in conjunction with the whole people." Curious situations sometimes arise out of this article of faith of present-day Russia. Here are the workers, "owning" their industries, yet as a rule dissatisfied with the collective agreements which they conclude with themselves concerning wages and hours. Sometimes they even run away from "their own" factories, and all kinds of methods of persuasion and compulsion have to be applied to keep them at their jobs, or more correctly, at "their" property. The confusion is even greater than that. The workers, as the "owners" of the factories, are thus logically the real "employers." The technicians, the engineers, the managers, are their "employees." No wonder that the Bolsheviks, as the defenders of the oppressed, take all the possible care of the "hired men," that is, the managers and technicians, and pay them much more than they do the "owners."

But there is a hitch somewhere. The ballyhoo is too crude—it could be believed only by naive "liberal" innocents four thousand miles away but not by the uneducated workers on the spot. As a result it sometimes happens that the unsophisticated editor of a provincial paper complains that "labor discipline is deteriorating in the Irkutsk district, and that the workers do not consider the industries as their own."[8] Even Lazar Kaganovich, a man of steel second only to Stalin, occasionally would make a slip in the presence of that mystery. In a speech reported by the Moscow *Izvestia* of June 8, 1930, he mentioned that the "proletariat begins to realize the fact that it is the owner of the production, the owner of industry." So it took the proletariat thirteen years to "begin to realize" that it is the master of the country. . . .

The "thaw" which followed Stalin's death in 1953 failed to justify the hopes of those who expected an essential departure from Lenin's and Stalin's totalitarianism. To be sure, some of the harshest features of Stalin's despotism were mitigated. The secret police was shorn of some of the unlimited power it had wielded prior to the tyrant's death. It became an instrument of the Communist party rather than the dictator's Damocles' sword suspended over communists and non-communists alike. The slave labor camps were liquidated, or so the world was told. Novelists are now permitted to hint that some men in authority are abusing their power, but they cannot afford to write that it is the very system which breeds these abuses, lest they suffer the fate of Pasternak, Russia's greatest poet. Some satellites, as in the case of Poland, were allowed a modicum of cultural freedom, and the names of some of the purge victims were vindicated, while the body of the Great Butcher was removed from Lenin's tomb . . .

However, the basic features of Soviet totalitarianism have remained unchanged. The one-party system of government is still in full force. The press remains a government monopoly, while all cultural activities are under strict control. And military intervention and massacre, as in the case of Hungary, are held in store for any "people's democracy" which would attempt to assert its independence.

Chapter VII

TOOLS AND DUPES

THE COMMUNIST INTERNATIONAL

At its outset the movement centering around the person of Lenin was specifically Russian in character, concerned exclusively with the Russian Revolution. To be sure, during World War I Lenin had launched the slogan that the carnage could be stopped only by converting the imperialist conflict ino a civil war throughout the world. But considering the absence of any really revolutionary elements outside of Russia, this slogan was more in the nature of a propaganda phrase than a serious attempt at any action for achieving a definite social change in the direction of a communist society.

It was only after the Bolshevik Revolution of 1917 that the task of survival in a hostile capitalist world brought to the fore the idea, originally launched by Trotsky in 1905, of carrying the revolution to the countries of the West. What only a few years before had been considered a fantastic pipe dream of a lone Marxist free-lance journalist now became a concrete task. The Communist International, an organization destined to further the cause of the "proletarian revolution" in the West, was launched in 1919. Leon Trotsky, between 1917 and 1923 second only to Lenin in the councils of the Communist party and of the Soviet government, wrote during that period all the official appeals of the organization.

At first the parties of the Communist International outside the U.S.S.R. were comparatively small sects of enthusiasts or fanatics, representing the extreme left wing of the socialist parties and a number of former anarchists and syndicalists. The human material of the affiliated organizations was not different from that of other revolutionary bodies that had sprung up in the course of the nineteenth and twentieth centuries. Soon enough, however, a very important difference became quite apparent. The communist organizations abroad were organized along the same lines as the parent body: as a strictly disciplined army of professional revolutionists following instructions given from above. "Above" was the Executive Committee of the Communist International, which for all practical purposes was a branch of the Commissariat for Foreign Affairs. It was the Soviet government which supplied all the funds necessary for the functioning of those organizations. Thus, the German, the Hungarian, the French, the Chinese, and all other communist party leaders became de facto paid functionaries of a foreign government, except in those rare cases where they were able to raise the funds in their own country. This was something new in the history of revolutionary movements, and it was bound to have disastrous effects upon the moral integrity of the communist leadership the world over. From bodies of revolutionary enthusiasts interested in the seizure of power in their respective countries, the communist parties gradually became what was at first called "frontier guards" and later "fifth columns" of the Moscow regime—in utter disregard of the interests of the working masses of their own countries. The preservation of the Soviet government and later the strengthening of its position on the chessboard of international diplomacy became the only criterion for the activities of all communist parties.

When, shortly before the outbreak of World War II, Soviet Russia concluded its fateful alliance with Hitler, communists the world over repeated Molotov's famous phrase about Fascism being "a matter of taste" and used an "ultra-revolutionary" vocabulary to the effect that there was no difference between "capitalist democracy" and Fascism—as an excuse for their "neutrality" during the first two years of World War II, which they called an "imperialist war." They kept echoing the assertions of the Moscow press that the Allies were the aggressors, since after the partition of Poland between Nazi Germany and Soviet Russia in 1939, France and England insisted upon continuing their war against Germany. And they maintained their opposition to the Allied war efforts against the Berlin-Rome Axis until the moment when Russia was attacked by the Nazis.

Not all communists outside Russia were ready to accept without questioning all those changes of policy dictated by the interests of Russia's ruling bureaucracy. Many of them bolted, either to withdraw completely from political activity, or to join various groups of the moderate or ultraradical Left.

After Russia's invasion by the Nazis in 1941, the Communist International was officially dissolved in 1943 as a gesture of complete harmony with the capitalist powers. This implied opposition to strikes and to pressure by the workers against their employers in capitalist countries. When the relations with the West cooled off, another organization, called the Communist Information Bureau (Cominform), was formed in 1947. That was the period of the preparation for world conquest through the establishment of communist-controlled "people's democracies" in all satellite countries, of the struggle against Titoism in Yugoslavia and in the satellite countries, and of the "fifth columns" in all other countries. The Cominform has for all practical purposes ceased to function. When Premier Khrushchev wishes to make his views known to outlying communist parties, he simply summons them to a conference of "the socialist world."

At variance with the various democratic socialist parties—each of which as a rule conducts a policy of its own independent of any outside body, such as the Socialist International—the communist parties of the various countries have always submitted to instructions from Moscow or from any other center housing a bureau entrusted with issuing instructions to the organizations either openly using the communist label or hiding their identity under another name.

An exception to the rule of absolute submission were the first two leaders of the German communists who were by no means blind followers of Lenin and Trotsky. Karl Liebknecht and Rosa Luxemburg, who represented the extreme left wing of German democratic socialism, had opposed the kaiser's government and their own party during World War I. The "Spartacus Bund," which embodied their views, hailed the Bolshevik Revolution and in December 1918, shortly after the establishment of the German Republic, constituted itself as the German Communist party. The majority of its membership consisted of ultraradicals who insisted upon an immediate uprising aiming at the establishment of a German soviet republic. Their views were not shared by the two leaders, who were convinced that an undertaking of this kind could not possibly succeed. Most German workers still followed the leadership of the two democratic socialist parties then at the helm of the German democratic republic. Liebknecht's and Luxemburg's counsel of prudence was not heeded by the majority. The uprising, staged in the middle of January 1919, was crushed and the two leaders who had opposed it were murdered by the monarchist soldiers who arrested them.

At a convention held in 1920 those responsible for the hapless Berlin revolt were expelled from the party, whereupon they constituted themselves as the Communist Workers' party (Kommunistische Arbeiter-Partei).[1]

In the meantime a process of disintegration took place within the Independent Socialist party, a minority Social-Democratic organization which had seceded from the main body in protest against its support of the war. At a convention held by the "Independents" during 1920, the majority of the delegates decided to join the Communist party.

However, there was no smooth sailing for the Communist party after that merger. Between 1919 and 1922, during the period of the Russian civil war and postcivil war dangers, the Communist International encouraged uprisings all over Europe, even if they were hopeless either because of the weakness of the communists or because of the passivity of the bulk of the working masses. These adventures were undertaken to show the wavering and exhausted Russian masses by some practical sign that the European revolution against capitalism was stirring and that the wealth of the West would soon come to their rescue. Characteristic in this respect was the so-called "March action," which the German communists were ordered to undertake in 1921. The Central Committee of the party, composed of Kremlin stooges whose livelihood depended upon obeying the orders from Moscow, could apparently not afford to protest, but its leaders showed so little enthusiasm that the appeals urging their followers to rise had to be written by *non-German* agents of the Communist International—they were later called "die Turkestaner"—who gave themselves away by the atrocious German in which those documents were couched. The useless bloodshed of the abortive revolts called forth violent protests on the part of Paul Levi, the outstanding intellectual of the party who refused to play the role of an obedient tool. He was expelled from the party to which he no longer cared to belong. It was he who arranged for the posthumous publication of Rosa Luxemburg's now famous pamphlet *The Russian Revolution*, in which she attacked the dictatorial methods of the Bolshevik regime.

Heinrich Brandler, Paul Levi's successor as the leader of the party, found himself in the dual position of a man who dreamed of winning the consent of the masses for the formation of a leftist government that would include both communists and socialists as a transition to the establishment of a soviet regime, and had to cope with a rapidly deteriorating economic situation which reached its lowest point in 1923. In this situation the *masses*—and not merely small groups of extremists —embittered by a runaway inflation were at last psychologically prepared to rise. What followed was one of the most controversial chapters in the international communist movement. An uprising, which had some chance of success, was slated for October 1923. Ostensibly endorsed by the Communist International, it was called off by Brandler and the other leaders of the German Communist party. It is an open question whether by doing so they followed the promptings of their own lack of heroism or the secret orders of the Kremlin.

There are those who suspect that the Soviet regime, by that time more or less stabilized as a result of the New Economic Policy, was afraid to risk its existence in case of a *successful* uprising. For such a contingency might have called forth an armed intervention on the part of France, and a war with the Western powers was the last thing the Soviet leaders were eager to provoke at that time.

Be that as it may, the calling off of the uprising caused Brandler's fall from power and his replacement by Ruth Fischer, who represented the left wing of the party. There were no uprisings at the time of her ascendency—except one against her authoritarian methods in ruling the party. After her expulsion in 1928, Ernst Thaelmann, an impressive personality with a gift for popular oratory, but an intellectually insignificant stooge of the Moscow bosses, was imposed by the Comintern as the leader of the party.

As Hitlerism was rising in Germany, the communists were ordered to go through the motions of fighting the Nazis. Yet their hostility was directed mainly against the still powerful Socialist (Social-Democratic) party with which they refused to co-operate against the National-Socialist peril. On many occasions they went so far as to form a united front with the Nazis, as in 1931, when they voted with the Nazis in a referendum directed against the Prussian government then controlled by the socialists; and again a year later, when the Nazis joined the communists in supporting a strike of the transport workers directed against the Social Democratic municipal administration of Berlin. Throughout these years the communists never ceased hurling insults at the socialists, calling them "Social-Fascists" and "main supporters of capitalist dictatorship." It was not sheer suicidal insanity, prompted by factional hostility towards their moderate-leftist "step-brothers." It was a deliberate policy aiming at preventing collaboration between the socialist and the communist rank and file against the Nazi menace. It was a subtle Machiavellian game of the Moscow Foreign Office, at that time afraid of a possible Western bloc directed against Russia. For this reason it preferred a Nazi regime in Germany, from which it expected militant opposition to the Western powers.[2] These, however, were reasons which could not be publicly admitted; hence the argument that the socialists were the main enemies of the working class, that their destruction as a party by the Nazis was not to be regretted, that the rule of the Nazis would be a short-lived one, and that the communists were bound to take over as soon as the Nazis had their brief fling.

Those leading German communists who did not cherish the prospect of their country and their own organization coming under Hitler's heel were either expelled or called to Moscow, where they were eventually "purged." Hitler showed no gratitude to the communists for the services which most of them unconsciously rendered to his success. He persecuted them just as he did his other opponents. After the conclusion of the Moscow-Berlin pact (1939), the German communists, just as did their comrades in all other countries, tried to justify Stalin's policy. As long as the alliance between the two totalitarian powers lasted, their attacks were directed exclusively against the Western powers. At the end of World War II, those of the old leaders—Pieck and Ulbricht—who had survived Stalin's purges and Hitler's executions were put in charge of the government of Eastern Germany where, together with the remnants of the Social Democratic party, who were forced to join, they formed the so-called Socialist Unity party. Communists were for a while active in Western Germany as well. Outlawed as agents of the

Soviet government and rejected by the masses who have not forgotten the exploits of the Red Army after the invasion of Germany, they have remained without any influence.

Total submission to Moscow's policies was also characteristic of the French Communist party. Formed in 1920, when the majority of the Socialist party decided to join the Communist International, the Communist party, headed by Maurice Thorez, Jacques Duclos, and André Marty, showed its colors during the 1930's, when Moscow, after deliberately helping the Nazis to seize power by preventing a united front between communists and socialists, began to realize that Hitler might turn against Russia rather than against the West. As a result, the Communist International dropped its previous hostility to the socialists and began to advocate a "united front" with the former "Social Fascists" (that insulting epithet was dropped, of course) and even a "popular front" with all middle-class parties of the Western countries, provided they were opposed to the Nazis. The French communists, who until that time had been staunch antipatriots, suddenly became most vociferous in professing their devotion to their country, going so far as to top their posters with the legend "France for the French!"—a slogan which, a few decades before, had been coined by Edouard Drumont, leader of the French anti-Semites. They even pursued the policy of the "outstretched hand" with regard to the Catholic Church. During that period the communists became the right wing of the labor movement, trying to tone down bread-and-butter conflicts in the democratic countries, extolling the defense of democracy and civil liberties (outside of Russia), and denouncing those ultraradicals who spoke about overthrowing the capitalist system.

During the Moscow-Berlin Pact period (1939-41), the French communists refused to support those who tried to resist the Nazi invaders, and their leader, Thorez, deserted to Moscow when he was called to the colors. It was only after the invasion of the U.S.S.R. by Hitler's armies that the French communists joined the Resistance, in which they fought valiantly side by side with the socialists, the Free French, and other anticollaborationists. They did it, to be sure, not for the sake of defending France, but as part of their defense of their "Soviet fatherland." This participation in the Resistance enabled them to regain their earlier popularity among the working masses. This popularity they owed chiefly to the revolutionary tradition of the French workers which led them to see in the "Great" Russian Revolution a "proletarian" sequel to the French Revolution. The largest political organization in France, the French Communist party, regularly polled about one-quarter of the vote in parliamentary elections. Party membership, however, has been steadily decreasing, falling from one million in 1945 to one quarter of that number in 1961.

Aside from the top leader, Maurice Thorez (born 1900), a self-educated former miner who deserted to Moscow immediately after the Nazi invasion of France, but was nevertheless permitted to join General de Gaulle's Cabinet after the liberation of the country, the most colorful personality of French communism was André Marty (1886-1956). A sailor on a French battleship sent to the Black Sea in 1918 to help the Russian "Whites" against the Soviet regime, Marty organized a mutiny of his fellow sailors, a gesture which resulted in the withdrawal of the French navy from

Russian waters. Sentenced to twenty years' imprisonment, he was pardoned after four and a half years. He was repeatedly elected to various legislative bodies, including the Chamber of Deputies. After his release he was active in campaigns against the French occupation of Morocco and Syria. He was in Moscow during the period of the Popular Front, a policy of collaboration with the socialists of which he did not approve. During the Spanish Civil War (1936-39) he was entrusted by Moscow with the organization of the International Brigades. In the course of this activity he became notorious for his cruelty, which was no doubt a manifestation of insanity. He had hundreds of revolutionary fighters shot for breaches of "revolutionary discipline," and any one suspected of being a Trotskyist suffered the same fate. Ernest Hemingway depicted him as a homicidal maniac in a special chapter of his *For Whom the Bell Tolls*—a novel sympathetic to the republican side of the Spanish civil war. When, after the occupation of France, the Nazis attacked the U.S.S.R., Marty went underground and became one of the organizers of the Resistance. A few years before his death, he was expelled from his party because he disapproved of its "soft" policy.

Like the French communists, their Italian brothers-in-arms have succeeded in winning the adherence of a great body of working masses to their support. Their success is to be explained largely by the great poverty of vast regions of Italy. The Italian communists take advantage of the prevailing longing for salvation among the masses by combining the cult of Lenin with that of Garibaldi and . . . Francis of Assisi. And as "practical" politicians, out to get the vote of the devout peasantry at any price, they bent over backward trying to disprove the accusation that they were enemies of religion. In the pursuance of this policy they aligned themselves with the clerical Christian Democratic party in voting in Parliament for the recognition of the Catholic Church as the state religion.

This happened shortly after Italy's liberation from Fascist and Nazi rule at the end of World War II, when the communists participated in the newly established democratic regime headed by the Christian Democrats. It was doubtless their intention to do in Italy what their comrades did at about the same time to the democratic regimes established in Eastern Europe after the defeat of the Nazi armies. However, Italy was not in the same predicament as Poland or Czechoslovakia. It was not occupied by Soviet troops. So the Christian Democratic Premier De Gasperi could easily eliminate the communists from his cabinet shortly after they had disgraced themselves by throwing to the winds the principle of the separation of church from state.

Since that time the communists were in the opposition attracting large masses by the "eclecticism" of their "principles." By 1961, their party, with a membership of over 1,700,000, was the largest communist organization outside the Soviet orbit. And with the votes it garnered (6,700,000 at the national elections of 1961) it has become the second largest political factor in the country. Its leaders were consistently toeing the Kremlin "line," and Moscow has shown its appreciation by subsidizing its unofficial agency to the extent of $20,000,000 annually, if one is to accept the figures of the usually well-informed correspondent of the New York *Reporter* (January 4, 1962).

With its thousands of functionaries, four daily newspapers, nearly three score periodicals, the control of the municipal administrations of large cities like Bologna and countless smaller communities, with the appendant opportunities to grant favors, not to speak of the many profit-making enterprises, the party has evolved into something resembling a cross between a "regular" prewar democratic socialist mass party, German style, with a very radical political vocabulary, and a political machine not unlike Tammany Hall. As a result it has attracted large numbers of careerists and plain job-hunters as anxious to risk their lives in revolutionary adventures as any respectable politician; yet at the same time not averse to the idea of taking over the government in case an international conflict resulted in their country's occupation by the Soviet army.

However, as this hope is waning, the party leaders are becoming more and more anxious to stand altogether on their own feet and to become independent of any possibly embarrassing instructions they might get in the future from the Moscow center. The Soviet-China-Albania rift within the communist orbit and the recurring squabbles for power among Stalin's inheritors have caused some of the leaders of the Italian Communist party to raise the question of "polycentrism," a euphemism for independence from the strict discipline hitherto requested by the Moscow paymasters.

Ever since the early 1920's Palmiro Togliatti has been the outstanding figure among Italian communists. However, Stalin's posthumous disgrace has greatly shaken the prestige of his proconsul within the Italian party.

THE SMALL FRY

None of the other Leninist parties in Europe attained any importance—except possibly the Spanish communists who, quite insignificant at first, became the front for Stalin's secret police during the Civil War of 1936-39.

Most striking of the attitudes of the smaller communist parties was the position adopted by the Norwegian party during the Nazi occupation of their country at the time when the Moscow-Berlin Pact was still in operation. In a manifesto published by that party —its text was printed in the communist New York *Daily Worker* of April 17, 1940—the invasion of their country by the Nazis was justified as follows: "German troops have occupied several important points in our country, including Oslo. The German military authorities declare that the aim of the occupation is defense of the country and to prevent the possibility of its becoming transformed into a theater of military operations. The situation created in this connection depends on the strivings of the Anglo-French military bloc to extend the imperialist war and also to disarm Scandinavia."

As this was the way the Nazis, too, justified the invasion, the Norwegian communists and their press did not have to go underground.

GREAT BRITAIN

The Communist party of Great Britain was founded in 1920 out of the merger of the British Socialist party (which had evolved out of the old Social Democratic Federation), and of the Socialist Labour party, a small Scottish organization professing the ideas of the American Socialist theorist Daniel De Leon. (That group had seceded from the Social Democratic Federation in 1903.) A few other ultraradical groups, some of them with a syndicalist slant, likewise participated in the merger. As pointed out by F. Borkenau in *World Communism*, the comparative tolerance and absence of splits within the Communist party of Great Britain can be explained by the fact that it was formed not as a result of secession from a larger organization, but by the unification of several small groups of radicals professing different views. The British communists differ from the communists of other countries in that they have been trying, ever since the formation of their party, to be admitted as a body to the British Labour party, while in other countries the communists were as a rule trying to split or destroy the established socialist parties. These attempts, which have been consistently rejected by the Labour party, were made on instructions from the Communist International. The Soviet regime, for reasons of diplomatic expedience, was trying to win the sympathies of the British trade unions constituting the Labour party. There is no doubt that these attempts of the Communist party to become affiliated with the Labour party—a sacrifice imposed upon them in the interest of Russia's foreign policy—worked against the communists in the eyes of the rank and file of the British workers; for if the Labour party was good enough for the Communist party, there was apparently no point in joining the communists. It would also seem that the improvements which the British workers have attained as a result of the gradualist methods of the trade unions, the Labour party, and the Labour government have inoculated them against the propaganda of the communists.

Communist propaganda occasionally stimulated leftist tendencies within the trade unions and the Labour party. But these tendencies, while contributing to a certain "radicalization" of the rank and file, added little to the strength of the Communist party. In some unions, however, whose workers have had grievances of long standing—as was the case with the coal miners and the electrical workers—the communists did succeed in gaining influence and in having officers elected to leading posts.

At the elections of 1924 the communist vote was 55,345. It rose to 74,824 in 1931 and to 91,753 in 1950.

The vote garnered in 1951 was only 21,640, when the party put up candidates in a much smaller number of constituencies. Neither in 1951 nor in 1950 was the Communist party able to elect a member of the House of Commons, although during previous elections it usually succeeded in sending one or two of its leaders to Parliament.

Communist influence reached its height among British intellectuals during the Popular Front period of the 1930's, but has since been greatly weakened. The conclusion of the Berlin-Moscow Pact of 1939 was a serious blow to the prestige of the party whose general secretary, Harry Pollitt, resigned his post in protest. (He was later readmitted to the party.) The most serious defections occurred after the publication abroad of the secret speech delivered by Nikita Khrushchev at the 20th Congress of the Communist party of the Soviet Union, February 25, 1956, in which all the criticisms of Stalin's cruelties were confirmed. The suppression of the Hungarian Revolution (1956) by Soviet tanks seems to have driven the few remaining intellectuals out of the party. Some procommunist trade union leaders likewise turned their backs on the party.

A valuable prop to the cause of communism in England were some paradoxical pronouncements of Bernard Shaw, which were attributed partly to his predilection for outrageous statements, partly to his admiration for "strong men" (he also admired Mussolini and Hitler).

THE SATELLITES

A peculiar role, different from that of most communist parties of Europe, was played by Lenin's followers in Hungary. After the break-up of the Habsburg

dual monarchy, those sections of the Hungarian kingdom inhabited by Slovaks, Ukrainians, Romanians, and
Croats were given by the victors to Czechoslovakia,
Romania, and Yugoslavia, respectively—"rounded out"
with regions inhabited by Hungarians (Magyars)
proper. In despair over the fate of his country, Michael
Karolyi, the liberal anti-Habsburg prime minister and
later president, resigned his post and in March 1919
transferred his power to a combination of socialists and
communists. Eventually, the regime was taken over entirely by the communists, who were headed by Foreign
Minister Bela Kun. After four months the Hungarian
Soviet regime fell before the onslaught of Romanian
troops under whose auspices a counterrevolutionary,
"monarchist" government, headed by Admiral Nicolas
Horthy, was established. Those communist leaders who
escaped went to Russia, where some of them, including
Bela Kun, were executed during the purges of 1936-38.

In 1925, Matthias Rakosi, acting commissar of
trade during the Bela Kun regime, returned secretly
to Hungary to revive the communist movement. Arrested soon afterward he was sentenced to eight and a
half years of imprisonment for communist propaganda.
After completing the sentence he was indicted again and
sentenced to life imprisonment for his participation in
the Soviet regime of 1919. Rakosi was not released until
late in 1940, after fifteen years in jail, when he went to
Russia again. His release was effected as a result of the
Berlin-Moscow Pact of 1939, when friendly relations between the Kremlin and the Fascist governments were
established. (During the "Pact" period the term "Fascism" practically ceased to exist for the communists, and
after his release, Rakosi, in an article published in the
New York *Daily Worker* of February 17, 1941, in speaking about his imprisonment and his release, referred only
to "Hungarian capitalism" although the regime had

been outspokenly Fascist.) After the conclusion of World War II and the occupation of Hungary by the Soviet Army, Rakosi returned to his country of which he became the virtual dictator, or, more correctly, Stalin's proconsul.

One of the most sensational events that took place under Rakosi's dictatorship was the frame-up and "purge" of Laszlo Rajk, next to the "boss" the outstanding figure among the Hungarian communists. Suspected of "Titoism" he was arrested in 1949, forced to "confess," and executed.

The Hungarian Revolution of October 1956, largely caused by the general hatred incurred—even among the communists—by the despotic rule of Rakosi, forced the latter to resign and to go to Moscow once more. Supported by the enormous majority of the population, including most of the members of his party, the leader of the anti-Rakosi opposition, communist Prime Minister Imre Nagy aimed at obtaining for his country the same status as had been won by Tito for Yugoslavia; or at least some autonomy, such as had been achieved by Poland during the same year in the wake of the partly successful anti-Moscow resistance offered in Poland by Wladyslaw Gomulka and other anti-Stalinist communists. To Khrushchev, yielding to Budapest right after the Warsaw events apparently meant the beginning of the end of his satellite empire. He sent his tanks to crush the revolt. Nagy, who had sought refuge in the Yugoslav Embassy, was delivered, upon Tito's orders, to the Russian executioners. Janos Kadar, an ex-supporter of Nagy's, having turned traitor, became Khrushchev's proconsul.

About a decade before the Budapest massacre— shortly after the conclusion of World War II—leading communists of Moscow's Balkan satellites hoped to form a Balkan federation of Soviet republics. George Dimitrov, top Bulgarian communist, Stalin's loyal henchman, was suspected by the Kremlin dictator of fostering such separatist plans. He was called to Moscow, where his death was reported soon afterward. It is generally believed that he was the victim of a secret purge, after which he was honored by a state funeral. After his death, his successors, handpicked Stalinists, publicly tried and executed Traicho Kostov, next to Dimitrov the outstanding leader of the Bulgarian communists. He was indicted of, and forced to "confess" to, the crime of what was later known as Titoism, which can be defined as an autonomist or separatist tendency on the part of those territories which, at the end of World War II, had come under the domination of Moscow. It was named after Tito (Josip Broz), a Yugoslav communist guerrilla leader during that war, who, having become the dictator of Yugoslavia, objected to his country's economic exploitation by the U.S.S.R. and eventually succeeded in achieving complete independence from Moscow. That separation did not affect the nature of the regime, which remained as totalitarian as its Moscow prototype, except that some of its compulsory features were mitigated. Collectivization of agriculture was practically abandoned, and a sort of "market economy" within a decentralized system of planning was substituted for the old method of economic supercentralization.

Tito's autocratic rule was challenged in the late 1950's by his former friend and collaborator Milovan Djilas who, converted to the cause of democratic socialism, in his volume *The New Class* (1957), attacked communism as the rule of a "new class"—the officeholders, managers, party leaders, and army officers. It was not a new discovery; it had been predicted by Michael Bakunin in 1873 and again by Waclaw Machajski in 1898.

Djilas was sentenced to nine years' imprisonment for criticizing the regime he had helped to establish. This was a comparatively mild punishment as compared with what might have happened to any one attempting a similar criticism in Czechoslovakia. The communist rulers of that industrialized and culturally advanced "people's democracy" had covered themselves with glory, immediately upon assumption of power, by assassinating—through defenestration—the Czechoslovak democratic diplomat Jan Masaryk, the son of the founder of the Czechoslovak Republic. A few years later they pandered to the latent anti-Jewish prejudices of the masses by staging "Moscow trials" of such of their own leaders as happened to be Jews, forcing them to "confess" to alleged crimes committed against the Czechoslovakian people because they were "Jewish bourgeois nationalists." The execution of these scapegoats served the non-Jewish leaders as an alibi for all the shortcomings against which the masses were grumbling; shortcomings caused by the colonial exploitation of the country by the Stalin regime. Even as late as 1961, after they had destroyed Stalin's monument on Khruschev's orders, they refused to vindicate the Jewish "traitors," lest even the most gullible of the rank and file get some ideas about the ethics of their communist masters.

Unlike Czechoslovakia where centuries-old hatred of the German oppressors and fear of a German revanche have caused the communists to become the most abject flunkeys of the great Russian "protector," sentiment in Poland, even among most communists, was anything but friendly toward the powerful eastern neighbor who had been the chief beneficiary of their country's partition at the end of the eighteenth century. However, the initial success in the struggle for some sort of autonomy achieved in 1956 by the courageous stand of the anti-Stalinist communist leader Wladyslaw

Gomulka was not followed up in the direction of total independence, Yugoslav style, or at least real cultural liberty demanded by the revisionist wing of the communist intelligentsia. On the contrary, the permanent threat of the Kremlin's military intervention or of its economic sanctions, as well as the opposition of the die-hard Stalinists within the regime, resulted in the restriction of many of the cultural liberties obtained in the first flush of that near-revolution of 1956.

FIDELISMO

A role unlike that of the Kremlin's European satellites is held by Cuba which, for all practical purposes, has "annexed itself," so to speak, to the Soviet orbit. Until 1898 a colonial possession of Spain, Cuba became formally an independent republic as a result of the war between the United States and the Madrid regime. That independence had many galling strings attached to it, particularly a provision called the Platt Amendment (1901), which was part of its Constitution, and in the opinion of most Cubans actually nullified the country's independence. That amendment was abrogated in 1934, but this concession did not put an end to the economic power of those American businessmen who in the course of decades had acquired control over a very substantial part of Cuba's national wealth, such as sugar lands, mines, and so on.

No wonder then that the propaganda of all movements of radical anticapitalist protest was invariably permeated with strong ingredients of anti-Yankee chauvinism—particularly as the American administrations as a rule lent their support to even the most tyrannical and the most corrupt dictators, such as Batista, the last president prior to Castro's revolt.

That revolt, undertaken with a handful of men, resulted in 1959 in the capture of power by an erratic, though heroic, leader who ostensibly owed no allegiance to any of the traditional political groupings—until, late in 1961, he admitted that he was, or had become, a Marxist-Leninist, that is, a communist. It was no doubt with an eye to winning the sympathies of an important section of the Latin American populations that Castro engaged in that noncommunist masquerade while gradually adopting and enforcing communist-like measures in the field of economics and abolishing all political and cultural liberties in the time-honored totalitarian manner. And it was, possibly, part of that masquerade that at the outset Cuban communists posed as his critics and adversaries.

Castro undoubtedly enjoys the support of both the workers and the peasants of his country. For his expropriation and nationalization measures have given them hope. Sooner or later they will find out that the real beneficiaries of his upheaval are the educated young scions of the middle and lower middle classes, who, as members of a new officeholding and managerial elite have become the real masters of the country. This, in turn, may become one of the Kremlin's drawing cards in its endeavor to get a foothold in the southern part of the Western hemisphere. For the young men with education and without well-rewarded jobs are just as numerous in Latin America as they are in all other underdeveloped countries.

However, it remains to be seen what effect Castro's humiliation in connection with the missile incident will have upon the future of Fidelismo.

The communist movement in the United States was an outgrowth of the pro-Bolshevik left wing within the Socialist party, which was formed shortly after the conclusion of World War I. Immediately after the foundation of the Communist International, early in 1919, the left wing of the Socialist party, composed to a large extent of immigrants from Europe, issued a manifesto containing the customary accusations, inspired by the Russian communists, against the socialist parties because they "stultified working-class political action by limiting political action to elections and participation in legislative reform activity." At its national conference held in the same year, the left wing adopted a program which denounced all existing socialist and labor movements. Speaking about the state, the manifesto said: "The bourgeois parliamentary state is the organ of the bourgeoisie for the coercion of the proletariat. The revolutionary proletariat must, accordingly, destroy this state. But the conquest of political power by the proletariat does not immediately end capitalism, or the power of the capitalists, or immediately socialize industry. It is therefore necessary that the proletariat organize its own State for the coercion and suppression of the bourgeoisie." And so on, for over ten thousand words of classical Leninism.

Simultaneously with the "political expropriation" of the bourgeoisie there was to be effected the economic expropriation of that class, the scope of the measures adopted "being determined by industrial development and the maturity of the proletariat." These measures, at first, were to include:

a) Workers' control of industry to be exercised by

the industrial organizations of the workers, operating by means of the industrial vote.

b) Expropriation and nationalization of the banks, as a necessary preliminary measure for the complete expropriation of capital.

c) Expropriation and nationalization of the large (trust) organizations of capital. Expropriation proceeds without compensation, as "buying out" the capitalists is a repudiation of the tasks of the revolution.

d) Repudiation of all national debts and financial obligations of the old system.

e) The nationalization of foreign trade.

f) Measures for the socialization of agriculture.

Two Communist parties emerged from the expulsion of the left wing elements from the Socialist party. They called themselves Communist party and Communist Labor party, respectively. The former, which claimed a membership of 58,000—it is believed that the figure actually did not exceed 35,000—consisted almost exclusively of the members of the foreign language federations. Its guiding spirit was Louis Fraina,[3] an American of Italian descent. The other group, which was much less numerous, consisted largely of native Americans and English-speaking immigrants. Its most popular leader was John Reed, well-known American journalist and magazine writer, and author of *Ten Days That Shook the World*, a vivid description of the Bolshevik uprising of November, 1917. As Benjamin Gitlow, the outstanding orator of the early communist movement, put it in his *I Confess:* "The difference between the Communist Party and the Communist Labor Party was evident in the desire of the Communist Labor Party to apply what it believed to be Bolshevism to American conditions. The Communist Party, on the other hand, was oblivious of America. Its heart was in Russia and its head full of Bolshevik abstractions." The groups professed the same theories and both were in favor of affiliation with the Communist International. Only personal rivalries, the question of who was to control the movement, prevented the formation of a single communist party. The group calling itself "Communist party," banking on its numerical superiority, would have no dealings with its competitor short of unconditional surrender, which meant acceptance of the heads of the foreign-language groups as leaders of the American Communist party. It also meant the control of all the jobs which the party, and eventually the diplomatic and trade representatives of the Soviet government, would have at their disposal.

While the quarrel between the two groups was going on, the Department of Justice swooped down upon both, arresting all the radical non-citizens it could find. The Communist party and Communist Labor party were forced to go underground, whence, in their illegal publications, they advocated armed insurrection, civil war and other tactical methods of Russian Bolshevism. After various attempts at unification, which were followed by new splits, the group which called itself Communist party remained as the only underground organization—until its dissolution in 1923 when underground activity was no longer considered necessary.

In 1922-23 the anti-communist hysteria was abating and many communists considered the idea of an "open party," that is, an organization that could function like any other bona fide political party. A number of such organizations sprang up, employing more or less restrained language and refraining from using the communist label which was still tabu. Eventually, all these organizations, including the leaders of the underground Communist party, organized the "Workers'

Party of America." The party statement of principles read as follows:

1. The Workers' Republic: To lead the working masses in the struggle for the abolition of capitalism through the establishment of a government by the working class—a Workers' Republic in America.

2. Political Action: To participate in all political activities including electoral campaigns in order to utilize them for the purpose of carrying our message to the masses. The elected representatives of the Workers' party will unmask the fraudulent capitalist democracy and help mobilize the workers for the final struggle against the common enemy.

3. The Labor Unions: To develop the labor organizations into organs of militant struggle against capitalism, expose the reactionary labor bureaucrats, and educate the workers to militant unionism.

4. A Fighting Party: It shall be a party of militant, class-conscious workers, bound by discipline and organized on the basis of democratic centralization, with full power in the hands of the Central Executive Committee between conventions. The Central Executive Committee of the party shall have control over all activities of public officials. It shall also co-ordinate and direct the work of the party members in trade unions.

5. Party Press: The party's press shall be owned by the party, and all its activities shall be under the control of the Central Executive Committee.

The program adopted at the convention was comparatively moderate and could have been subscribed to by any progressive party. It demanded the withdrawal of American armed forces from the Caribbean area and the Philippines, it insisted upon workers' rights to strike and to picket, it demanded that municipalities should supply the trade unions and the organization of the unemployed with funds for the support of the jobless, and championed the cause of the Negroes. When the program was adopted, the underground Communist party was still in existence, and its leaders, who got their instructions from the representative of the Communist International, actually controlled the Workers' party, which was not formally affiliated with the Comintern.

There was friction between the underground party, which was called "Number One," and the Workers' party, known as "Number Two," as well as between that faction of "Number One" which insisted upon the continuation of the underground organization, and its opponents who were bent upon scrapping it. A secret convention held in 1922 in the Michigan woods was raided by the police, who succeeded in seizing all documents, including the real and party names of all delegates. It was a disaster which contributed to hasten the decision to liquidate all conspiratorial activities.

Between 1922 and 1924 the Workers' party changed its previous communist attitude of refusing to collaborate with "gradualist" or "reformist" elements. This was the period in which the Soviet regime, having overcome its opponents and established diplomatic and trade relations with various capitalist countries, lost interest in revolutionary activities. Therefore, the Communist International declared, the capitalist world had entered upon a period of stabilization. As a result, it recommended to the communist parties a policy of the "United Front," which implied collaboration with socialist and labor organizations. In the United States, this policy took the form of participation or attempted participation, in the formation of a nation-wide Farmer-Labor party, as well as attempted participation in the "Third party" movement aiming at the election of Senator Robert LaFollette. Both actions ended disastrously for the communists. The convention had been organized by various trade unions and farmer organizations for the creation of a Farmer-Labor party. It was captured by the communists with the result that the noncommunist elements would have nothing to do with the so-called Federated Farmer-Labor party, and it soon disappeared. The communists did not fare better with their hope of jumping on the bandwagon of the Third party. They cynically and naively revealed that they intended "to enter the third party wherever the opportunity presents itself, to form a left wing within it and split it away from the third party." The Conference for Progressive Political Action, which nominated La-Follette, refused to admit the representatives of the Workers' Party to its deliberations. The communists thereupon nominated William Z. Foster as the presidential candidate of the Workers' party. Their ticket received hardly more than 33,000 votes. Four years later in 1928, running again as the presidential candidate of the communists—this time the official name of the party was "Workers' (Communist) Party of America" —he obtained 75,000 votes.

WILLIAM Z. FOSTER AND HIS RIVALS

The self-taught son of an unskilled Irish-American worker, William Z. Foster (1881-1961) had no formal education and worked at various manual occupations. At first a member of the Socialist party, he joined the quasi-syndicalist Industrial Workers of the World in 1909. He later became converted to the original, French version of syndicalism which opposed the formation of competing or "dual" unions. Hence he turned against the I.W.W. and founded the Syndicalist League, which was to "bore from within" the American Federation of

Labor and win it over to the syndicalist cause. After becoming general organizer of the Brotherhood of Railway Carmen, a union affiliated with the A.F. of L., he gradually receded from his ultraradical position and in 1918 was placed in charge of organizing the unskilled workers in behalf of the A.F. of L. As a leader of the great steel strike of 1919, he became a national figure. The disappointments he met with during his activities as organizer of the A.F. of L. made him susceptible to the fascination exerted on many radicals by the rising star of the Soviet regime. He became a communist—at first unofficially, later openly, when his participation in the raided secret party convention of 1922 lifted his incognito. After that his career was closely connected with the history of the American Communist party.

During the period between the two elections there were violent struggles within the trade union movement and bitter wrangles within the Workers' party. The Trade Union Educational League, a subdivision of the Workers' party headed by William Foster, was out to infiltrate the trade unions and permeate them with the radical spirit and to gain control of them as a first step on the way toward getting control of the country itself. The unions struck back by expelling the communists, and the only permanent acquisition made during that period was the Furriers Union, headed by the Communist Ben Gold. Simultaneously with the campaign within the trade unions, there was a permanent factional war within the Workers' party. Like the early struggles of 1919 between the Communist party and the Communist Labor party, this was not a clash of principles, but sheer rivalry for power between two groups of leaders and would-be leaders. The faction led by Foster consisted mostly, though not exclusively, of former workers with trade-union experience. It looked askance at the other group—led first by Charles Ruth-

enberg, and after his death in 1927 by Jay Lovestone—
which consisted chiefly of young college graduates who,
as one of their opponents put it, "had leaped directly
from New York City College into leadership of the
party without any intermediary steps in the turmoil of
the class struggle." In other words, it was a "class
struggle" between self-educated upstarts from the working class and college-bred déclassés from the lower
middle class. They were competing for the glory of
leadership and its material rewards; though the total
membership of the party at that time hardly exceeded
13,000, the organization had on its roster a relatively
large number of functionaries. The point on which
there was real disagreement was the question of the
"third" or the "farmer-labor" party. The Fosterites were
dead set against communist participation in such ventures. Whatever "theoretical" arguments they advanced,
the real reason for their opposition was their fear lest
the college-bred politicians of the opposing group gain
predominance in a mass party which included middle-
class elements as well as workers.

The two factions were not permitted to compete
for power on their merits. The Foster group, which had
gained control of the party in 1924 and which had a
majority of delegates at the convention of 1925, was deprived of its control by the representative of the Communist International, which preferred the Ruthenberg-
Lovestone group of white collar men at the helm.
Possibly it did not trust Foster because of his syndicalist
past and because of his sympathies for Trotsky, then on
his way out. The newly installed minority group headed
by Ruthenberg, Lovestone, and Gitlow gradually succeeded in winning the majority of the party to its side.
At the party convention of 1929 the Lovestoneites had
ninety seats as against one "Fosterite"—Foster himself
—plus half a dozen dissenters fom his own former

group. However, at the convention itself, on receipt of a telegram from Moscow, the Lovestone majority was deprived of power and ordered to yield leadership to Foster.

The ostensible reason for Lovestone's disgrace was his theory of "Exceptionalism," according to which capitalism in America was still on the upgrade and not declining as in the other countries. This theory was decried as a heresy by the theorists of the Comintern. The real crime committed by the Lovestone group was that in the conflict then raging between Stalin and the Russian communist right-wing group headed by Bukharin, the leader of the American communists had banked on the victory of Bukharin, then at the head of the Communist International but soon to be shorn of all power by his cunning antagonist. Lovestone's fall from power was followed by the expulsion of himself and his closest followers from the party. The rest of his associates, and practically all of the rank and file, turned their backs on the losers and joined the victorious Foster group.

The victory of the Foster group was soon followed, ironically enough, by Foster's removal from leadership, and his replacement as secretary general by one of his lieutenants—sometimes called his "errand boy"—Earl Browder, who was to wield unchallenged power until 1945.

THE "THIRD PERIOD"

One aspect of the ultrarevolutionary character of communist policy between 1928-35—the so-called "Third Period"—was the attempt of American communists to organize "unemployment councils" and to stage "hunger marches" the real purpose of which, as they frankly admitted, was to "Build Party Through Hunger March." Their championship of the cause of the unemployed sometimes assumed the aspects of inadvertent humor. In its issue of August 29, 1931, the *Daily Worker* listed a number of demands which—as the organ of one of the Communist splinter groups put it—included a demand that a jobless worker "should get more than twice as much when he is unemployed as when he is employed."

During that period the communists outdid themselves in harping on the alleged "social-fascism" of the socialists and on the imperialistic tendencies of the United States and of all other countries allegedly threatening the safety of Soviet Russia. Here are a few samples of their style: "This pamphlet will indeed help to strike the mantle from [Norman] Thomas and reveal him as the social-Fascist—socialist in words, Fascist in deeds—that he is" (*Daily Worker*, September 24, 1932). "We must blast the pretensions of the Socialist party that it is a party of the working class and show that its program is dictated by the needs of American imperialism in this period of deepest crisis and imperialist war preparations" (*The Communist*, June, 1932). "The policies of the government at Washington have one purpose . . . to establish fascism at home. The Socialist Party supports every particular policy of the New Deal" (from Earl Browder's book *Communism in the United States* written in 1934, but published in 1935). This antisocialist and anti-Roosevelt policy was scrapped the same year by the Communist International, to be replaced by one that was the very opposite of it.

Particular targets of communist press insults during the period were Franklin D. Roosevelt and Henry A. Wallace, both of whom, a few years later, were to become almost as popular with them as were Stalin and

Browder: "Roosevelt, leader of the corrupt, anti-labor Tammany Hall" (*Daily Worker*, June 8, 1929), "Roosevelt 'Helps' the Farmers to Ever Greater Destitution" (*Daily Worker*, May 11, 1933), "Roosevelt's 'New Deal' supported by the A.F.L. leaders as beneficial to the workers, and by the Socialist Party leaders as a step toward socialism, is only the embodiment of the war and fascist program of the Wall Street bankers" (*Daily Worker's* Tenth anniversary issue, January, 1934), "Seeds of Fascism Sprout in New Pamphlet by Secretary Wallace" (*Daily Worker*, January 24, 1934).

Another feature of the period was catering to Negro chauvinism, as expressed in the slogan of "self-determination of the Black Belt," and the demand for an independent Negro republic in the United States. To win the Negroes they devoted enraptured editorials to the victories of Negro prize fighters and contenders at the Olympic games. They even established a united front with a self-anointed Negro messiah, Father Divine, in spite of the fact that he was opposed to trade unions and was known to exploit the poorest among the poor, who turned over their earnings to him.

The period was also characterized by a display of unbounded Soviet patriotism. The communists continuously repeated the slogan "Workers, Your Fatherland, the Socialist Fatherland of All Workers, is in Danger! Demonstrate!" alternating it with "Defend the Soviet Union!" (*Daily Worker*, July 19, 1929).

The American advocates of communism did not yet consider it necessary to parade as champions of democracy. In a book entitled *Toward Soviet America*, written in 1932 by William Z. Foster, there is the following revealing passage: "Under the dictatorship all capitalist parties—Republican, Democratic, Progressive, Socialist, etc.—will be liquidated, the Communist party alone functioning as the Party of the toiling masses.

Likewise will be dissolved all other organizations that are political props of bourgeois rule, including chambers of commerce, employers' associations, Rotary Clubs, American Legion, Y.M.C.A., and such fraternal orders as the Masons, Odd Fellows, Elks, Knights of Columbus, etc." The book has since been withdrawn from circulation and even repudiated by Foster himself, when the Communist International changed its tune.

"POPULAR FRONT"

The ultraradical phase of American communism was followed by one—it lasted until 1939—in which the party assumed a most conciliatory attitude toward all those it had attacked before. The expression "social-Fascist," flung at the socialists during the preceding period, disappeared entirely from the communist vocabulary. This was in line with the new "popular front" policy inaugurated by the Communist International in 1935. The Soviet government, having temporarily given up hope of reaching a friendly understanding with the Nazi regime, embarked on a policy of friendly relations with the Western powers, which were likewise threatened by new Germany's expansionist tendencies. To cement friendly relations it was necessary to establish the broadest possible front of all anti-Fascist elements, from the communists to the Catholic Church.

In line with this policy, the American communists sought to establish friendly relations with the socialists, to work toward the organization of an "anti-capitalist Labor Party," to scrap the Red trade unions—formed to compete with the A.F. of L.—and to invite their members to join the A.F. of L. Every point of this program was the direct antithesis of the policy followed between 1928 and 1934.

Communist desires to placate the Church went to such lengths that the Convention of the Young Communist League held in New York adopted a resolution "addressed to the young Catholics of the State of New York bearing condolences on the death of Pope Pius XI and calling for co-operation in the fight 'against the common enemy, fascism' " (*Daily Worker*, February 13, 1939).

Less outspoken was their technique with regard to President Roosevelt. Moscow preferred the re-election of the Democratic chief executive at the impending election of 1936 because there was no doubt as to Roosevelt's hostility to the Hitler regime. As open support of the Democrats by the communists would have endangered rather than helped their success, they continued in 1935 and 1936 to attack Roosevelt by having the *Daily Worker* (January 1, 1936) print such headlines as "Support of Roosevelt Plays into Hands of Reaction," and by declaring that "A big vote for a Farmer-Labor Party [a Communist fiction that never made its appearance] in 1936, even if Roosevelt is defeated, will go a long way toward putting a crimp in the union-busting, liberty-strangling drive of the Wall Street corporations." But they made it clear to their followers that they wanted Roosevelt to be elected. Unable to say so outright, they launched the slogan "Defeat Landon [the Republican candidate] at all costs!"—which of course could be done only by voting for Roosevelt. For the sake of a "popular front" of all democratic, progressive elements, the communists completely eschewed the question of socialism. "Our election platform," Browder said in an address printed in the *Sunday Worker*, September 27, 1936, "proposes, *not socialism* [emphasis in the text]—which can only come *through revolution*—but a *progressive* platform of aims to be fought for under the *present capitalist system* by such a [still nonexistent phantom] Farmer Labor Party, etc. . . ."

In their endeavor to reach the masses, the communists were favored by a number of circumstances. One was the conflict within the American Federation of Labor, which resulted in the withdrawal of a number of large unions and the formation of the Congress of Industrial Organizations. The new trade union body was headed by John L. Lewis, president of the coal miners' union, who accepted communist agitators and organizers, although in his own union he had never tolerated them. As it transpired, however, it was Lewis who, for a multiplicity of reasons, left the C.I.O., while the communists remained firmly entrenched in it for many years. Not only did they obtain outright control of about one-third of the federations affiliated with the C.I.O., they exerted their influence on the very center of the organization, the views of the editor of the C.I.O.'s main organ and the legal adviser of its president being very close to those of the Communist party.

Another circumstance which benefited the Communist movement was unemployment among manual and intellectual workers and the feeling of insecurity which accompanied the great depression of the 1930's. College students without prospects, writers, teachers, actors, chemists, engineers—in short, white-collar and professional men in all fields—began to lend an ear to communist propaganda. They heard there was no unemployment in Russia and that with the removal of men of property, it was the professionals, intellectuals, and men of education in general who became the privileged stratum—implying that the same could happen in the United States. That the Communist party leaders, the secret police, and the army officers were the real masters under the new dispensation the new converts were never told. The communist trend impressed many members of such successful groups as Hollywood writers and actors, who were willing to make generous contributions to the Communist party treasury. They had grievances against their employers, who earned millions while writers' earnings rarely exceeded hundreds of thousands. The adherence of these glamorous elements had an effect on many neurotic members of the leisure class on the lookout either for a new religion or for the latest fashion in art, literature, and politics.

There were also many well-intentioned and capable intellectuals among the new converts; the seemingly hopeless impasse of capitalism, as demonstrated by the depression, made them susceptible to the charms of a system whose champions employed such alluring catchwords as "planned economy," "production for use," "abolition of the profit system," "classless society," etc. Many of these intellectuals succeeded in infiltrating various government departments, and some may have thought that they were serving a good cause when they tried to influence America's foreign policy in the direction desired by Moscow. From that attitude to the betrayal of state secrets and outright spying was only one step. There were also cynics and ambitious adventurers who saw in the rising power of communism the possibilities of a swift, if dangerous political career, a short cut to the power and the privileges of a new elite.

The Communist party went to great lengths to placate the conservatives so as to overcome their opposition to an alliance with Russia in case of an attack by the Nazis. Communist leaders catered to the patriotic feelings of the American public by calling communism "Twentieth Century Americanism," and by glorifying the great names of American history. Their party school was named after Jefferson, and the troop of volunteers sent to Spain to further Russia's designs was called the "Lincoln Brigade."

With the re-election of Franklin Roosevelt in 1936, the Communist party bent over backward to insist on its law-abiding character and its devotion to democracy and American principles of freedom. By 1939 the party's respectability was—at least in the opinion of its leaders—so firmly established that according to the N.Y. *Times* (May 12, 1939) Browder could openly come out for a third term for Roosevelt without fear of giving him the "kiss of death."

THE MOSCOW-BERLIN PACT INTERLUDE

A few weeks prior to the conclusion of the Soviet-Nazi Pact in August 1939, rumors concerning the possibility were repulsed by the party's leader, Earl Browder, in an address at the Institute of Public Affairs, Charlottesville, Virginia (July 5, 1939). Browder declared that "there is about as much chance of such an agreement as of Earl Browder being elected president of the American Chamber of Commerce." The actual conclusion of the agreement was described as follows by the *Daily Worker* of August 23, 1939: "German fascism has suffered a serious blow in prestige in its own country as well as in the world." A week later, on August 30, the same paper reported Browder as saying that "the United States and world peace [were] aided by Soviet blow to Axis." During the twenty-two months between the conclusion of the pact and the invasion of Russia by the Nazis (June 22, 1941) the American Communist party maintained an attitude of hostility toward the Western powers, referred to as the "so-called democracies." Over and over again the *Daily Worker* insisted that "the outbreak of the war in September removed all practical differences between the Allies and German fascism as far as 'democracy' is concerned" *(Daily Worker, April 24, 1940)*, and in a pamphlet entitled *The Jewish People and the War,* Browder argued that it made no difference to the Jews whether the Nazis or the Allied imperialists won. During the first week after the conclusion of the pact the *Daily Worker* (August 31, 1939) soothed its Jewish readers by arguing that "the nonaggression pact is a triumph in the fight against anti-Semitism" and that "the blow which the Soviet pact has dealt to anti-Semitism in Germany, is being felt by every anti-Semitic force in the United States."

In line with these pronouncements the Communist party of the United States was absolutely opposed to any help that the United States might give to England, then bearing the brunt of the struggle against Hitler. And it was, of course, still more opposed to any direct American intervention. "The Yanks are not coming," was its slogan of the period.

THE TURN-ABOUT

On June 22, 1941, when the Nazis invaded Russia, the American Communists performed a one hundred and eighty degree turn with regard to their attitude toward America's war policy. It was no longer an "imperialist war" in whose outcome the masses were not interested. In a statement issued by the National Committee of the Communist Party, U.S.A. *(Daily Worker,* June 30, 1941), it was declared that "the involvement of the Soviet Union has changed the character of the war" and that the invasion of Russia "has immeasurably increased the menace of Hitler and facism to the national existence of all peoples, to the social and national security of the people of the United States." (Hitler's previous occupation of Poland, France, Belgium, the Netherlands, Denmark, Norway, Hungary, and Yugoslavia was apparently no menace to the national existence of the peoples inhabiting those countries—as long as the Soviet-Nazi Pact enabled Moscow to swallow the three Baltic countries, half of Poland, and a large section of Romania.) Now that American friendship and assistance to Russia was needed and expected, the Communist party of the United States again went through all the motions of what between 1935 and 1939 was called either "popular front" or "people's front." The manufacture of war equipment became a national duty, and strikes in defense industries were condemned. Russia's immediate interests demanded that the American communists should bend over backwards in proving their 100 per cent American patriotism, including support of profiteering and exploitation. American workers were urged to produce as much war material as possible, and to disregard their own interests as against those of their employers. "The employers," the *Daily Worker* wrote on January 17, 1942, "have a right to reasonable profits; have a right to manage their own plants; have a right to make contributions to the war program out of their own experience; have a right to press their own point of view."

In the same spirit American communists bitterly attacked Walter Reuther and other trade unionists who were opposed to the no-strike pledge and to what was called "incentive pay," an attempt to induce workers to overexert themselves to the detriment of their health. Harry Bridges, the party's chief spokesman within the trade-union movement, spoke in favor of national service legislation, which would reduce the workers to the status they are "enjoying" in the totalitarian countries. And in a speech delivered in San Francisco on May 25, 1944, he suggested, in agreement with the official opinion of the Communist party on that subject, that strikes should be ruled out "not only for the duration of the war but after the war."[4] This attempt at bartering labor's most elementary rights for the sake of the expected postwar credits to Russia of course met with definite resistance on the part of the noncommunist labor leaders, who thus showed up the communists as agents of a foreign power parading as champions of the underdog.

The communist policy of ultramoderation grew in intensity as long as the war lasted. The dissolution of the Communist International, pronounced in 1943, was logically followed by the self-liquidation of the Communist party in the United States early in 1944. It was suggested by the party's leader, Earl Browder, who, at a meeting held at Madison Square on January 10, 1944, declared that "the American people are so ill prepared, subjectively, for any deep-going change in the direction of socialism, that post-war plans with such an aim would not unite the nation, but would further divide it." In place of the party, a new body called the Communist Political Association was organized. Its constitution called for "the advancement and protection of the interests of the nation and its people" and it threatened with expulsion from the Association those endeavoring to "subvert, undermine, weaken or overthrow any or all institutions of American democracy."

CHANGING THE LINE AGAIN

As victory in Europe neared, the Kremlin decided that control of the "liberated" territories might turn out to be a greater boon to Russia's power than American credits and peaceful co-operation with the Western powers. In other words, the time had come to take over not only Hitler's spoils in Eastern and Central Europe but his dream of world conquest as well. This meant that the policy of communist self-liquidation in America for the sake of obtaining credits was to be scrapped as an unnecessary and unprofitable piece of humiliation. This, of course, meant the liquidation of Browder's leadership to the accompaniment of a barrage of abuse and vituperation which put all the "theoretical" blame on a man who was simply carrying out the instructions of his paymasters.

The first indication of things to come was contained in an article from the pen of France's No. 2 communist, Jacques Duclos, published in the April 1945 issue of *Les Cahiers du communisme*, theoretical organ of the French Communist party. Written after Duclos' visit to Moscow, the statement was the official view of those who determined the policies of the international communist movement. The gist of the article was that Browder's advocacy of dissolution of the Communist party of the United States represented "a notorious revision of Marxism on the part of Browder and his supporters, a revision which is expressed in the concept of a long-term class peace in the United States, of the possibility of the suppression of the class struggle in the post-war period and of establishment of harmony between labor and capital." The article also "revealed" that William Z. Foster, almost alone, had opposed the adoption of Browder's proposal to dissolve the party and to abandon the class struggle. (Owing to the monolithic character of the communist parties, such opposition was not made known at the time and was denied when allusion to it was made in the noncommunist press.) It is beside the point whether or not Foster's "opposition" at that time was genuine or directed by the same representative of Stalin who had inspired

Browder's attitude. Foster's "opposition" quite naturally slated him for the post of Browder's successor.

At the time when Duclos' article appeared in *Cahiers du communisme*, the American Communist party reached its peak with some 80,000 members. Within a few years this reservoir of support disappeared, and the Communist party was left high and dry, exposed, for those who cared to look, in its pathetic nakedness as a hapless instrument of the Kremlin.

At first it seemed that the popularity won during the war years when it was outdoing itself in ultra-patriotic, class-harmony phrase-mongering, would not be impaired by Moscow's sudden change of policy and the ensuing duty of the American Communist party—or more precisely of all communist parties—to attack "American expansionist plans for the enslavement of Europe." The plan was to attack the Truman administration not in the name of class warfare, as good old Marxism or Leninism would have demanded, but in the name of "peace." As standard bearer in the struggle, they decided to use Henry A. Wallace, former secretary of Agriculture and vice-president in earlier Roosevelt administrations. Wallace was not a communist, to be sure, but his disappointment with having missed the chance of becoming President after F.D.R.'s death induced him to accept a third party (it was labeled "Progressive Party") candidacy which was supported—some say masterminded—by the communists. The result was a dismal fiasco. Instead of the hoped for ten million votes, Wallace received only 1,156,000, half of which came from New York, the traditional stronghold of the communists and of their sympathizers and dupes.

By opposing the candidacy of Truman, who enjoyed official labor support, and by supporting Moscow's policy in the cold war, the communists eventually forfeited both the sympathies and the tolerance they had been enjoying during the war years. Their men were gradually pushed out of the influential positions they had held in the Congress of Industrial Organizations, and those few unions whose rank and file stuck to their communist leaders were ejected from the C.I.O. After the Wallace campaign of 1948, far from influencing events in any way, the communists were continuously on the defensive politically and legally, operating in an environment which was increasingly hostile. The anticommunist Smith Act, passed in 1940 during the Nazi-Soviet Pact period, was applied to harry communist officials. (Ironically, during their days of wartime patriotism, the communists had demanded that the act be applied against a Trotskyist group in Minneapolis, as indeed it was.)

It is hard to assess to what extent Senator Joseph McCarthy's crusade (1950-54) actually hurt the communist movement. By attaching the Red label to many noncommunist leftists and by victimizing those who more often than not had been the communists' innocent dupes, that campaign more likely than not invested the communists with a halo of martyrdom which they did not deserve.

In 1956 the American communists, like communists throughout the world, were shaken by the secret speech of Khrushchev, condemning Stalin's atrocities, and later in the year the Hungarian revolt, crushed by Soviet tanks, further added to the depletion of communist ranks, which were reduced to a hard core of less than five thousand cynical functionaries and innocent superdupes.

The only real success the American communists actually achieved after more than four decades of mischievous futility is the spurt they gave and the pretexts they supplied to the ultrareactionary neo-Mc-Carthyites.

THE BIG FOUR OF THE ASIAN ORBIT

In Asia the Leninist version of anticapitalism made its appearance very soon after the organization of the Communist International in 1919. One of the first areas in which communist parties began to operate in the early 1920's was India, then still under British domination. In the country of Nehru and Gandhi, communism was at its outset the most extreme expression of the intelligentsia's nationalist protest against foreign rule, just as the social radicalism of the Poles, the Czechs, and other national minorities was always closely connected with the idea of nationalist revolt against the empires of which they were the unwilling subjects. Those who combined anticapitalist ideologies with nationalist protest were as a rule representatives of the educated déclassés, the underpaid or unemployed members of the lower middle-class intelligentsia. That stratum was and is particularly large in underdeveloped India where the supply of college graduates greatly exceeds the demand for their services. No wonder then that in that country many educated malcontents hailed the ideas and the methods of the Bolshevik Revolution as a way out of their economic predicament, for power meant jobs and a full dinner pail.

The outstanding champion of communism in India was at the outset Manabendra Nath Roy, whose disciples began their activities around 1921. The concrete aspects of those activities were strikes, food riots, and other forms of violent protest. At that time they also began to infiltrate the All-India Trade Union Congress, which eventually came under their domination. Because of its revolutionary activities the Communist party, which had been officially constituted in 1925, was outlawed in 1933.

During the Moscow-Berlin Pact period (1939-41) of World War II the Indian communists took the same position as the communists the world over, who refused to take sides in the conflict. It was only after the U.S.S.R. had been invaded by the Nazis in 1941 that the Indian communists changed their attitude. As a result the party was permitted in 1942 to come out from the underground, and its imprisoned leaders were released by the British. The fact that they had thus become, so to speak, the allies of India's British rulers, while the leaders of India's liberation movement were still in prison, was to hurt their prestige and thus to slow their growth.

After the proclamation of India's independence in 1947, the Communist party was outlawed in a number of provinces, and some of its leaders were arrested in connection with the turbulent events that followed in the wake of their activities. However, the party gradually abandoned its violent methods when the results of its propaganda among various sections of the population opened prospects of victory by parliamentary methods. At the elections held in 1957 the Communist party garnered 11,838,000 votes, or 9.9 per cent of the total vote. With the 29 seats which it thus obtained it became the second largest party in the House of Representatives. Another symptom of its strength is the control of the All-India Trade Union Congress, the second largest labor federation in India, not to speak of the great appeal which the party has to the unemployed or underpaid college graduates and intellectual workers in general. Its great handicap, however, is the fact that so far it has not found a method of winning the rural population which in India forms the immense majority.

A spectacular success was achieved by the party in 1957 when, with the help of an independent group, it got control of the government of the state of Kerala, at the southernmost end of the peninsula. During the almost two years of its rule the party carried out various reforms which had been contemplated but not enacted by the preceding regime. As a result, its appeal to the electorate was not weakened, even though in 1959 it was removed by the central government because of misrule. A united front of their opponents prevented the communists from regaining power in the elections of 1960, but the number of votes they received increased. The success of the communists in Kerala is doubtless to be explained by the unemployment and poverty afflicting a very large section of the population.

For all its victories at the polls the Communist party was weakened during the late 1950's and early 1960's by the impact of Khrushchev's "secret" speech about Stalin, by Moscow's dispute with Peking, and most of all, by the Chinese invasion of India. By the middle of 1962 it was rent by factional conflicts. There were those who sided with Khrushchev against Mao and aligned themselves with Nehru against the invaders. These "rightists," as it were, were opposed by a strong Maoist faction, and there were also those who, like the Kerala communists, would not commit themselves for either of the two sides in this controversy. There is no doubt that general popular resentment against Chinese aggression has greatly reduced the effectiveness of communist propaganda.

The early history of Japanese communism is a record of savage persecutions at the hands of a reactionary government that was obviously scared by the Bolshevik Revolution. Founded in 1922, the Communist party won many followers within the ranks of the malcontent intelligentsia. However, all attempts to spread its gospel among the masses were frustrated by the police which kept arresting, one after another, successive batches of leaders who, indoctrinated in Moscow, were continuously trying to revive the movement. During the 1930's progress of the communist movement was also impeded by the rise of Japanese military Fascism, which offered the educated malcontents an imperialist substitute for social revolution.

It was not until the collapse of the regime in 1945 at the conclusion of World War II, that the Communist party became a political factor. With its leaders released from prison by the Allied occupational authorities, the Communist party set out to carry on its activities as a legal political party. Its propaganda for the removal of all remaining restrictions, its implicit protests against foreign occupation, and its radical demands in general proved very popular at first. The very small number of party members notwithstanding, they were able to poll almost two million votes in the elections of 1946. Encouraged by this success, the communists made several attempts to call nation-wide strikes—attempts which failed largely due to the presence of the Allied military forces. As a result of these activities the Communist party was practically suppressed, most of its leaders having been driven underground, although it was not officially outlawed. Its decreasing influence was reflected in the considerably lower number of votes polled in the 1952 elections— only 891,000, as against two million in 1946. Eight years later, in 1960, the party, having in the meantime adopted less violent tactical methods, polled 1,156,000 votes, or 2.9 per cent of the total, which netted it three seats in the House of Representatives. This, however, was not a spectacular increase, considering that in the same elections the Socialist party polled nearly 11,000,-000 votes (27.6 of the total) and obtained 145 seats.

The growth of the Communist party of Japan has been largely handicapped by two circumstances: the fact that the Socialist party (particularly its left wing) has been championing many demands for radical reforms and also successfully stealing much of the communist thunder in other ways; and an aversion among the people in general to an organization which too obviously was taking its cue on all questions from a country that was not very popular with the average Japanese.

As in most countries, the communists of Japan are trying to conceal their identity in the guise of various front organizations. But unlike the Western communists, they prefer not to take sides in the conflict between Moscow and Peking. The Russians had been their original teachers and "angels," but Mao seems to be closer to their heart because of his ultra-radicalism, and, incredible as it may seem, for "racial" reasons as well. In their propaganda against Allied occupation the Japanese communists had actually used the "race" argument. It would seem that anything goes in politics, whether "regular" or revolutionary.

The Communist party of Indonesia was founded in 1920. During the stormy initial period its activities were behind numerous strikes and uprisings all of which failed to achieve their goal of a general uprising against Dutch rule, which they had in common with the Indonesian nationalists. Outlawed in 1926 because of these activities, the Communist party did not come out in the open until nearly two decades later.

During the later 1930's the threat of Japanese imperialism bent on the conquest of all of Asia, and the Soviet Union's opposition to these ambitions caused the Indonesian communists to modify their attitude toward the Dutch government, while Sukarno and other nationalist leaders sided with Japan. When in

1940 The Netherlands were occupied by the Nazi army and two years later the Japanese invaded Indonesia, the communists went underground to fight the invaders.

After the expulsion of the Japanese, when Indonesia achieved near-independence with the Dutch still officially in power, the communists made an attempt to seize power for themselves. The nationalists who, led by Sukarno, continued to fight for full independence, crushed the communist uprising in 1948, and some of the outstanding communist leaders were killed in the process.

Indonesia obtained full independence in 1949. Soon after, the communists began to organize local uprisings and strikes, their activities reaching a peak in 1951. In 1952 they at last had their day when a conflict broke out among the various parties and factions within the noncommunist camp. The communists supported Sukarno, and since that time their influence grew so enormously that the Indonesian Communist party has become the largest outside the U.S.S.R. and China, its membership having risen to over 2,000,000. They garnered more than 6,000,000 votes in the local and provincial elections in 1955. The trade unions under their control are believed to have a membership of about 3,000,000; and there are additional millions enrolled in peasants', students', and women's front organizations.

Since the early 1960's the Communist party of Indonesia has been playing the exceptional part of being one of the main props of a noncommunist dictatorial government. The regime headed by President Sukarno is supported both by the army and by the communists, two mutually hostile factors which hold each other in check, while the majority of the population seems to be opposed to the system of "guided democracy," a euphemisn for Sukarno's virtual dictatorship. It is in line with this "realistic" policy that the communists supported Sukarno's purely imperialistic or colonialist claim to Dutch New Guinea.

So far the Communist party has taken no sides in the conflict between the U.S.S.R. and the Chinese communists. The great amount of economic assistance received by Indonesia from Moscow, and the pro-Chinese sympathies of a certain section of the party may have something to do with that neutrality.

In the Philippines, the Community party, which was founded in 1930 and which, in 1938, merged with the Socialist party, was repeatedly outlawed both before and after the proclamation of the country's independence. It played a certain role in the history of the archipelago in that after the Japanese occupation during World War II, it organized a guerrilla army against the invaders. After the expulsion of the Japanese, these guerrillas, mostly peasants who were kept in dire poverty and virtual serfdom by their semifeudal landlords, formed a sort of revolutionary partisan army, known as the Hukbalahaps or Huks. Their struggle for agrarian reform was exploited for their own purposes by the communists, who became the leaders of that campaign. The fact that the legitimate demands of the peasants were ignored by the Philippine government after the establishment of the country's independence in 1946 kept the partisan warfare alive for many years until it was greatly weakened but not completely suppressed by a large-scale military campaign against the guerrillas and by the surrender of its leader, the communist Luis Taruk.

LATIN AMERICA AND AUSTRALASIA

In the Latin-American orbit, Leninism, for all its claims to being the gospel of the working class, has a very strong appeal to the numerous stratum of under-paid or unemployed intellectuals. This is particularly true of Mexico and Venezuela, where the communists are not very influential in the labor unions.

The communists are firmly entrenched in Brazil, where they control the main association of the university students and where their position in the labor unions is likewise very strong. In Chile the communists succeeded in polling 11.7 per cent of the total vote in the elections of 1961. There they also have a large following among the industrial and agricultural workers whose trade unions they dominate. Suppressed as a political party in Argentina, the communists cannot run any candidates of their own. But like their Brazilian comrades, they have been successful with their propaganda both among the students and the organized workers.

A place apart is held by Australasia—New Zealand and Australia. In the former the number of communists is estimated as about 500 with about 3,000 sympathizers. At variance with New Zealand, where their influence is insignificant, the communists in Australia have succeeded in obtaining and holding positions of authority in some of the largest and most important trade unions. Did they attain this influence at the price of leaving the field of politics to the powerful Labor party? In the elections of 1958 the communist candidates polled only 0.5 per cent of the total vote.

CURIOSITIES

The communist parties in Africa, the Middle East and some sections of Southeast Asia are of little or no significance due mainly to the extreme economic back-wardness of those areas and to the absence of any *sizable* stratum of unemployed or underpaid intellectuals, who constitute the main driving force of modern anticapitalist movements.

However, it may not be amiss to mention, as a curiosity, the case of Ceylon where the communists—deriving their inspiration from Trotsky rather than from Stalin and Khrushchev—polled in 1960 7.4 per cent of the total vote, as compared with the 3 per cent obtained by the "regular" communists. Even more confusing for the radicals concerned is the situation in Bolivia, where the traditional communists have to contend with the competition of a Trotskyist party and a third group which likewise claims to be the sole possessor of proletarian truth as revealed by Lenin. There is also the case of Israel, where the communists with 4 per cent of the total vote in 1961 had an even slighter following in the labor unions (2.8 per cent), while the crypto-communist left-wing socialist Mapam party participates in the coalition government headed by the anticommunist Prime Minister Ben Gurion, the leader of the Labor party (MAPAI). Ben Gurion's next-door neighbor and archenemy, the Egyptian dictator Nasser, has stolen much of the communist thunder by nationalizing most of the country's wealth and providing jobs for the potential communists among his nation's malcontent intellectuals. And Madagascar, the giant island off the southeastern coast of Africa, is reported to have a Communist party whose members call themselves "Titoists."

Chapter VIII

THE COMPETITORS

Factional strife within the Soviet Union's ruling body was bound, sooner or later, to result in the creation of a party of dissident communists. It was primarily a struggle for power, directed against the predominance of Stalin, the boss of the party machine for nearly three decades. The character of that struggle is illustrated by the fact that during the 1926 campaign against the Stalin-controlled majority, the Opposition was unwilling to publish its platform prior to the party convention, lest Stalin steal its thunder. The leadership of the Opposition, though headed by Leon Trotsky, consisted of many elements which prior to 1926 had vigorously attacked all the views the great tribune had held before and after the Revolution of 1917. And Trotsky himself, to placate many of his new allies, publicly renounced those views which in the past had been in contradiction to those of Lenin.

The "Opposition" was expelled from the party in 1927, and its leaders were arrested, forced to recant, and eventually exterminated as "traitors" and "Nazi agents." Destroyed in Russia, opposition to the official party policy remained alive abroad. The monolithic character of the parties affiliated with the Communist

International outside of Russia resulted in frequent schisms, due either to differences of opinion or to personal rivalries. Those dissenting "outs" who were more radically inclined usually rallied around the glamorous name of Trotsky and eventually formed their own international organization, called "The Fourth International."

International Trotskyism viewed itself as representing the gospel of undiluted Marxist-Leninist intransigency toward the capitalist system the world over. (It was one of Trotsky's personal tragicomedies that, for reasons of propaganda, he had to bow to Lenin's prestige, even though in reality it was the founder of Bolshevism who had accepted Trotsky's idea of an anticapitalist revolution "in our time," which the latter had advanced as far back as 1905.) It was equally intransigent with regard to the socialist and communist parties, attacking the former as the flunkeys of capitalism, and the latter as the mercenaries of the treacherous, parasitic Soviet bureaucracy.

However, the hostility of the Trotskyists towards the communist parties and the ruling bureaucracy of the U.S.S.R. did not extend to the social system established in Russia by the November Revolution of 1917. The Soviet Union, Trotsky explained, was still a "workers' state," a system which had abolished capitalist exploitation and therefore in case of war should be defended as the "workers' fatherland."

The Trotskyists did not, and do not, ignore the glaring economic inequalities existing in the Soviet Union. They admit that the ruling stratum of officeholders, experts, and managers enjoys a privileged status and consumes an enormous and disproportionate share of the national income. However, in their opinion, Russia's new masters do not constitute a new class of exploiters; for, according to the Marxian concept, only landowners and capitalists could be included in that category. Once these two groups had been eliminated, the Russian masses—according to all communists, including the Trotskyists—have actually become the owners of their country's national wealth. If, in spite of it, there is a deep cleavage between the standard of living of the majority and that of the ruling upper stratum, it is due to the low productive level of the Soviet Union and to the consequent backwardness of the masses which are cruelly disadvantaged by the Soviet bureaucracy. However, the latter is merely *swindling* the masses, not *exploiting* them. A revolution and civil war will eventually dethrone those cheats and parasites and put in their stead a new administration of honest men who would have the interests of the masses at heart.

"Un-Marxian," as this "good-man" theory may seem, Trotsky was on good Marxian ground when he took this naive position. Marx could never visualize the simple fact—pointed out to him by his confused, yet sometimes inspired, heretical disciple and rival, Michael Bakunin—that an upper stratum of educated men, whether they be college-bred professionals or upstart ex-workers, could constitute themselves as a new ruling class. Such an admission would have broken the edge of Marx's contention that the elimination of the capitalists was equivalent to the emancipation of the working class.

Shortly before his death, Trotsky made a statement which amounted to a reversal of his dearly cherished position. In an article published in *The New International* (November, 1939), immediately after the beginning of World War II, he expressed his "firm belief" that this war would "provoke a proletarian revolution" which would "inevitably lead to the overthrow of the bureaucracy in the U.S.S.R. and to the regeneration of

Soviet democracy." "If, however," he added, "it is conceded that the present war will provoke not revolution, but a decline of the proletariat. . . ." and "in the event that the proletariat of advanced capitalist countries, having conquered power, should prove incapable of holding it and surrender it, as in the U.S.S.R., to a privileged bureaucracy," and again, "if the world proletariat should actually prove incapable of fulfilling the mission placed upon it by the course of development, nothing else would remain except openly to recognize that the socialist program based on the internal contradictions of capitalist society, ended as a Utopia." In that case it would have to be admitted, in Trotsky's opinion, that "the Stalin regime is the first stage of a new exploiting society" and "then, of course, the bureaucracy will become a new exploiting class." And he concludes the paragraph with the words that if this should happen "it is self-evident that a new 'minimum' program would be required—for the defense of the interests of the slaves of the totalitarian bureaucratic society."

By having his old rival assassinated, Stalin relieved Trotsky of the melancholy necessity of revising his Marxian principles, considering that World War II did not bring about the "proletarian revolution" in whose coming Trotsky so "firmly believed." Most of Trotsky's followers, however, still cherish the hope of succeeding the Communist party in the leadership of the working class and have chosen to ignore Trotsky's admission by the ingenious device of declaring that the World War is not over yet. The myth of the working-class character of the Soviet system (for all its temporary counterrevolutionary deviations, as the Trotskyists would put it), with the fascination it exerts upon all malcontents who never had any direct contact with it, is too valuable a propaganda asset to be given up wantonly for the sole reason that it is . . . a myth.

MAO TSE-TUNG

The Chinese Communist party was founded in 1921 during the Chinese civil war and grew in influence when, during the early 1920's, the Soviet government granted political, financial, and military assistance to Sun Yat-sen and Chiang Kai-shek, then fighting for survival against the "War Lords," who were supported by the various imperialist and colonialist interests. That assistance was the only alternative to total defeat in an unequal struggle. It was particularly hailed by the great mass of destitute students, the sons of the impoverished lower middle classes. They had hitherto been ardent democrats and nationalists in revolt against Manchu and militarist despotism and against imperialist encroachments and foreign capitalist privilege. Now they accepted the Russian communist gospel of hostility against capitalism in general, particularly as they realized that a successful struggle inspired by the new philosophy would raise them to the top of the social pyramid of China. The communists sought and found a mass following among the industrial workers whose strikes and parades against their foreign and domestic employers were repeatedly countered with machine guns—the best way of driving both students and workers into the camp of Russian communism.

Chiang Kai-shek who, after Sun Yat-sen's death in 1925, became the head of the new nationalist regime in the making, was opposed to communism and hoped for a new China built on the model of the Western powers. But he had to tolerate the communists within the Kuomintang—the party of the Chinese nationalist revolution—and he even sometimes indulged in their vocabulary as witnessed by his remark that "the Chinese Revolution was part of the world revolution." For both Russia's help and the support of the communist students and their following among the workers were necessary in his military campaign against the "War Lords."

No sooner was Chiang Kai-shek sure of his success in 1927, after he had seized control of the entire southern half of China, than he not only expelled the communists from his party, but also organized a massacre of all communists—intellectuals and workers—that he could lay hands on. Chiang may have felt justified in proceeding that way, since the Chinese communists, in a mixture of cynicism and naiveté, openly boasted at the Fourth Congress of the Comintern in 1922 that they were going to use their association with the Kuomintang to win its mass following and to destroy that party.

After that the Chinese communists went underground. There was a conflict in their ranks as to the tactics they were to pursue. The Communist International, that is, Stalin, and the official leaders of the Chinese Communist party—the so-called "28 Bolsheviks," that is, Chinese students who had been indoctrinated in Moscow—insisted on the time-honored policy of concentrating all efforts on winning the support of the industrial workers—the urban masses. Mao Tse-tung took a different position. He was out to win and realized that he could only do so with the support of the peasants who constituted 85 per cent of China's population. It is possible that the shock of the atrocious massacre engineered by Chiang Kai-shek in 1927 had somehow affected his Marxist orthodoxy. From now on Marx's well-nigh liturgical "the emancipation of the working class will be effected by the working class itself," was replaced, consciously or unconsciously, by the idea that the overthrow of the bourgeoisie would be effected by the peasant masses under the leadership and in the interests of the students and other propertyless members of the educated lower middle classes.

The idea of starting a peasant rebellion went not only in the teeth of Marxist orthodoxy. It also went against the interests of the Soviet regime, as Stalin saw them. As a practical politician, not chasing the wild goose of a *Communist* China, the Soviet dictator had accepted the idea of a bourgeois-nationalist Chiang Kai-shek regime opposed to and by the imperialist powers which were Soviet Russia's enemies as well. A peasant rebellion, Stalin apparently feared, might have weakened Chiang Kai-shek's efforts to oppose the encroachments of the hostile powers which supported the "War Lords." He went so far in his acceptance of Chiang's national revolution as to send him his (Stalin's) autographed picture which, to the gloating of Stalin's Trotskyist opponents, arrived at its destination shortly after the anticommunist massacre.

Mao Tse-tung's heresy at first cost him his standing in the party. He was removed from its top steering committee (Politbureau) and, according to some reports, from the party itself. However, his counsel prevailed in the end, and under his leadership the remnants of the party, instead of working underground among the urban masses, undertook a guerrilla war at the head of about 6,000 partisans. In the course of that campaign they built up an army composed of peasants whose allegiance was won by canceling their indebtedness to the bankers and usurers in all territories which they occupied. In 1931 a Chinese Soviet Republic, with Mao as president, was proclaimed in the territories held by the communists.

When during the 1930's Japanese troops invaded China and began to occupy large sections of its territory, a sort of popular front was established between the two warring Chinese camps. The communists showed their patriotism by declaring, in the words of Mao Tse-tung, that "the property of rich farmers would not be confiscated by the Communists if these wealthy men supported the movement to resist Japan" and "that the property and factories of merchants and of larger and smaller capitalists will not be confiscated."[1]

Pressed from all sides, Mao and his partisan Red Army left central China and undertook in 1934 what has come to be called the "Long March" to Yenan in the northwesternmost corner of the country, where Mao was well beyond the reach of both Chiang Kai-shek and the Japanese. The following year Mao took control of the Communist party.

A rapprochement between the communists and the Kuomintang took place in 1936 after what is called the "Sian incident," when Chiang Kai-shek was captured by a Northern "war lord," and an alliance against the Japanese invaders was concluded between the two warring parties. It lasted until the total defeat of Japan in 1945.

During that period the Chinese communists, under Mao's unquestioned leadership, never flinched from their support of all of Stalin's policies. Mao glorified the Soviet dictator and found nothing objectionable in what was later to be called the "cult of personality." He himself gradually became the object of a similar cult.

At the conclusion of World War II in 1945, the question arose as to whether China should be ruled by a coalition of the two hitherto hostile parties. That idea, by the way, was supported by the United States government which wanted to put an end to the civil war and its devastations. The communists were ready, and Mao even went to Chunking, Chiang Kai-shek's capital, to meet his old foe. However, no agreement was possible—largely because of Chiang Kai-shek's absolute refusal to make concessions to the peasants at the expense of the moneyed interests of the Chinese bourgeoisie. This attitude alienated a large section of the progressive intelligentsia which hitherto had been opposed to the communists. In the civil war which was resumed, Chiang Kai-shek's forces—composed mostly of poor or landless peasants—as a rule melted away by joining the communists when they heard that the financial burdens oppressing the peasants were removed by the rebels.

According to the White Paper published by the United States Department of State, on August 5, 1949, "the Nationalist [Chiang Kai-shek] government had received U.S. aid worth U.S. $2,254 million since Japan's surrender, but had failed to use that help efficiently." The unwillingness of the Chiang Kai-shek crowd to use American subsidies "efficiently" and its reluctance to win the peasants by the method of relieving them of their debt burden is believed by many to have contributed even more to the victory of the communists than their military valor.

There was also another circumstance which greatly helped the communists. In 1948, one year before Mao's final victory, the *New York Times* of June 30, 1948, reported that "25,000 young men and women will receive degrees in Nationalist China this month. Only a few thousand will obtain positions." One suspects that most of those who did *not* "obtain positions" joined the communists.

It goes without saying that the Chinese communists belied the arguments of those of their sympathizers and apologists who were bending over backwards to persuade their listeners that Chiang Kai-shek's opponents were mere "agrarian reformers," anxious to alleviate the lot of the peasant, but otherwise in no way to be equated with the regular communists.

In 1949 the communist armies were in possession of all of Chinese territory—except the island of Formosa where Chiang Kai-shek had taken refuge. In September of that year Mao Tse-tung, secretary general of the Chinese Communist party, became the head of the government of what henceforth was to be called the "People's Republic of China." Mao's promise not to dispossess the capitalists, made at the time of his anti-Japanese "popular front" with Chiang Kai-shek was kept for a few years. As under the New Economic Policy in Soviet Russia (1921-28) many small enterprises could continue their operations without government interference. As for the larger plants, they became "joint state-private enterprises" managed by their former full owners, who "received a fixed rate of interest on their investments." (By making this concession, instead of resorting to complete expropriation, the new regime protected those industrial undertakings from being sabotaged by their managers, as the state had apparently no technicians of its own on whom it could rely.) This period, corresponding to the "NEP" phase in Soviet Russia, came to a close in the course of 1955-56, when the privately owned enterprises were nationalized.

It took the new regime much less time than the Russians to tackle the collectivization of agriculture (1954-55). Three years later Mao decided to show the world that his communism was more "advanced" than that of the Moscow pattern. The collective farms had to make way for the so-called "communes" which were a cross between a colonial superplantation and a military barracks, reducing family life and personal liberty to an absolute minimum. Those "communes" were meant to stimulate the output to make up for the shortages incurred due to natural causes, such as drought, inundations, and overpopulation. What this measure actually stimulated, however, was the resistance of the long-patient peasantry. As a result this scheme—an involuntary confirmation of Herbert Spencer's "coming slavery" nightmare—had to be abandoned, although this was never officially admitted.

This attempt at "liberating" the masses by the "dialectical" method of totally enslaving them met with no approval on the part of the communists of the Soviet orbit. They were apparently afraid lest such a treatment of the majority of the population nullify much of the propaganda effect of their opposition to the status quo among the masses of the noncommunist world.

The Chinese communist leadership was not deterred by this deleterious aspect of their "communes." At the helm of an enormous territory with a low standard of living affecting not only the masses but also to a certain extent its communist upper crust, they were ready to adopt any measure that in their opinion would relieve their economic plight—regardless of whether from a purely humanitarian point of view the remedy was not worse than the disease. Even before resorting to the expedient of the "communes," they had tried something that was even worse than that form of slavery. It was war. In 1950-51 they sent a large army of "volunteers" to fight alongside the communist North Koreans for the conquest of the southern part of that peninsula. The conflict ended in a stalemate. Had the communist side won, it would have meant Chinese political and economic exploitation of the conquered territory, but even without winning, they "benefited" by the loss in manpower, thus "heroically" relieving population pressure.

After the Korean adventure the communist regime

turned its attention to Tibet which, though formally under Chinese suzerainty, had for centuries enjoyed complete autonomy, amounting practically to independence. The communist invaders succeeded in overcoming the armed resistance of the Tibetans and in adding a large chunk of territory which they hoped to settle with their surplus population. It was only the outright threat of war on the part of the United States which prevented the Peiping regime from attacking Formosa (Taiwan). The idea that the Formosans may have the right to be—as most of them would prefer—independent of either Mao Tse-tung or Chiang Kai-shek, is rejected as not worth discussing—just as is the idea of Ukrainian independence by the Russian communists.

Frustrated in their ambition to force their admission to the United Nations by completely annihilating Chiang Kai-shek, the Chinese communists began to encroach on Indian border regions which, they claimed, were Chinese territories illegally grabbed by England. There are those who see in this the first step toward an attempted conquest of India.

All these military actions and gestures were not merely manifestations of a nationalist or imperialist tendency which, paradoxically, has not infrequently been associated with an ostensibly internationalist outlook of nineteenth- and twentieth-century radicalism. They were the reflection of a tragic situation in which the Chinese communists found themselves after they had taken possession of the country. For all their intensive drive toward industrialization, the standard of living of the masses was bound for a long time to remain on a beggarly level, as compared not only with the Western countries but even with the Soviet Union. The communists were sufficiently hardboiled not to mind the poverty of their subjects as long as they—the ruling officeholders and managers—remained in power and could enjoy a higher standard of living. But they were not sure that under such conditions they would remain in power *indefinitely*. There were in their own ranks the dissatisfied, jealous, and ambitious rivals of the top "ins" who, at a propitious moment, might take advantage of the pent-up general dissatisfaction.

What was the way out of this situation? The obvious thing was extensive economic help from the outside world. But no such help could come from the wealthier Western powers, particularly from the United States, which, both politically and economically, had been too deeply engaged in assisting Chiang Kai-shek; and which was certainly not interested in helping to his feet a sick giant who, once restored to health, might prove an even greater menace than Soviet Russia. Nor was any considerable help forthcoming from the European Soviet orbit. For the masters of the Kremlin have been no less aware of the sinister potentialities of a healthy and vigorous supercolossus whose population was at least three times as large as their own. The profession of the same political or religious creed has never yet been a sufficient guarantee against attack by an ambitious or hungry neighbor.

In this desperate situation, Mao took recourse to an exceedingly subtle, yet incredibly naive stratagem in whose success he hardly believed himself. He assumed the air of an orthodox believer in the immortal and immutable truth of Lenin's dictum to the effect that a final violent conflict between capitalism and anticapitalism was unavoidable. And in the name of that dogma, he engaged in an ostensibly theoretical offensive against Khrushchev who on various occasions had spoken of the possibility of co-existence between capitalism and what communists call either socialism or communism. The Soviet premier was accused of "revisionism"—the worst heresy a man professing

Marxism-Leninism could be accused of. This heresy, moreover, equated the Kremlin's top man with his Yugoslav counterpart in Belgrade. Years before, Mao had shown his animus by refusing to be impressed by Khrushchev's "secret" speech against Stalin. The latter—as far as the Chinese communists were concerned—remained a worthy successor of Lenin and the embodiment of the noble cause of communism. Since that time Mao and his followers have been lending the support of their prestige to those communists, both in the Soviet Union and beyond its borders, who have been opposing Khrushchev's ascendancy.

Behind the argument about the "inevitable" clash between the two social systems lurked, of course, Mao's unspoken ar.d unspeakable wish for a nuclear war in the course of which the United States and the U.S.S.R. would mutually destroy each other, whereupon China, more or less unscathed, could inherit what was left. As Tito is reported to have said, Mao is ready to sacrifice even 300,000,000 of his subjects, since he would still have as many subjects left with whom he could get along much better than with the rapidly multiplying 600,000,000.

At any rate, whether or not he actually expects to be able to bully the Soviet people into a nuclear war or whether he himself hopes to start one as soon as he can produce his own H-bombs, the fact is that he has rejected birth control as a remedy for his country's population explosion—an obvious blackmailing threat to the rest of the world, in order to obtain economic help, or admission to the U.N.—or both. It may not be amiss to recall that during the 1930's the dictators of all so-called "proletarian" nations, Stalin, Hitler, and Mussolini, openly encouraged unrestricted procreation —not as a remedy for labor shortage, but as a means of increasing their supply of cannon fodder.

Mao's rejection of the idea of co-existence—as expressed in his utterances in 1960 and 1961—was in outright contradiction to what he had said in his famous "Let a Hundred Flowers Bloom" speech of February 27, 1957, on the same subject. In the last sentence of that long oration he had said: "As for the imperialist countries, we should also unite with their peoples and strive to co-exist in peace with those countries, do business with them and prevent any possible war, but under no circumstances should we harbor any unrealistic notions about those countries."[2] The last thirteen words were apparently meant as a mere ritualistic repetition of the Leninist dogma of the "inevitable" hot war between capitalist and socialist-communist countries, for if that war was actually inevitable, there was no point to "strive to *coexist* in peace . . . and to *prevent* any *possible* war" (emphasis added). Three years later, either because he had become impatient with the slow progress achieved in the economic field, or for other reasons, he dropped the "strive to coexist in peace" as a betrayal of the sacred principles of Marxism-Leninism.

He also dropped something else in that speech—his reputation of a pure-in-heart idealist, or a man of honor. The most famous passage, the one about the "blooming of a hundred flowers," which promised full freedom of criticism by both communists and non-communists, turned out to be a trap—like the tsarist Constitutional Manifesto of October 1905, which lured the revolutionists out of the underground and facilitated the work of the police in arresting them. Mao, no doubt familiar with Russian history, repeated that stratagem with the same murderous effect. Such is the ethics of communism—in China and everywhere else.

Need one be astonished that Mao, who insists upon his own independence from the Kremlin, had only expressions of the sternest condemnation for the Yugoslavs and the Hungarians who felt exactly the way he did? And that his Peking *People's Daily* of November 5, 1956, called the Budapest massacre "the Great Victory of the Hungarian People."

EPILOGUE

The fascination which the Soviet regime has had for a great number of the foremost intellectuals of our day constitutes one of the spiritual tragicomedies of history. Early in the last century dissatisfaction with feudal reaction induced most European liberals outside of France to hail the new tyranny of the Corsican usurper. Similarly, the growing insecurity under a system of recurrent depressions in our day reconciled many progressive intellectuals outside Russia to the new despotism of Lenin's successors. They behold the abolition of unemployment and are willing to suspend judgment on the undemocratic features of a regime which, in their opinion, has done away with exploitation. They forget that unemployment had been abolished in Nazi Germany as well, and they apparently assume that the Russian workers are no longer despoiled since the high incomes formerly pocketed by the now dispossessed capitalists are distributed among the new bourgeoisie of officeholders, technical experts, and writers and scholars defending the new regime.

The inability to see in their true shape things that are a few thousand miles away, particularly if cherished hopes and illusions attach to them, may serve as an excuse for some of those to whom the Russian version of totalitarianism still seems to hold out the promise of a better world. Honest and self-deluded malcontents, or tormented souls in quest of a noble "cause," they are unable to understand that the concept of a "higher" form of production is devoid of any progressive meaning, if it is coupled with the sacrifice of personal and cultural freedom which has been the great achievement of the modern age. They are on a level with those who turned their indignation only against the Roman emperors who persecuted the Christians, but closed both eyes to the autos-da-fe of Torquemada or Calvin. And they naively believe in the necessity of a dictatorial supertyranny as a precondition for the realization of the Kingdom of Freedom, just as the pious Abd-al-Aziz, we are told, believed that it was necessary to make a hell of this world in order to enjoy paradise in the next.

There are also admirers of the Soviet regime whose attitude has nothing to do with honest delusion or sincere passion. These are the professional communists and some of their not quite disinterested hangers-on. They anticipate the impending world triumph of Soviet totalitarianism and prefer a seat on its bandwagon to internment in its concentration camps.

Communists and their sympathizers violently object to the inclusion of the so-called Soviet system among those forms of government which are labeled totalitarian. Their objection is based on the ground that totalitarianism is a form of capitalist oppression and exploitation, while the dictatorial methods of the communists have helped to destroy capitalism and to abolish exploitation. Communist "abolition of exploitation" consists of the substitution of a new bureaucratic aristocracy for a capitalist aristocracy, just as the latter had in its day replaced the old feudal aristocracy. The communists and their friends are equally wrong in their contention that the Fascist regimes represent a capitalist form of oppression. Wherever the Fascists were or have been in power long enough, they left no doubt that they were, or are, bent upon the elimination of private enterprise, first through government control and later by means of government ownership. In contradistinction to the Russian experiment, theirs has been a gradual process, carried out in the form of restrictions, levies, assessments, and heavy taxation. That process was attempted by Perón in Argentina; having learned his lesson from the Russian Revolution, the gifted disciple of Mussolini and Hitler wanted to avoid the chaotic confusion that would follow a sudden and simultaneous expropriation of all property owners. Perón and his following of army officers and officeholders, preferred to get their "roast pig"—that is, all the wealth of the capitalists and big landowners—without burning the barn. Prior to Perón, there was during the 1920's and 1930's the example of the nationalization of all large enterprises by Kemal Ataturk, and later, to a certain extent, by the Japanese militarists. It is also the expropriation and nationalization policy of Nasser.

Historically, the real difference between the two totalitarian camps was in the strategic approach. As steppingstones to power the communists used the war weariness of a defeated country, anxious for peace at any price, and the land-hunger of an exhausted peasant soldiery; while the Fascists exploited the postwar depression and the Bolshevik bogey in order to get the support of large sections of the impoverished middle classes and of the frightened capitalists at home and abroad. As a result of the different circumstances under which they were operating, the communists suddenly dispossessed the rich and gradually enslaved the rest of the population; the Fascists reversed the process, by first destroying all independent organizations and only gradually proceeding with the dispossession of the capitalists.

Thus, the first large-scale experiment in authoritarian collectivism, as conducted in Russia, which is erroneously called "communism," has been revealed as the original form of modern totalitarianism carried to its final conclusion both in the political and economic field. The democratic, libertarian, and internationalist coloring of its ideological superstructure need not deceive anybody—for it has no counterpart in reality.

The thinking man of today has been placed before a cruel choice: either the preservation of the status quo guaranteeing a certain amount of personal and cultural freedom at the exorbitant price of insecurity and unemployment, or a plunge into the dark ages of a "security" which has, once and for all, substituted unquestioning obedience and martial law for the right of criticism and civilized democratic procedure.

To find a way out of this double impasse, to combine the advantages of a planned economy with the blessings of liberty, will be a challenge to the best minds and a task which will require the collective effort of all those who are not willing to accept either of these alternatives.

NOTES

NOTES TO CHAPTER I

1. In Plato's opinion, as Bertrand Russell put it somewhere: "The State should teach a religion which he himself regarded as false, and [that] men should be persecuted for throwing doubt on it."
2. Anton Menger, *The Right to the Whole Produce of Labour* (London, 1899), p. 119.
3. It had, of course, nothing to do with what some American opponents of organized labor understand by this term today.

NOTES TO CHAPTER II

1. Max Nomad, *Aspects of Revolt* (New York, 1961), pp. 19, 91–92, 142–44, 158.
2. For a biography of Blanqui, cf. Max Nomad's *Apostles of Revolution* (New York, 1962).
3. Wilhelm Weitling, *Garantien der Harmonie und Freiheit* (1842). Quoted from the new edition (1908), pp. 238, 253.
4. See pp. 77-81.
5. See pp. 82-97.
6. For more details of this point, see Max Nomad's *Apostles of Revolution* and *Aspects of Revolt*.
7. The authorship of the *Catechism* has been attributed by Marxists to Bakunin, while most anarchists attribute it to Bakunin's wayward disciple Nechayev, with whom Bakunin had broken all relations. However, another famous disciple of Bakunin's, Michael Sazhin ("Armand Ross") in his *Reminiscences*, published in 1925 on the occasion of his eightieth birthday, declared that he himself had seen the manuscript of the *Catechism* in Bakunin's handwriting.
8. That term had achieved currency after the publication of Turgenev's novel *Fathers and Sons* in which the purely philosophical individualism of Russia's rebellious but by no means revolutionary youth of the 1860's was designated as "nihilism." In the West—but *not* in Russia—where the Russian *nonpolitical* nonconformists of the 1860's were confused with

the *political* revolutionists of the 1870's and early 1880's, the term "Nihilist" was henceforth applied to the democratic terrorists who killed the tsar in 1881. In Russia these rebels are called *Narodovoltzi*, i.e., members of the *Narodnaya Volya* ("the People's Will"), the name of their organization.

NOTES TO CHAPTER III

1. In his *Das Recht of den vollen Arbeitsertrag* (Stuttgart, 1886), published in English (London, 1899) under the title *The Right to the Whole Produce of Labour*.
2. Pages 218-19 of Vol. XIV of Proudhon's *Correspondance*, quoted in Max Nettlau's *Der Anarchismus von Proudhon zu Kropotkin* (Berlin, 1927), p. 15.
3. A contemporary of Proudhon, the German individualist philosopher Max Stirner (1806-56), who did not call himself an anarchist, was the author of *Der Einzige und sein Eigentum* (*The Ego and His Own*), which is often mistakenly called the fountainhead of anarchist philosophy. Stirner's gospel of ultraegoism, generally ignored by the anarchists—whether of the Proudhonian, Bakuninist, or Kropotkinist denomination —was at the turn of the century, a frequent topic of conversation among French and German parlor anarchists and Nietzscheans. It also served as a rationalizing philosophical cloak for some professional crooks who did not want to be confused with the common run of underworld characters. For more about these "anarcho-bandits" see Max Nomad's *Rebels and Renegades* and *Aspects of Revolt*.

NOTES TO CHAPTER IV

1. For more about Lassalle, see *Aspects of Revolt* by Max Nomad (1961).
2. The father of Karl Liebknecht (see p. 113).
3. *Die Zeit* (Vienna, 1895), Nos. 36 and 37.
4. Page 52 in the German original (*Voraussetzungen des Sozialismus*), or pp. 49-50 in the English translation (*Evolutionary Socialism*).
5. Many of the former "Allemanists" became later, jointly with some anarchists, instrumental in initiating the revolutionary current known as "syndicalism."
6. The split was accompanied by a break within the trade union movement, the pro-communist elements seceding from the "reformist" General Confederation of Labor (C.G.T.) and forming a new trade union organization called Unitary General Confederation of Labor (C.G.T.U.). The new trade union organization was also joined by the old guard of the revolutionary syndicalists who, in the early 1920's, carried away by

the revolutionary prestige of Soviet Russia, joined the communists, only to leave them a few years later.

7. They were neither radicals nor socialists, but very moderate left-of-center progressives.

NOTES TO CHAPTER V

1. For more about Sorel, see Max Nomad's *Aspects of Revolt* (1961).

2. Browder, for many years the head of the party, was expelled in 1945; Cannon, expelled as far back as 1927, became the leader of the Trotskyists; Elizabeth Gurley Flynn is at this writing the chairman of the party once headed by the ex-Wobblies Foster and Browder.

3. Pronounced Vatzlav Makhaysky. For more about Machajski see Max Nomad's *Aspects of Revolt* (New York, 1961), pp. 96-117.

NOTES TO CHAPTER VI

1. In his *Ob Oppozitzii* (p. 269) Stalin argued that in Lenin's works "the formula 'dictatorship of the party' is used but very rarely." There was a girl who insisted that she had not lost her virginity since her baby was so very, very tiny.

2. Did Marx deliberately use obscure and unintelligible verbiage in presenting his views on the subject? The well-known Marxist historian, Franz Mehring, in his biography of Marx, frankly admits that the *Critique* went over the heads of the delegates to the socialist convention to whom it was addressed.

3. *Daily Worker* (New York), April 5 and 12, 1947.

4. It is possible that some of these monstrosities have been or will be abrogated by Stalin's successors. But they existed for decades under a system maintained by the Soviet Communist party and defended by communists and fellow travelers abroad.

5. It is in line with this attitude toward personal freedom that Soviet women who married foreigners were forbidden to leave the country with their husbands and that in 1947 a law was passed—unheard of in the annals of any civilized country—forbidding marriage between Russians and foreign citizens.

6. It is reported that the slave labor camps have been abolished since Stalin's death. But Stalin was in power for twenty-nine years, and during his regime outright slavery was part of the Soviet version of—socialism.

7. The italicized passage was omitted in the "full text" printed by the Communist *Daily Worker* of New York, of March 6, 1936. Apparently it seemed to the editor too incongruous to be swallowed by the more intelligent readers. But the missing words were contained in the full text printed in the Moscow

Izvestia of March 5, 1936, and in the Basel *Rundschau* (organ of the Communist International) of the same date, p. 412.

8. V*last Truda* ("The Power of Labor"), Irkutsk, Jan. 26, 1930.

NOTES TO CHAPTER VII

1. The KAP, which eventually disappeared, was opposed to parliamentary action and believed in the seizure of power with the support of workers' councils. It showed some superficial similarities with syndicalist tendencies.

2. In the *New York Times* of March 2, 1933, Walter Duranty, a correspondent friendly to the Soviet regime, inadvertently (or cynically) let slip at the time of Hitler's assumption of power: "It is beyond question that Moscow would welcome even a one hundred per cent Hitler regime on the grounds it would conjure away the nightmare that has harassed the sleep of Soviet statesmen for the past five years: namely, an anti-Bolshevik European coalition or a 'holy war against the Red Peril.' "

3. Later to become widely known as the economist Lewis Corey, when he no longer was a communist.

4. Irving Howe and Lewis Coser, *The American Communist Party* (1957), p. 412.

NOTES TO CHAPTER VIII

1. Quoted in Mary A. Nourse's *Short History of the Chinese* (New York, 1943), p. 344.

2. Mao Tse-tung, "Let a Hundred Flowers Bloom," *New Leader* (New York), Sept. 9, 1957.

INDEX

Wood, Clement, 182
"Work book" in U.S.S.R., 266
"Workers' Conspiracy," 238-41
"Workers have no country," 132, 213
Workers' Party of America, 296-300
"Workers state," 326
Workingmens' party of the United States, 177
World Communism, 285
Wroblewski, General, 86

"Yanks are not coming, The," 310
Young, Art, 182
Young Communist League, 306

Zamiatin, Eugene, 37
Zeno, the Stoic, 12
Zimmerwald Conference, 161
Zoar settlement, 176
Zoshchenko, M. M., 268
Zwischen zwei Weltkriegen, 125
Zyromski, Jean, 139